COME HERE TO ME!
Vol. 2

COME HERE TO ME!

Vol. 2

More Unexplored Dublin Histories

Donal Fallon

Sam McGrath

Ciarán Murray

NEW ISLAND

COME HERE TO ME! VOL. 2
First published in 2017 by
New Island Books
16 Priory Hall Office Park
Stillorgan
County Dublin
Republic of Ireland

www.newisland.ie

Print ISBN: 978-1-84840-633-9
Epub ISBN: 978-1-84840-634-6
Mobi ISBN: 978-1-84840-635-3

Typeset by JVR Creative India
Cover design by Karen Vaughan

New Island Books is a member of Publishing Ireland.

Contents

Donal Fallon

To Leagues O'Toole.
The pleasure, the privilege is mine.

I have had the good fortune to work with many people in this city who are passionate about history.

Trevor and the entire team at the Little Museum of Dublin have been great supporters of this blog and project, and great champions of Dublin history in their own way. I would also like to thank all in Dublin City Council, in particular all in Dublin City Public Libraries, who have provided me with many opportunities to engage with Dubliners about the past.

I am grateful to all those who have provided me and the blog more generally with a platform over the years. My thanks to *Rabble*, Lois and Sam at *Dublin Inquirer*, all at Newstalk Drive and RTÉ's *The History Show* and the inimitable Tommy Graham of *History Ireland*. I am also grateful to all at the UCD Access and Lifelong Learning Programme team, who have allowed me to teach over many years.

I am grateful to the community of writers and fellow historians who I call friends. In particular, I thank the historians Brian Hanley and Pádraig Óg Ó Ruairc.

My thanks to everyone who has given their time to our 'Dublin Songs and Stories' nights in the Sugar Club, in particular the great Brian Kerr who captivated the room and who embodies all that is great about this city. There are too many people to name individually, but my thanks to all artists, musicians and others who have supported the nights.

Lastly, I am beyond indebted to friends and family who kept faith through an incredibly turbulent period of depression and difficulty. All things pass. Gabhaim buíochas libh go léir.

Ciarán Murray

*To those who continue to support the blog
almost eight years since its inception.
Keep the Faith.*

Thanks to:

Dan and all at New Island for giving us the opportunity to bring more of Dublin's stories to light. To the Gutter Bookshop, the Winding Stair, Books Upstairs, Designist and Hodges Figgis and the many stores who keep plugging us, six years on from our first book.

To Johnny Moy and the Sugar Club, and all those who have spoken, played at or attended our Songs and Stories events. These singers, songwriters, poets, playwrights, authors, artists and activists are the personification of what we strive to be as a blog. Thanks for the great nights and spectacular moments.

Those who have provided the inspiration for or assistance with articles in this book, not least Frank Hopkins, Harry Warren, Noel Redican, Aileen O'Carroll and Cormac O'Malley. In particular I'd like to thank Jelena Djureinovic for helping me cross the finish line.

My friends and the extended Murray clan. Ma, as always and forever in my thoughts, Da.

Last but not least, the other two authors of this book.

Sam McGrath

To my one and only Ciara Ryan.
For turning a black-and-white world into colour.

Since our first book was published five years ago, I've had the privilege to work with many brilliant archivists and historians. I'd like to take this opportunity to thank the following people: Tony at the Archive of the Irish in Britain, all at the National Library of Ireland and the National Archives of Ireland; Becky and Chris of U2's archive; Gordon and Lucinda of the Joe Strummer archive, and Dick and Hughie of The Atrix. Also to Brian, Paul and Ger of Eneclann; Mark at Arcline; Martin Bradley and finally to Cécile, Niamh, Michael and Rob and all at the Military Service (1916-23) Pensions Project and Military Archives.

Community history groups dotted around the city continue to inspire us and make history accessible for all. Special shout-out to Joe (East Wall), Ado and Cieran (Cabra), Fin, Stew, and Alan (Smithfield and Stoneybatter) and the *Gernika80: then and now* project. Also my gratitude to Brian and all at Saothar.

Thanks to a number of people who provided additional comments and information for pieces originally published online. 'The White Horse' article – Eanna Brophy, Hugh McFadden, Dunster, Freda Hughes, Fearghal Whelan, Niall McGuirk, Alan MacSimon, Des Derwin, Stompin' George, and Shay Ryan. 'Rice's and Bartley Dunne' article – Tony

O'Connell, Mark 'Irish Pluto', Mark Jenkins and John Geraghty. 'Four Corners of Hell' article – John Fisher, Seán Carabin and Brendan Martin. 'Max Levitas' article – Manus and Luke O'Riordan and Rob and Ruth Levitas.

Lastly, I'd like to convey my deepest gratitude to my parents Billy and Carolyn, my family and all my friends for all their encouragement and guidance.

A Divided Rathmines

Sam McGrath

For more than seven decades, only a couple of streets in Dublin 6 separated the affluent Georgian homes of Mount Pleasant Square and the poverty-stricken slum of Mount Pleasant Buildings.

Architect Susan Roundtree wrote in her 2006 article 'The Georgian Squares of Dublin: an Architectural History' that Mount Pleasant Square has 'justifiably been described as one of the most beautiful early nineteenth-century squares in Dublin'.

Developed in the early nineteenth century by English speculative developer Terence Dolan and his sons, the square comprises of 56 terraced houses overlooking a small public park and Mount Pleasant Lawn Tennis Club, which dates back to 1893.

The 1911 census shows that 387 people lived on the square that year, including 149 Catholics and 214 Protestants. A sample included a wine merchant (at no. 10), a landlord (no. 18), an electrical engineer (no. 22), and a secondary-school teacher (no. 40). These middle-class residents enjoyed access to squash, badminton, and tennis courts, as well as a private garden on their doorstep.

It was a different world altogether in Mount Pleasant Buildings, just a stone's throw away. The block of ten large

1

flats, situated in a small area on the hill between Ranelagh and Rathmines, later became a by-word for poverty and bad planning.

Rathmines Urban District Council started building the blocks in 1901 to provide accommodation for the local working class. The township of Rathmines was incorporated into the City of Dublin in 1930, and its functions were taken over by Dublin Corporation (now Dublin City Council). The blocks were completed in 1931, and contained 246 flats: 60 one-roomed, 150 two-roomed, and 36 three-roomed residences.

Widespread unemployment among residents and a lack of basic sporting and community facilities soon led to anti-social behaviour. The former caretaker of the buildings told *Irish Times* journalist Maev-Ann Wren, according to a 5 March 1979 article, that 'things really started to come apart in the late '40s'. Petty crime and anti-social behaviour increased, and the area began to get a bad name. Large families were moved into very small flats, and overcrowding became a problem. In the same 1979 piece, Wren wrote that:

> Poor quality housing will inevitably deteriorate, become low demand, achieve open area status and so a ghetto will be created ... If all these inadequate or problem families are placed together it seems inevitable that a problem area will result.

Families who were evicted from other social housing around the city were moved to Mount Pleasant Buildings while they paid off their rent arrears. An RTÉ documentary from the late 1960s, which is available to view online focused on the buildings. It interviewed a young couple who lived with their four young children in one room. Their flat was beside the continuously overflowing communal toilet that was shared by fourteen people. The mother told the interviewer, 'it's like punishment for not paying your rent … no decent person should have to live in this condition'.

A frustrated man who lived in a one-room flat with his wife, his brother and his sister-in-law asked the reporter, 'There's five thousand on the housing list. Why can't they house them? They're building office blocks overnight. What's more important? Office blocks or human beings? If this is what they call a Roman Catholic country, I'm disgusted.'

Resident Lee Dunne wrote a fictionalised account of growing up in Mount Pleasant Buildings in his book *Goodbye to the Hill*, which was published in 1965. Banned due to some sexual content, it went on to sell over a million copies. Another famous resident was the Limerick-born film star Constance Smith, who lived there with her family in the 1940s.

Journalist Michael Vinny in the 28 April 1966 edition of the *Irish Times* described Keogh Square in Inchicore, Corporation Buildings off Foley Street in the north inner city, and Mount Pleasant Buildings as 'the three Dublin ghettos … used by the corporation as dumping grounds for problem families'.

The *Trinity News* reported on its 29 January 1970 front page about a group of students who were 'attacked, terrorised and beaten up by hooligans' who tried to gate-crash a house party that they were holding in Ranelagh. The students were attacked with bottles, frying pans, belts, and metal bars. Two of their windows were put in. The article noted that the 'attackers disappeared into the nearby Mount Pleasant Buildings, a corporation house area popularly known as "The Hill" [which] is notorious for gang violence'.

A column titled 'Living in fear in Ranelagh' by Eileen O'Brien in the 10 December 1971 edition of The *Irish Times* was particularly harrowing. She talked to a number of frightened residents, including an old woman who, after coming home from a short stay in hospital, found her flat wrecked. Her clothes, coal, and a statue of the Sacred Heart that had belonged to her father had been taken.

A former resident who had recently moved into new corporation flats in Fenian Street, told the *Irish Times*, according to its 29 June 1973 edition, that:

> [It] was an awful place. We had only a communal toilet and wash-house. You had to go down a passage for water and the windows were getting broke all the time. It was a woeful place to live in, woeful … [It] was not too bad at first. I was there 17 years, and at first they left you alone. Lately there are gangs there … You could not go out.

In the early 1970s, the buildings were 'deemed unfit for human habitation', and the first block was demolished in October 1972. By July 1977, only ten families remained – six were squatting.

Only one block was still standing by March 1979. Wren wrote in the *Irish Times* that:

> the community is now scattered. Tenants in condemned blocks receive priority on the corporation waiting list. They are all over the city: in York Street, Holylands, Ballymun, Clondalkin. Many would

prefer to be rehoused locally but there is very little corporation housing in the area. Rathmines is one of the few mixed areas in the city, but to a decreasing extent. Property values rise as the more affluent move back into the city and the poorer must move out to new corporation estates and less mixed areas.

The flats were replaced with low-density corporation houses based around the new streets of Swan Grove and Rugby Villas.

Unsurprisingly, the area's problems did not vanish overnight. Anti-social behaviour still plagued the community, and career criminal Martin Cahill (aka 'The General') was one if its more infamous residents in the 1990s. Having lived in the rundown Holyfield Buildings in the 1970s, he had moved to a house at 21 Swan Grove. He was shot dead by the Provisional IRA in August 1994 just around the corner, at the junction of Oxford Road and Charleston Road.

Sandwiched between Ranelagh and Rathmines, this small working-class enclave with a chequered history was a stark example of extreme poverty and extreme wealth attempting to cohabitate.

Drunken Vagabonds and Lawless Desperadoes

Ciarán Murray

Dublin has always had its fair share of troublesome groups, from the Pinking Dindies, the Liberty Boys and the Ormond Boys of the eighteenth century, through the various fracas of the Animal Gangs, on to the Black Catholics in the 1970s and '80s, and now today's variant. The notion of gang warfare here isn't exactly a new one.

Riotous behaviour was a regular occurrence in the eighteenth century, but one event that stands out is a three-day riot involving both the Liberty Boys and the Ormond Boys that brought Dublin to a standstill in May 1790. Accounts of Dublin from the turn of the nineteenth century are rarely without mention of the two groups, both whose notoriety still rings true to this day. Injuries, maimings and deaths are all purported to have taken place in this particular encounter though, making it one of their bloodiest.

According to J.D. Herbert's *Irish Varieties, for the Last Fifty Years: Written from Recollections*, the Ormond Boys were the 'assistants and carriers from slaughter-houses, joined by cattle drivers from Smithfield, stable-boys, helpers, porters, and idle drunken vagabonds in the neighbourhood of Ormond Quay', whilst the Liberty Boys were:

> a set of lawless desperadoes, residing in the opposite side of the town, called the Liberty. Those were of a different breed, being chiefly unfortunate weavers without employment, some were habitual and wilful idlers, slow to labour, but quick at riot and uproar.

The Liberty Boys' infamy spread further than Dublin. References to them can be found in several newspaper articles from across the water, including one in the *Leeds Mercury* from January 1867 that referred to them as French Huguenots who had 'degenerated physically'.

> They are the Liberty Boys of Dublin, the dwellers in 'The Coombe', or hollow sloping down to the river, famous for their lawlessness, their strikes, and their manufactures of poplin and tabbinet. They do not seem at all favourable specimens of humanity as you watch them leaning out of windows in the tall, gaunt, filthy, tumble-down houses around and beyond St Patrick's.

The hostility between the two gangs often led to full-scale riots involving upwards of 1,000 men, and these occurred several times a year, but especially in the run-up to the May Day festival. The city would be brought to a standstill, with businesses closing, the watchmen looking on in terror, as battles raged for the possession of the bridges over the Liffey. John Edward Walsh's *Rakes and Ruffians* reports the Lord Mayor of Dublin, Alderman Emerson, as saying of the riots: 'it is as much as my life's worth to go among them'.

The battle this piece refers to began on Tuesday 11 May 1790 and lasted several days. It coincided with an election in the city, although an opinion piece in the *Freeman's Journal* on the Thursday of that week described the violence as wanton, saying:

> The situation of the capital on Wednesday night was dreadful in the extreme; it was shocking to civilisation, for outrage was openly and without disguise directed against the civil protection of the city. On other occasions, grievance, from sickness of trade, from injury by exportation of foreign commodities, from the high price of provision and the low rate of labour, grievances from the want of employ and a variety of other causes were usually alleged for the risings of the people, but on the present occasion, no grievance exists, and the fomenters of disorder are without such a pretension. 'Down with the police' is the cry, and demolish the protection of the city is the pursuit.

The article continues:

> In different parts of the town, prodigious mobs of people were assembled and the avowed purpose of their tumultuous rising was declared in the vehemence of their execrations against the police. 'Down with the police, five pounds for a policeman's head.' They were the shouts which filled the streets. In Mary Street, no passenger could escape the shower of brick bats and paving stones intended for the police. In St Andrew's Street, the scene was if possible more dreadful, for the mob, not content in driving the police watchman

before them, proceeded to pull down the watch house in which he took refuge … [The men] were obliged to fire and three of the rioters fell.

The riot only concluded on the Thursday, due to military intervention, when:

a party of men on horse dispersed the rioters and stood guard for the remainder of the night, which prevented more bloodshed and massacre … The blood of the unfortunate wretches who met their unhappy fate rests at the door of those few incendiaries who stimulated by their playful insignias unthinking persons to destruction.

A Forgotten Tragedy on Hammond Lane, 1878

Donal Fallon

On Church Street in Dublin 7, a memorial marks the location where two tenements collapsed in September 1913, killing seven people and injuring dozens more. Flowers are left beside it on occasion, and in 2013 the Stoneybatter and Smithfield People's History Project organised a local commemoration to remember those who had lost their lives there a century ago.

Numerous plaques on Church Street and in its environs also record the area's strong links to Ireland's revolutionary past. The Fianna Éireann activist Seán Howard, shot delivering dispatches during Easter Week, is remembered by a plaque unveiled by the National Graves Association, in addition to a more recent memorial from the Cabra Historical Society unveiled during the 1916 centenary. At St Michan's Church, a plaque remembers John and Henry Sheares, prominent members of the Dublin Society of United Irishmen, who were hanged at the Newgate Prison for their role in planning insurrection in 1798.

In an area so rich with history, and in which history is so well marked, it is curious that nothing remembers one of the greatest industrial accidents in the history of the city, and the dreadful events of 27 April 1878. On Hammond Lane, which sits between Church Street and Bow Street, a powerful boiler explosion within Strong's iron foundry was enough to bring tenements, public houses and industrial buildings crashing to the ground, while also resulting in the loss of fourteen lives. One newspaper described the day as 'a catastrophe, perhaps exceeding in its calamitous nature and deplorable consequences, any event which happened in Ireland within recent years'.

The Poverty of St Michan's

Hammond Lane sat within the parish of St Michan's, which was long regarded as one of Dublin's poorest and most densely populated parishes. One early nineteenth-century guide to the city warned that the residents of this district were 'all of the poorest classes of society; and so proverbial is this parish for its poverty, that the advertisement of the annual charity sermon is headed by the words 'the poorest parish in Dublin'. Nugent Kennedy, speaking to the Social Science Association in Dublin in 1861, referred specifically to the parish of St Michan's as being among the very worst districts in the city, insisting much of it was 'only fit to be demolished'. To him, 'the people inhabiting these localities look as though stricken by the plague'.

By the time of the 1862 *Thom's Almanac*, a year after Kennedy's comments, Hammond Lane was home to a grocer, stables and two provision dealers, but it was clear who the primary employers were. At number seven, James Tyrell operated an iron mills. At numbers eight and nine, John Strong and sons operated a 'foundry and ironworks, millwrights and engineers'. Amid these centres of work were tenements: numbers four to six, numbers eleven to fourteen and numbers seventeen to twenty-five were all tenement accommodation. This would remain the urban fabric of the street for decades to come.

Iron foundries were a significant employer of working-class Dubliners throughout the nineteenth century. While there were thirteen iron foundries in Dublin in 1824, the number had risen to twenty-nine by 1850.

The Explosion of 27 April 1878

At around half one on 27 April 1878, an explosion in the area of Hammond Lane caused panic and confusion. The *Freeman's Journal* noted that rumours abounded in the city, as:

> a terrific explosion was heard in the neighbour-hood of Arran Quay and Church Street and in the Four Courts. Reports spread rapidly, and were, it is needless to say, of a very varied character. One was that the Bow Street Distillery had been blown up; another that four houses had fallen. Those in the vicinity of Hammond Lane knew too well what had happened.

At Strong's foundry, the steam boiler had exploded, bursting with a force that led *The Irish Times* to describe how 'one of the front walls of the foundry was rent into pieces, and literally blown into the street'. A part of the boiler was described as having been 'violently hurled into a gateway opposite. Had it struck one of the houses filled with alarmed men, women and children, a terrible addition might have been made to the dreadful calamity.'

The risk of such boiler explosions at the time was well-known. Publications like *The Engineer* repeatedly wrote of the risks of such incidents occurring, and in Britain lives were lost in such industrial accidents. Fifteen lives were lost at the Town and Son Factory at Bingley in West Yorkshire in June 1869 owing to a boiler explosion there, while an earlier explosion at Fieldhouse Mills in Rochdale had claimed ten lives in 1855. In New York, the dreadful Hague Street explosion in 1850 had claimed more than sixty lives. In Dublin, the *Freeman's Journal* was furious that 'of late years, boiler explosion has followed boiler explosion with alarming and increasing frequency'.

The loss of life on Hammond Lane could have been worse, as many men had left Strong's at one o'clock on their break. At the time of the explosion, the lane was described as 'deserted, save by a few passers-by and some children playing in front of the ill-fated walls'. One premises destroyed by the powerful blast was Duffy's public house, opposite the foundry, where the proprietor, Patrick Duffy, and two of his children were killed.

Mr Duffy was a well-known figure in Dublin, having held the position of warder in one of the Metropolitan convict depots, and having been employed by Dublin Corporation in the past. His public house, after the blast, was described as 'a shambles, having collapsed like a pack of cards, burying those inside'. Two of the tenement buildings on the street were destroyed too – three-storey buildings that housed some of the poorest workers in Dublin.

The Response to the Blast
In the immediate aftermath of the explosion, the Dublin Fire Brigade arrived on the scene and began seeking survivors in the rubble, as well as removing remains. Under the stewardship of James Robert Ingram, a veteran of the New

York Fire Department, the fire brigade provided an important service with very meagre resources. The first task for firefighters was removing those members of the public who wished to assist from the scene of the carnage. More often a hindrance than a help to a rescue operation, the distraught public would remain a sight on the street in the days that followed. One hundred men from the 91st Highlanders arrived from the nearby Royal Barracks and assisted the firefighters in removing debris.

When the tragedy came before the coroner's court, details of how the fourteen had lost their lives emerged: twelve had suffocated and two were crushed. There were also more than thirty people who were injured in the blast, some of whom were maimed for life. Dr Robert Martin, the resident surgeon of the Richmond Hospital, detailed the horrific sights that followed the tragedy, while others recounted the scenes of people alive under the ruins of the blast, fighting for survival.

Yet if there was hope for answers, people were to be left disappointed. Dublin Fire Brigade historians Geraghty and Whitehead note that:

> The engineer's report stated that the boiler was not properly maintained and was weakened by corrosion. No independent engineer had examined the boiler in the previous two years ... There were no statutory regulations under the Factories Act 1875 for the inspection of boilers, although such provision had been demanded from parliament by engineers throughout the United Kingdom.

In the end, nobody was found negligent. Instead, it was found that 'the explosion was the result of a defective condition of one of the boiler plates, which was externally corroded to a dangerous extent … We cannot attribute any criminal negligence to the Messrs Strong, who appear to have taken all reasonable care to keep the boiler in effective condition'.

In the immediate aftermath of the tragedy, there was an outpouring of support for the families of the victims, and the dozens of people left homeless. The Grafton Theatre of Varieties, a popular institution in the city, raised hundreds of pounds for those who had lost so much, and the Lord Mayor of Dublin appealed to the people of the city to reach into their pockets. Still, the tragedy quickly disappeared from the pages of Dublin newspapers, leaving the people of Hammond Lane to put the pieces back together again.

Today, there is no trace of the foundry. In 1973, the Hammond Lane foundry closed, resulting in the loss of just under two hundred jobs, and in recent years much of Hammond Lane has been behind hoardings, awaiting ever-delayed redevelopment and plans for a new family law courts building. Memorials like that to the victims of the Church Street tenement collapse serve to remind us of the challenges and struggles of working-class people in history, and it is undoubtedly time the victims of the foundry explosion were remembered in some way.

From Grandeur to Ruin: the Story of Sarah Curran's Home in Rathfarnham

Sam McGrath

The ruins of a Georgian home lie hidden in the middle of a 1970s housing development in Rathfarnham. Known as the Priory, this house, which stood for at least 150 years, played an integral role in what has been called 'the greatest love story in Irish history' – that of Sarah Curran and Robert Emmet. Its journey from a beautifully well-kept homestead to a vandalised ruin is yet another example of the Irish state and other bodies failing to preserve buildings of historical interest.

The house was linked to secret societies, wild parties, underground passages, fatal accidents, ghosts, secret rooms, and a long-running quest for a forgotten grave. Its story has all the hallmarks of a fantastic melodramatic thriller.

In 1790, the famed barrister and politician John Philpot Curran took possession of a stately house off the Grange Road in Rathfarnham. He renamed it the Priory after his former residence in his hometown of Newmarket, Co. Cork. A constitutional nationalist, Curran defended various members of the United Irishmen who came to trial after the failed 1798 rebellion.

William O'Regan described the view from the second floor of the Priory in his 1817 biography of Curran as:

The mystical entrance into The Priory from the book
Footprints of Emmet by J.J. Reynolds (1903).

of interminable expanse, and commanding one of the
richest and best-dressed landscapes in Ireland, including the Bay of Dublin, the ships, the opposite hill of
Howth, the pier, and lighthouse, and a long stretch of
the county of Dublin …

O'Regan described the house as 'plain, but substantial, and
the grounds peculiarly well laid out and neatly kept'.

Curran was a founding member of an elite patriotic
drinking club called the Monks of the Screw (aka the
Order of St Patrick), which was active in the late 1700s.
The membership, numbering fifty-six, included politicians
(Henry Grattan), judges (Jonah Barrington), priests (Fr
Arthur O'Leary), and lords (Townshend). Many were noted

View of The Priory ruins in 1988 in the Hermitage housing estate, Rathfarnham (Image: Patrick Healy (southdublinlibraries.ie))

for their strong support of constitutional reform and self-government for Ireland. The club used to meet every Sunday in a large house on Kevin Street owned by Lord Tracton.

Named the 'prior' of the Monks, Curran used to chair their meetings, at which members wore cassocks. It was he who wrote their celebrated song, the first verse of which is:

> When Saint Patrick this order established,
> He called us the Monks of the Screw
> Good rules he revealed to our abbot
> To guide us in what we should do;
> But first he replenished our fountain
> With liquor the best in the sky;
> And he said on the word of a saint
> That the fountain should never run dry.

Curran also used to host the Monks at his home in Rathfarnham, in a special room situated to the right of the hall door. The two outside legs of the table at which they would sit were carved as satyrs' legs. Between them was the head of Bacchus, god of the grape harvest and winemaking, and the three were wound together by a beautifully carved grapevine. An 18 September 1942 *Irish Times* piece said an elegant 'mahogany cellarette in an arched recess in another part of the room was capable of holding many dozens of wines'.

The parties, as can be imagined, were all-night affairs. Wilmot Harrison, in his 1890 book *Memorable Dublin Houses*, wrote that: 'Ostentation was a stranger to [Curran's] home, so was formality of any kind. His table was simple, his wines choice, his welcome warm, and his conversation a luxury indeed ...' The house was allegedly haunted by a mischievous ghost, who spent most of his time in a secret room of the house, which was eventually closed up by Mrs Curran.

Tragedy struck on 6 October 1792, when Curran's youngest daughter Gertrude accidentally fell from a window of the house and was killed. Devastated at the loss of his favourite child, Curran decided to bury his daughter not in a graveyard but in the garden adjacent to the Priory, so that he could gaze upon her final resting place from his study in the house. A small, square brass plaque was put on the grave's stone slab reading:

Here lies the body of Gertrude Curran
fourth daughter of John Philpot Curran
who departed this life October 6, 1792
Age twelve years.

Historian Richard Robert Madden, in his 1842 book *The United Irishmen: Their Lives and Times*, wrote that Sarah Curran's last request on her deathbed was to be buried 'under the favourite tree at The Priory, beneath which her beloved sister was interred'. However, her father did not agree to this. Lord Cloncurry told Madden that this was because he had been criticised for burying Gertrude in unconsecrated ground. The fact that Curran also disowned and essentially banished his daughter Sarah no doubt had something to do with it as well.

The story of Robert Emmet and Sarah Curran is known to many. In a nutshell, the Irish nationalist Emmet was introduced to the beautiful Sarah through her brother Richard, whom he knew from Trinity College. They fell madly in love, but Curran's father did not approve of their relationship. After clandestine meetings and many love letters, they secretly got engaged in 1802. Following his abortive rebellion against British rule the following year, Emmet fled to the Dublin Mountains but was caught after he tried to visit Sarah at the Priory. From his cell in Kilmainham Gaol, he wrote a letter – addressed to 'Miss Sarah Curran, the Priory, Rathfarnham' – and gave it to a prison warden whom he thought he could trust to deliver it. Instead, it was handed to the authorities, and Curran's cover was blown. The Priory was raided by the British, and Sarah's sister Amelia only just succeeded in burning Emmet's letters.

Emmet, aged 25, was hanged and beheaded on Thomas Street in Dublin 8 on 20 September 1802. Curran, disowned by her father, moved to Cork, where she married a captain in the Royal Marines. Accompanying him to Sicily, where he was stationed, she contracted tuberculosis. They returned to Kent, England, where she died in 1808, aged just 36. She was laid to rest in the family plot in Newmarket.

John Philpot Curran, a broken man after the deaths of two of his daughters, was pushed further to the edge when his wife left him for another man. From all accounts, he cut a lonely figure, wandering the gardens of the house at all hours of the night, and weeping by his daughter's grave. He lived in the Priory on his own until his death in 1817.

What follows is the story of the once magnificent Priory's slow journey into nothingness. Under the name 'Swart', a journalist had a long article in the 14 October 1922 *Irish Independent* titled 'John Philpot and the Priory – Some Incidents Recalled':

> Nestling amidst its groves of beech and chestnuts, the Priory still bravely shows a semblance of its former prosperous condition. What tales of revelry or love its old walls might repeat! What days of joys and sorrow in the lives of its occupants has it beheld!

Swart continued:

> We approach it through an open drive, guarded by old-fashioned gates of evident antiquity. Standing on the now moss-grown carriage-sweep before the front door one is conscious of a delicious air of mystery of breathing over all. The grove of tall beech trees flank-ing the eastern gable, the great dark cedar beside them, shading the door which leads to the gardens at the rear, the spreading timbers of chestnut outside the western gates are silent sentinels which will never betray the secrets of the days that are gone.

Apparently able to gain access to the house easily enough, he wrote that, looking from the front windows:

> over the high tree tops in the fields beyond, a misty vision of the city stretches far below, and the distant outlines of Howth Summit and the northern coast become faintly visible. At night the tiny beacons from the harbour bar glow like fair lanterns through the dark

Clearly deeply interested in the house itself as well as the Curran family, Swart wrote that:

> the years have dealt ruthlessly with the gardens of the Priory. Once the fond care of the great orator, he converted them into a veritable Eden. Often when touched by the melancholic depression which seems inseparable from the Irish character, he would wander out at midnight to pace a fitful hour through chosen leafy haunts.

Gertrude's grave marker was still visible in 1922, Swart writing that:

> in a tiny grove … a desecrated tombstone still marks a hallowed spot. It is the last resting place of one who in a short life brought great sweetness to those held her most dear … When she died in her twelfth year, he could not bear the thought of separating her from the surroundings to which she had so much gladness. They buried [her] in sight of the old house and with it much of the worldly hopes and aspirations of her sorrowing father.

The *Sunday Independent*'s 'Special Commissioner' focused his weekly column on 23 November 1924 on the Priory:

> Car No. 16 or 17 will take us … to Rathfarnham for 4d. … About three-quarters of a mile [past Loreto Convent], we meet … 'The Priory' on the left-hand side. The old house is about a hundred yards from the road, and we find it to be a long low building typical of the cottage type of country residence fashionable in the eighteenth century … [it] has changed so little during all those years that it does not require a very long stretch of imagination to see Ireland's heroine, the gentle Sarah Curran, standing at the door of 'The Priory' impatiently waiting for some message from her sweetheart, Robert Emmet.

In a letter published 9 May 1927, historian John J. Reynolds wrote to the *Irish Times* about his disappointment that nothing was being done to preserve the Priory, and especially Gertrude's grave:

> An inscribed stone was placed over the grave, and a circular group of shrubs was placed to enclose it. These in the course of years had risen sentinel-like to guard this simple tribute of paternal love. The familiar group of trees, together with the fine trees which stood at the entry of 'The Priory', has now been felled and nothing save a few ugly stumps remain. Just now when war memorials – of battles ranging from China to Peru – are fashionable, we have, apparently no time to think of a touching memorial left by the fearless

advocate of Catholic emancipation, the defender of Hamilton Rowan, Wolfe Tone, and the Sheares.

As the years went on, things went from bad to worse for the Priory. A decade later, James Hegarty of Glensk, Rathfarnham, wrote to the *Irish Press* in a letter published in its 9 June 1936 edition about Gertrude's tomb:

> The plate no longer exists but three of the four brass screws by which it was attached to the stone are still there. The little grave formed the centre of two concentric circles of beech trees probably planted by Curran's own hand. Vandalism and war-time avarice demolished these conspicuous reminders of a stirring period of Ireland's history. Less than five years ago the tombstone, a large slab 5ft by 4ft was still intact. It, too, has yielded to the desecrating and destructive spirit of the age. The sacrilegious hand of wanton profanation has broken the stone into four or five fragments and time is actively engaged in removing all traces of a prominent landmark of our history.

The following year, the celebrated political campaigner Hanna Sheehy-Skeffington asked readers of the *Irish Press*, in its 16 February 1937 edition, to take the 1903 book *The Footsteps of Emmet* and stroll with it around Rathfarnham. She questioned why there hadn't been more done to help salvage the historic sites associated with Emmet, writing that 'Surely the house in Butterfield Lane might have been acquired and set up as an Emmet museum like Goethe's in Weimar, the Brontë house at Haworth or Shakespeare's in Stratford-on-Avon.'

In 1939, James A. MacCauley of the Revenue Department visited the Priory and 'went around the rooms and in a study he saw a wall safe of solid granite, with a double door of metal and wood, where Curran kept his papers and valuables'. The staircase, door and windows were intact. However just three years later, they all had disappeared and the house was a 'gaping shell'. Obviously, the war years were not kind to the house, with individuals stripping it of its wood for fuel.

A few years later, an *Irish Times* reporter was sent out to visit the house as a result of reports that part of it had been demolished. His 12 September 1942 article stated that:

> Even from a distance he could see that the house was a ruin. A two-storey building of early eighteenth-century type, half of it is without a roof, and there is a big enough hole in the other half to bare the rafters. Window frames are empty and partially rotted, and the main entrance is without a door … Inside the house, in the drawing room, there were obvious signs of the cattle from the neighbouring fields having the right of way.

The writer was fully aware of the historical significance of this drawing room, in which:

> Curran probably discussed with his friend, Grattan, their plans to forward Catholic emancipation, and where, alone, he probably studied the briefs from which he defended the long succession of '98 men, from Rowan Hamilton to Napper Tandy. In the back part of the house, in a room which was probably once a pantry, our reporter found a cow stabled.

However, one sign of remembrance of things past did comfort the reporter:

> When he was looking for the house, [he] met on the road two little barefooted boys of 7 or 8 years of age. 'What is that house in the middle of the fields?' he said, pointing to the ruin. 'Sarah Curran's house,' they both replied, almost together.

An 18 September 1942 *Irish Times* article offered some new information into the house's deterioration:

> After the house became empty it was impossible to keep it in good repair, for it was continually raided by seekers after firewood ... the slab that covered the grave of Curran's favourite daughter was shattered under maliciously dancing feet, and now has disappeared. The garden is a wilderness, and the cattle find difficulty in browsing here.

In regard to the house's furniture, the article said that it all had seemed:

> to have disappeared, though a figure of St Patrick, once the occupant of a niche in the Monks' meeting place, was seen some years ago in a Dublin public house. The knocker of the door was sent some thousands of miles away to a descendant of Curran. The timber of the house has largely helped to warm some of the more unscrupulous poor, and the house is a complete ruin.

The well-known writer Mervyn Wall wrote to the *Irish Times* in a letter published in its 13 September 1950 edition to say that he had visited:

> last Saturday with the object of checking reports of recent further destruction there. Some high pieces of wall still remain, and some heaps of fallen stone, very much overgrown. The rest is stubbly fields. Within the past twelve months the main doorway (which gave character to the ruin) and most of the front wall have been overthrown – by local children, who we were told … use the place for play.

In regard to the grave of Gertrude Curran, Wall wrote:

> What is thought … is the grave was pointed out to us. It was completely unidentifiable from the surrounding ground, as the whole area has been recently subjected to intensive agricultural operations. The gravestones have been smashed in pieces, and, we were told, had been last seen some years ago in a neighbouring ditch. Despite diligent search, we were unable to find it.

Wall was informed that the gable and chimneys of the house were to be torn down in a fortnight's time as there was reason to believe that they were structurally unsound and could fall on the children who played in the ruin. He was bitterly frank in his views about how it was a disgrace that such a historic building was left to wither away:

Indeed some with a sense of retributive justice may regret that persons other than unschooled children will not be standing under that wall the next time the wind is in the west. This is an uncharitable thought, but Saturday was a hot day, far too hot to be searching for the violated grave of an eighteenth-century girl, and to be carrying in one's mind the greatest love story in Irish history.

Professor Felix Hackett, chairman of the council of the National Trust of Ireland, told the *Irish Times* that 'it was not part of their function to repair the errors of the past, and that the dilapidation of the building had gone so far as to make it impossible to renovate', according to the paper's 14 September 1950 edition.

The *Irish Press* published a story on 11 November 1953 about the Priory and the continuing quest to identify the exact place of Gertrude's grave. Patrick O'Connor, assistant librarian in the National Library, brought an *Irish Press* photographer to the Priory, and showed them the spot where he believed the grave lay. The journalist hoped that the 'long-forgotten grave ... [would be] marked and saved from obscurity'. O'Connor told the newspaper:

It was fifteen years ago since I had been there. But it was many years before that I saw the trees and the stone. In 1924 only the stumps of the trees were there. The stone had been smashed it is thought, and thrown into a ditch.

The *Irish Independent* on 23 June 1962 announced that the Priory was to be sold by public auction. It was described

as an 'unusual Tudor-style red-brick detached residence
... [standing] over 12 statute acres and a road frontage of
almost 1,100 feet'. By 25 February 1964, according to the
Irish Press, the Robert Emmet Society had decided to 'pro-
ceed with the proposed memorial to Robert Emmet and
Sarah Curran at the Priory', which was to consist of 'twin
evergreen oaks and a plaque in a lawn plot beside the ruins
of the house'. This plan unfortunately never came to frui-
tion.

In 1976, it was revealed that a new housing development
would be built on a site that included the Priory. This
gave local resident Bernadette Foley, a member of the Old
Dublin Society, the chance to search through the 'weed-
strewn patch of ground near her home hoping to find the
long-sought grave of Robert Emmet', according to the 9
October *Irish Press*. Local legend suggested that Emmett's
body had been smuggled out after his execution and buried
beside Gertrude's.

In her search, Foley was joined by a 'Mr Mooney', who
remembered seeing the grave, 20 years previously. Foley told
the *Irish Press*, according to its 12 October 1976 edition,
that 'he showed it to me, concealed under a ditch'. The
article expressed hope that Dublin Corporation would now
do all it could to help preserve the burial place.

Patrick Healy, who was involved in this 1970s
archaeological work, wrote in his 2005 book *Rathfarnham
Roads* that:

> a small group undertook to investigate the site ... a
> narrow trench 3 feet deep was dug through where
> the burial should have been. The result was a com-
> plete blank. A second and a third trench were cut at

intervals until a large area had been investigated without finding any burial, timber, brick, or stone.

Unfortunately, they were not able to find evidence of a grave even when the developers agreed to excavate a larger area.

Dubliner Seamus De Burcha told his own story in an *Irish Times* letter published on 16 November 1976:

> In 1956 the Priory stood as a roofless pile, and I was shown over it by my cousin, a Loreto nun. The square stone slab over Gertrude's grave remained, but the brass slab had already been removed … The Curran property was then in possession of the Loreto Order. The hall door had been removed when the house was unroofed, and had been erected as a stable door. With the permission of Mother General I replaced the door and, if I may be excused for saying so here and now, I rescued the door. I have it on a wall in Dame Street at this moment, where it was repainted by an artist friend …

Today quite amazingly, some ruins of the Priory can still be seen in the field around Hermitage Drive, Hermitage Park, and Eden Crescent. It is shameful that such a historic building does not even have a small plaque to tell people of its significance. The ruins today are popular with local teenagers as a place to hang out and drink. Litter, graffiti, and the smell of urine now blight what is the last remnant of Sarah Curran's house.

Admiral William 'Guillermo' Brown

Ciarán Murray

On Sir John Rogerson's Quay on the Liffey's south side stands a statue of Ireland-born Admiral William Brown. Unveiled nearby in September 2006 by then Taoiseach Bertie Ahern, the statue was moved to its present location, with an added plinth and plaque, in August 2012. It was lucky to have made these shores at all.

Two bronze statues were commissioned to be cast in Buenos Aires and transported here for unveiling: one in Foxford, Co. Mayo, where the admiral was born, and the other on Sir John Rogerson's Quay. They were a gift from the Argentine Navy to the people of Dublin and Foxford, as part of the 150th anniversary commemorations of Brown's death. However, a mix-up regarding who would pay for the transport of the statues meant that they almost didn't arrive in time for their official unveilings. Given that in Argentina over a thousand streets, several hundred schools, a couple of towns, and a football club bear his name, it would be a shame were he not celebrated here in the country of his birth.

Born on 22 June 1777, William Brown was brought to Philadelphia at the age of 9. Irish was his first language, with his early education having come from the parish priest in the

Admiral William 'Guillermo' Brown on his pedestal on Sir John Rogersons Quay. (Photograph by Ciarán Murray)

village, who happened to be William's uncle. Three years after arriving in Philadelphia, an area already heavily populated with Irish immigrants, he began work as a cabin boy.

Within ten years of this, his status had risen to captain of a US Merchant Marine vessel. He was press-ganged into the Royal Navy, and fought several battles against the Spanish. Respect for his skill at sea grew, and in his mid-20s, he was already the master of a large schooner.

Shortly before the Battle of Trafalgar, the French captured Brown's ship and imprisoned him. He was first placed in a prison in Verdun, where he contrived to escape, having charmed the governor's wife into handing over a warder's uniform. He was recaptured within hours, though, and transferred to Metz, where he managed to burn a hole in the roof of his cell using a hot poker, and escape using a rope of knotted bedsheets. He made his way via Germany to England, where he was heralded as a hero, fell in love with the daughter of a wealthy family, and married.

Brown and his family relocated to Argentina at a time when the South American colonies were in revolt. He made his base in the town of Ensenada, not far from the capital, Buenos Aires. His adventures at sea only beginning, he established several trade routes, but was constantly harassed by the Spanish Navy. This provoked Brown to take a hand in Argentina's revolt, and the Spanish quickly learnt they had made the wrong enemy. After several raids the Spanish impounded Brown's ship in an estuary off Montevideo. He made his way to shore, where he procured two small fishing vessels and rounded up as many English-speaking sailors he could – Irish, Scottish, and English. With a dozen or so men in each boat, he sailed out to where there was a well-armed Spanish cruiser anchored. The men boarded the unsuspecting vessel, overpowered its occupants and captured her.

His exploits earned him praise from the highest levels, and Brown was asked to take control of a small band of ships to lead the naval resistance against the Spanish. To say he succeeded in his role would be an understatement. Several times, in the face of adversity, with a small ragtag bunch of ships, he stood up to Spanish warships and was victorious, capturing many, burning others. Once, having taken control over a narrow estuary, he cut a new deck into one of his largest ships, lined the new deck with canon, ran her aground on a sandbank, and simply blasted an oncoming naval flotilla to smithereens.

On another occasion, on St Patrick's Day 1817, with the assistance of another Irishman, James Kenny, he forced the retreat of Captain Jacinto de Romarate, one of the Spanish Navy's prized officers. But it was not only on the sea that Brown helped the fight for independence. Any spoils he earned were sold via a businessman and friend by the name of William White, and the proceeds for these bought guns and ammunition for ground assaults. And while his battles are too numerous to mention, the ones that earned him the most plaudits were at Martín García and Montevideo. After the declaration of Argentine independence, he went on to help the Uruguayan cause, sailing against the Brazilian navy in his merchant vessels.

William Brown died on 3 May 1857. His funeral oration, delivered by Argentine President Bartolomé Mitré, read:

Admiral Brown bears with him the admiration of all patriots, and the love of all good men; and the

Argentine Navy remains orphaned of the old father who watched over its birth in the bosom of the River Plate; the Pacific, the Atlantic, the Plate and the Paraguay will be forever the immortal pages on which will be read his greatest deeds. And while one sloop floats on these waters, or one Argentine pennant flies above them, the name of William Brown will be invoked by every sailor as the guardian genius of the seas.

A Planned Massacre on Grafton Street, June 1921

Donal Fallon

In the coming years, we will undoubtedly be marking the centenaries of key moments in the War of Independence such as the firing of the first shots of the conflict at Soloheadbeg in Tipperary, the destruction of Dublin's Custom House, and, of course, Bloody Sunday in November 1920. A date that could have taken on such significance had things gone a little differently is 24 June 1921.

That's when the IRA planned a major attack in Grafton Street and its surrounding districts that was designed to take out every Auxiliary in the vicinity of one of Dublin's busiest streets. Encircling the area, they hoped to then move against uniformed and plain clothes Auxiliaries, with IRA intelligence officer Joseph Dolan remembering that 'the idea was to nail the whole lot in one blow'. In many ways, this operation would have been a second Bloody Sunday, and conducted in a much more open environment.

Looking at the memories of men who were involved that night, it is clear just how significant this date could have become. John Anthony Caffrey, a member of the IRA's Active Service Unit, remembered in his statement to the Bureau of Military History that:

One of the best known images of the War of Independence, this image is often said to show the so-called 'Cairo Gang' of British intelligence agents in Dublin, but it is more likely to be a separate gang of men. Number six is Leonard George Appleford, killed on 24 June 1921.

On an evening in June 1921, the entire Active Service Unit in conjunction with selected members of the Dublin Brigade were detailed to shoot every Auxiliary in Grafton Street, and at the same time one squad was to bomb Kidd's Buffet, which was one of the places chiefly frequented by members of the Auxiliary Division. The section to which I was attached was to operate on the top of Grafton Street, south King Street to Chatham Street. Our instructions were that the operation would commence at 6 or 6:15pm sharp.

Armed IRA men would be joined by an intelligence officer, such as Joseph Dolan, capable of pointing out Auxiliaries who were dressed in civilian clothes. Dolan recalled:

At the time great numbers of Auxiliaries paraded up and down Grafton Street in civilian clothes, and frequented Kidd's restaurant which was at the corner of Grafton Street. Michael Collins decided that there should be an attack on the Auxiliaries in this restaurant and in Grafton Street. The job was timed for the afternoon. This was the time the greatest numbers of enemy troops would be strolling in Grafton Street.

Rather bravely, a number of IRA men close to Michael Collins had begun frequenting Kidd's Buffet from October of the previous year. David Neligan, a leak within the British intelligence operation who was providing information to Collins and the IRA, introduced these men as informers. Frank Thornton, one of the IRA men who infiltrated this circle, was surprised by how little the Auxiliaries seemed to know about the IRA leadership, recalling that 'they actually had no photograph of any of us, and had a very poor description of either Collins or the three of us'. Kidd's was popular with more than just Auxiliaries and the Dublin Castle set, and contemporary menus promised 'the best Culleenamore Oysters in season ... Salmon, lobster, home-made pressed beef' and more besides.

Participating IRA man Padraig O'Connor remembered the manner in which the area around Grafton Street was subdivided for the operation:

from Suffolk Street to Wicklow Street; from Wicklow Street to Johnson's Court; from Johnson's Court to Harry Street and from Harry Street to South King Street. Parties were also taking in Stephen's Green,

Dawson Street, Nassau Street and Suffolk Street and a special party were going to Kidd's Cafe.

A number of factors worked against the IRA plans for the night. Dolan recalled that the plans were dealt a serious blow owing to what seemed to be an increased checkpoint presence on the streets of the capital, making it difficult for IRA members to take their positions. The men had even planned for a Ford Van to take away any wounded, 'and that couldn't turn up either, as it was also cut off. Because all these things happened it was decided to call the whole thing off.'

Still, some shots did ring out that night. Joseph McGuinness, one of the men who had gathered to attack Kidd's, remembered that 'the four of us loitered for some time and no shot was fired'. Yet, further up Grafton Street, at its intersection with Chatham Street, an opportunity presented itself, as two Auxiliaries wandered into the path of a waiting IRA unit. One participant recalled that 'one man fell on top of the other on the footpath. We fired against them and got away.'

By the time it was over, men were dispersing in all directions, and one remembered that 'we immediately ran up Grafton Street on to Stephen's Green, turned down a lane at the side of the College of Surgeons and into Camden Street, where we went into a barber's shop and dumped our guns there'. Some made for Harold's Cross, where pony racing was under way, remembering that 'we bought programmes which we marked up as an alibi for the night'.

The Auxiliaries killed were Leonard George Appleford and George Wames. Appleford, at 27, was the younger of the two men. From Essex, he held a commission in the Machine Gun Corps during the First World War. Wames, 29, came from Suffolk and had also served in the First World War with the Fifth Suffolk Regiment. These two young men had wandered into a set-piece ambush, which could have been much bloodier. In the end, individual IRA members had to account for their actions on the day, explaining why they fired on Appleford and Wames when the overall operation had been called off at the last minute. It demonstrated that sometimes men were forced to act according to circumstances of chance.

As historian John Dorney has noted, this was a time of enormous activity by the IRA on the streets of Dublin, as 'the Dublin Brigade recorded 67 attacks in the city in April 1921, 103 in May and 92 in June'. It was also the year the Thompson submachine gun made its first appearance in an IRA attack in the capital, a weapon that British intelligence acknowledged 'undoubtedly makes the IRA a more formidable organisation from the military point of view.' Had things come together, the 24 June 1921 operation would have sent a very clear message of what the IRA was still capable of, two years into the War of Independence.

Doran's of Castlewood Avenue

Ciarán Murray

On 20 April 1916, with days to go until the Easter Rising, and two days earlier than expected, the *Aud* arrived in Tralee Bay. The rebellion was imminent, and with this in mind, Pádraig Pearse and his brother Willie made their way to Rathmines. They turned down Castlewood Avenue and walked into Doran's Barbers. There they sat in silence as each got his hair cut for the last time; it's not so hard to believe that one of the brothers at least knew his fate. As John Doran recalled in an interview in the 28 March 1973 edition of the *Irish Independent*:

> They did not speak much as they awaited their turn in the chair: but then, they never did, he remembers; and, whatever thoughts were in the minds of Patrick and Willie Pearse, the 20-year-old John had no foreboding that he was giving the brothers their last haircut.

The Pearse brothers were only a small part of the history of a business stretching back over a century. James, John's brother, opened the shop on 2 January 1912, when he was 24. The 1911 census lists both James and John, then aged 15, as hairdressers. They were sons to Christina, who was listed as a widow on both the 1901 and 1911 census returns, and lived

41

in a house on Chancery Lane, not far from Christ Church Cathedral. Their father had been a hackney owner, and kept horses stabled nearby until his death sometime prior to 1901. John and James were just two of a family of thirteen.

Annual rent on the premises at Castlewood Avenue in 1912 was £52, and on opening, a haircut in the shop cost fourpence and a shave thruppence. Along with his wife, four girls, and two boys, James lived above the barbers until the early 1930s, when the family moved around the corner to Oakley Road. Born and reared above the shop, Jimmy and William would go into the family business. Their father James didn't retire until his late 70s, and it wasn't until then – in 1966, and at 50 years of age – that Jimmy took on the role of proprietor.

Born in 1916, Jimmy started cutting hair in 1930 at 14 years old, with Willy starting at the same age five years later. Castlewood Avenue was a different place then, the number 18 tram with its red triangle identifier passing the front door of the shop. The township of Rathmines existed as a separate entity to Dublin city until 1930, when it was amalgamated into the Dublin City Council area. In an interview with Rose Doyle that was published in the *Irish Times*' 16 October 2002 edition, Jimmy recalled:

> I was born upstairs eighty-six years ago, in 1916. I'm not a Dubliner though, I'm a Rathmines man. The oldest one around they say, though I'm not saying that. Dublin didn't come here, to Rathmines, until the 1930s. Rathmines Urban District Council made their own electricity until then.

The tramlines were taken up in the 1940s, but Jimmy and the shop remained unchanged. In the same manner as his father, Jimmy worked in the shop for sixty-eight years, only retiring in 1998, and passing on the mantle to the shop's current owner, Robert Feighery, who served his time in the Merchant Barbers, itself running for over half a century. Jimmy remained a regular visitor to the shop after retiring, dropping in a couple of times a week for a chat with Robbie and his customers until his death on New Year's Eve, 2010.

The shop remains largely as Jimmy left it, with a polished wood floor, benches lining two walls, two wash basins, and a large collection of historical memorabilia, including framed electricity meter reading cards dating back to the shop's opening, stamped with 'G.F. Pilditch, M.I.E.E. at the Electricity Works, Town Hall, Rathmines', as well as a picture of Jimmy and Willie with Brendan Gleeson, and various clippings about the shop from books and newspapers. Also on the wall is a large portrait of Pádraig and Willie Pearse, and a selection of Bohs newspaper clippings, including one from the day after the league win in 2001.

In the same interview with Rose Doyle quoted above, given in the shop in 2002, Jimmy said:

> Sometimes a fella comes in and says, 'You cut my hair 30 years ago.' Some are fifth-generation custom-ers, and there a number who are fourth-generation. Famous people come and go, but everyone's the same importance here. When a fella pays, and goes out the door, he's all the same!

The Waldorf stakes a brave claim that it is Dublin's oldest barbers, but I don't think it can beat that.

Dublin's First Gay-Friendly Bars

Sam McGrath

The social life of a gay man in Dublin in the early 1970s was summed up by one contributor to the 2003 book *Coming Out: Irish Gay Experiences* in this way:

> being gay in those days was a very lonely experience. There weren't many opportunities to meet gay people, unless you knew of ... Bartley Dunne's and Rice's ... there was no advertising in those days, and it was all through word of mouth.

Bartley Dunne's and Rice's proved to be critical points of social interaction and first emerged as gay-friendly pubs in the late 1950s and early 1960s. George Fullerton, who emigrated to London in 1968, was quoted in Diarmaid Ferriter's 2009 book *Occasions of Sin* as saying that, 'In 1960s Dublin the [gay] scene basically consisted of two pubs – Rice's and Bartley Dunne's.'

There are no traces left of either establishment. Rice's, at the corner of Stephen's Green and South King Street, was demolished in 1986 to make way for the Stephen's Green Shopping Centre. Bartley Dunne's, on Stephen's Street Lower beside the Mercer Hospital, was torn down in 1990 and replaced with the Break for the Border nightclub.

IN TOUCH

the newsletter of the
irish gay rights movement

CONTENTS

Front cover of *In Touch* magazine showing a group of Irish Gay Rights Movement members outside Bartley Dunne's in 1977.

Paul Candon, in the February 1996 edition of *Gay Community News*, labelled Bartley Dunne's 'the first gay pub as we know it in the city', and also referenced Rice's. He said there was a total of five regular gay-friendly bars to choose from in the 1960s in the Stephens Green/Grafton Street area. The other three were Kings, opposite the Gaiety, and the Bailey and Davy Byrnes, on Duke Street. An edition of the *Fielding's Travel Guide to Europe* from the late 1950s described 'the historic Bailey, entirely reconstructed' as being full of 'hippie types and Gay Boys'. It went on to say that neither it nor Davy Byrne's would be 'recommended for the "straight" traveller'.

Bartley Dunne's

In 1940, Hayden's pub on Stephens Street Lower was put on the market after the owner declared bankruptcy. The licence was taken over in August 1941 by Bartholomew 'Bartley' Dunne Sr. A native Irish speaker from the West of Ireland, he had returned to Dublin after nearly forty years of living and working in Manchester, where he had been a prominent member of the United Ireland League and the Gaelic League.

Bartley Sr ran the pub until his death in 1960. It was then taken over by his two sons – Bartley Jr (known as Barry) and Gerard (known as Gerry). They redecorated the place and built up its reputation for stocking exotic drinks from all over the world. Barry later recalled that 'there was a time when, if a customer wanted a particular drink and we didn't have it in stock, he got something else for free', according to the 7 September 1985 *Irish Times*.

It would seem that Bartley Dunne's (known to many as BD's), which had already been attracting Dublin's avant-garde and theatre crowd, started to become gay-friendly (by word of mouth) in the early 1960s. David Norris has written about visiting the pub as a schoolboy in his late teens circa 1961/62:

Towards the end of my schooldays I started to explore a little. I had a kindred spirit in school and we occasionally visited a city-centre bar called Bartley Dunne's, which was a notorious haunt of the homosexual demi-monde. It was an Aladdin's cave to me, its wicker-clad Chianti bottles stiff with dribbled candlewax, tea chests covered in red and white chequered cloths, heavy scarlet velvet drapes and an immense collection of multi-coloured liqueurs glinting away in their bottles.

The place was [full] of theatrical old queens, with the barmen clad in bum-freezer uniforms. While not being gay themselves, as far as I know, the Dunne brothers were quite theatrical in their own way. Barry would hand out little cards, bearing the legend 'Bartley Dunne's, reminiscent of a left bank bistro, haunt of aristocrats, poets and artists'. Whatever about that, Saturday night certainly resembled an amateur opera in full swing. There only ever seemed to be two records played over the sound system: 'Non, Je Ne Regrette Rien' by Edith Piaf, and Ray Charles' 'Take These Chains From My Heart'.

Brian Lacey, in his excellent 2008 book *Terrible Queer Creatures: a History of Homosexuality in Ireland*, noted that among the many characters who frequented the bar was the then virtually unknown Norman Scott, whose 1960s affair with Jeremy Thorpe, who was later to become the leader of the British Liberal Party, forced the latter to resign from the party in 1976.

We take it for the granted the range of drinks available in Dublin bars today, but Bartley Dunne's was really a trailblazer. It offered sake, tequila, and ouzo long before any other place in the city. A writer going by 'Endymion' in a 1968 Dublin guide book described Bartley Dunne's as the city's 'most unusual pub'. Its clientele was an 'an odd mixture of bohemians and down-to-earth Dubliners [that] creates an atmosphere which would have interested James Joyce'. It was described by Roy Bulson in 1969's *Irish Pubs of Character* as: 'one of Dublin's most unusual pubs, with its Continental atmosphere. Well worth a visit to mix with a variety of characters. Ask for the wine list which is one of the most reasonably priced and extensive in Dublin.'

Bartley Dunne's had a 'French bistro ambience', with prints on the walls by Cezanne, Monet, and Picasso, as well as Partisan theatre posters and photographs of film stars. It was also famous for its dimly lit nooks and crannies. Elizabeth Taylor and Richard Burton drank there regularly in 1965, during the filming of *The Spy Who Came in from the Cold*, as did other actors, including Kim Novak, Laurence Harvey and Noel Howard, and local characters like Brendan Behan (who seemingly drank in every pub in Dublin).

The younger Dunne brother, Gerry, passed away in 1981. Barry continued to run the place up until 1985, when the family put the pub on the market. It was bought by three Irish businessmen based in the United States. From around 1985 to its last days in 1990, the pub became the de facto headquarters for Dublin's goth, Curehead, and alternative metal scene. Drug dealing also became more open, and without the Dunne family behind the bar, things got wild.

A massive bar fight took place sometime in the late 1980s, after someone objected to a biker driving his motorbike into the pub and asking for a pint. An uncle told me it was the first pub in Dublin in which he ever saw someone shooting heroin in the toilets. A friend, Ado, has a story (as I'm sure many others have) of being served his first pint there while still in his school uniform.

The pub was sold in July 1999 for a record-breaking £1.7 million. It was knocked down and replaced by the super-pub Break for the Border.

Rice's

While Bartley Dunne's stood out as an alternative bar with an avant-garde clientele early on, Rice's was an unassuming traditional Dublin boozer. There was a pub on this site from at least the 1850s. Called the Grafton Bar (in the 1940s), the Four Provinces (mid-1950s), and Eamon Nolan's (late 1950s), it was taken over by publican Robert 'Bobby' Rice in 1960.

It seemed to have become gay-friendly from this point onwards, but only the inside of the Stephen's Green entrance. Tony O'Connell, who started visiting the place in 1965, remembers that if owner 'Bobby was on duty and a non-gay couple came into that bar he would usher them into the back lounge, lest they be contaminated'.

Ireland's most famous and accepted gay couple, Hilton Edwards and Micheál Mac Liammóir, founders of the Gate Theatre, drank in Rice's, as did actor Patrick Bedford.

Former patrons Anthony Redmond and Frank Meier wrote to the *Irish Times* in January 1986 to lament the closing and the tearing down of the pub. They described Rice's as having:

> great warmth, character and charm and there was nothing garish, brash or kitsch about its decor. If it

was a quiet drink or serious conversation you wanted, with the cacophony of raucous music, Rice's was the place to go to.

The Rice family later went on to open the Village Café in Rathmines.

*

From all accounts, the heyday of Rice's and Bartley Dunne's was in the 1960s, when they were the only shows in town, so to speak. They provided a very important early social space for gay men in the capital. Street harassment from the police or drunk revellers was almost non-existent during these years, as the gay community was still very much 'underground'.

The 1970s saw the establishment of Ireland's first gay-rights organisations and discos. The Irish Gay Rights Movement (IGRM) was founded in 1974 and Dublin's 'first proper gay disco' according to David Norris soon followed over a health-food store called Green Acres in Great Strand Street, with DJ Hugo Mac Manus. In 1979, the Hirschfeld Centre opened in Temple Bar as a gay community centre, and began running a disco on the weekend called Flikkers – see the chapter '"Fortress Fownes" and the Story of the Hirschfeld Centre' on page 74 of this book.

The Viking bar on Dame Street also opened its doors in 1979. Tony O'Connell remembers that this was an important 'stopping point on the "pilgrimage" between Rice's and Dunne's'. Other popular gay-friendly bars in the 1970s and early 1980s included the Pygmalion (now the Hairy Lemon), the South William (now Metro Café), the Parliament Inn (now the Turk's Head), the Oak on Dame

Street, the Foggy Dew on Dame Street and the Pembroke (now Matt the Thresher) on Pembroke Street.

Women-only lesbian nights were held upstairs at the weekend in JJ Smyth's on Aungier Street in the early 1980s. Davy Byrne's and the Bailey on Saturday mornings still remained popular. Dublin's longest-running gay bar, the George, opened on South Great George's Street in 1985, and so the next chapter of Dublin's gay social life began.

Rice's, and particularly Bartley Dunne's, remained popular with the gay community in the 1970s and 1980s. Though it was widely known that the two places were gay-friendly, the owners didn't seem to want to attract attention to that. In a *Sunday Independent* piece from 11 May 1975, one proprietor (later to revealed as Barry Dunne) said: 'It is known that a certain number of these people come in every now and again. Most people regard it as a bit of a laugh … This is a public house and people have certain rights.' Ten years later, when Bartley Dunne's was being sold by the family, Barry hadn't really changed his tune, telling journalist Frank McDonald in the 7 September 1985 *Irish Times* that the pub did attract a 'few who were that way inclined but it was really nothing like the rumours'.

While Bartley Dunne's and Rice's were extremely different places, some key dates overlapped. Bobby Rice took over Nolan's in 1960, the same year that the Dunne brothers took over the pub from their dad. The Dunne family sold their pub in 1985, while Rice's was demolished the following year.

A Spectre is Haunting Ballyfermot: the 1952 Co-op Scandal

Donal Fallon

The Ballyfermot Co-op of the 1950s, to quote one of its central activists, had the misfortune to 'fall foul of reaction'.

In Dublin's new suburbia, grocery co-operatives offered more than just affordable goods, providing people with inclusive local organisations and a sense of community. But in West Dublin a red-scare campaign forced the closure of one of these important local services.

The controversies around the Ballyfermot Co-op arouse from the belief it was a communist infiltration scheme, with a letter to the press denouncing its presence in the area signed by the secretaries of the local Fianna Fáil, Labour and Fine Gael branches. Much of the moral panic was whipped up by *The Standard*, a religious newspaper that didn't hold back in attacking the co-op, and even managed to evoke the name of Joseph Stalin in the process.

In his autobiography *Just Joe*, Joe Duffy recalled the power of the church in the Ballyfermot of the 1960s, and pointed back to the story of the co-op a decade earlier, writing that:

> Ballyfermot was run – in a very real sense of the word – by a big, gruff, silver-haired Kerryman, Canon

Michael Charles Troy … He was a larger-than-life country parish priest transplanted into a sprawling, uncontrollable, volatile urban area with the population of a small city. One of his first acts was to savagely quash attempts by a group of locals to open a co-op shop to bring down prices. Troy smelt a whiff of communism in the 'co-op' notion and bullied people into turning against it.

If Troy got a whiff of communism off the co-op movement in the locale, it should be noted that leftists were central to its foundation, though it became much broader.

One central figure in this story is Joseph Deasy. Born in Dublin in 1922, he was raised at The Ranch in Ballyfermot and later Goldenbridge Gardens in Inchicore. He devoted much of his life to politics, and was elected to Dublin Corporation as a Labour Party councillor in 1945, an impressive achievement at the age of 22.

It was a fellow Labour Party activist, Tim Graham, who initiated the co-operative movement in his area, and who brought Deasy into the fold. The first meeting was held in the Workman's Club on Emmet Road, which led to the establishment of a grocery shop on Grattan Crescent in Inchicore, before the opening of a larger presence on Decies Road in Ballyfermot, leased from Dublin Corporation.

Writing in the *Irish Workers' Voice* in November 1952, Deasy remembered:

In September, Ballyfermot and Inchicore witnessed one of the most scandalous and unscrupulous campaigns ever waged against a people's movement – the Inchicore-Ballyfermot Co-operative Society …

This society was founded in 1945 and was based on the democratic principles of all co-operative movements ... After a short period in existence the society purchased a small shop in Inchicore ... In 1951, through hard work and initiative, the allocation of one of the rented shops in Ballyfermot was secured from the housing committee of the Dublin Corporation. The membership had in the meantime increased considerably and reached a figure approaching 400 paid-up members, and 300 partially paid-up.

Deasy recalled that 'the Ballyfermot shop was a splendid, first-class grocery and provision store. By careful and conscientious management it was well on the high road to success and promised to be a real asset to the people of the area'.

While Deasy had been a member of the Labour Party at the time of the inauguration of the co-op, he then departed for the Irish Workers' League, a forerunner to the Communist Party of Ireland, which was frequently the subject of negative media attention from the Catholic newspaper *The Standard*. It was perhaps unsurprising when they mentioned him in a November 1952 edition, alongside more famous names:

Everybody who knows the slightest thing about communist technique knows that its first objective is contacts. What better contact, than the unsuspecting members of a co-op? It was Ballyfermot's misfortune to be selected for infiltration. How appropriate are the names of Ballyfermot? Sarsfield, Decies and Cremona? They might have been changed to Lenin, Stalin and, perhaps, Deasy Road.

In addition to being denounced in the Catholic press, the co-op was also condemned from the pulpit. The presence of members of the Irish Workers' League (IWL) on the committee of the co-op caused great concern, at a time of heightened anti-communism. Deasy remembered:

> Four of the committee of twelve, including myself, were members of the Irish Workers' League. Now it could be argued that having regard to the environment at the time we made ourselves rather vulnerable. The Cold War was heating up and a very strong anti-communist feeling prevailed. There were also several details about the nature of the attack which were personally upsetting. As a result of denunciations from the pulpit my parents couldn't go to Mass locally but had to go to church in the next parish.

Rumours spread through Ballyfermot, some of them outlandish. Deasy remembered that there was one that he 'had gone into the vestry and physically attacked Father Troy. This would have been rather unwise on my part considering the impressive physique of the man.' Troy, a former Kerry footballer, was not to be messed with.

In attempting to appease those who feared the communist influence of the co-op, the IWL members made it clear they were willing to resign from the committee of the group, but not the co-op itself. This wasn't enough for some. The members of the co-op sought outside assistance: Secretary Tim Graham met with the Civil Liberties Association, but he found them less than helpful. Deasy sought advice from the veteran socialist Peadar O'Donnell, who advised him to write to Paddy 'The Cope' Gallagher in Donegal, as he had successfully established a co-op there, but, fearful of communist association, Paddy refused to support the Ballyfermot activists.

In the pages of the national press, opponents of the co-op wrote that 'we would all like a genuine co-operative, but it is false to say that the movement arose in Ballyfermot by spontaneous desire'.

In the end, pressure on the co-op grew so great that it eventually closed, despite labouring on for a few difficult months after *The Standard*'s denunciation. Deasy would later wonder if there was more at play than anti-communism in the whole affair:

> Perhaps the whole campaign was sparked off by local shopkeepers who would have had a vested interest in preventing the progress of the co-op. The clergy did promise the people that they would start a Christian co-op based on Christian principles. This idea never materialised.

A Dublin Reimagined

Ciarán Murray

The 2016 occupation of the Moore Street terrace brought to memory previous struggles to save buildings and locations of historic interest in Dublin. The ghosts of Wood Quay and the Georgian Mile must have haunted the minds of those involved, and rightly so; a blatant disregard for public and historical interest has long been a feature of redevelopment in Dublin, with countless significant sites intentionally permitted to fall into disrepair and dereliction, and many more to disappear from our streetscape forever.

Mindful of this, it's interesting to think not only about what we've lost architecturally and historically, but about how this city might have looked had history played out a little differently. The rather ambitious plans to build the Hugh Lane Gallery across the Liffey, and the stunning landscape of Patrick Abercrombie's 1922 report 'Dublin of the Future' would feature prominently. But step back decades and indeed centuries further to some other projects, and it becomes apparent that we could be living in a very different city.

Prior to the construction of the North Wall, the East Wall, and the Great South Wall, the Liffey meandered as it liked, from source to sea. The construction of these walls, and the reclamation of land that this allowed, along with

Before the establishment of UCD in Earlsfort Terrace, there were plans afoot for a Catholic University in Clonliffe on Dublin's north side.

One of the more inventive transport schemes planned for Dublin involved a rail line running along a raised colonnade from Westland Row to Heuston Station, passing through buildings where necessary.

the construction of city quay walls, drastically changed the landscape of Dublin into something resembling what we see today. Seventeenth-century Dublin had looked very different, with the Liffey allowed to find its natural course.

Back then, Merrion Square sat considerably closer to the Liffey's muddy banks than it does today, and in 1685 it was the site for an audacious plan to replicate the Tilbury 'Citadel' Fort located on the Thames. The Dublin fort was originally planned in 1672 by 'His Majesty's Chief Engineer' Sir Bernard de Gomme to sit closer to Ringsend, but on his death, a man named 'Honest Tom' Phillips proposed a location covering large parts of Merrion Square, Mount Street, and Fitzwilliam Square.

Per Frank Hopkins' book *Hidden Dublin: Deadbeats, Dossers, and Decent Skins*, 'had it been built, the fort would have covered an area of thirty acres and would have been capable of accommodating seven hundred officers and soldiers'. The fort was to be brick-built, faced with stone, and encompass ramparts, ravelins, a curtain wall, and overhanging bastions. A prohibitive cost of over £130,000, along with the cessation of hostilities between the English and the Dutch, caused the idea to be shelved.

Merrion Square was also the site for a proposed cathedral in the 1930s. As late as 1934, Archbishop Byrne was quoted as saying, 'Merrion Square has been acquired as a site for the cathedral and on Merrion Square, please God, the cathedral will be built'. The park had been purchased from the Pembroke estate four years earlier for the sum of £100,000. Of course, the cathedral was never built on the site, and in 1974 the land was transferred to Dublin Corporation for use as a public park. The Pro Cathedral on Marlborough Street, which had been altered and extended in preparation for the Eucharistic Congress, remained the main Catholic cathedral in the city.

With the formal establishment of the Catholic University of Ireland in 1854 came a need for a site for an actual physical university. On 20 June 1862, a foundation stone was laid at Clonliffe, near Holy Cross College. The plans for what was to be known as St Patrick's University consisted of two large quadrangles, one consisting of the university and the other a residential block, Ruskinian in design and per Frederick O'Dwyer's *Lost Dublin*, 'not unlike some of the entries for the Whitehall Government Offices competition in 1857.' A contractor was employed but the project was shelved due to several constrictions on the site, and in time a Catholic university would open on Dublin's south side at Earlsfort Terrace: University College Dublin.

The Loopline Bridge has always proved a controversial, but necessary feature in Dublin's skyline. Built in 1891 with a view to improving the passage of British mail through Ireland, the main objection has generally been that the bridge spoils the views of James Gandon's Custom House. There were tentative plans in the early 1960s for the bridge's removal, alongside a major reconfiguration of Connolly Station, with some platforms moving underground. The plans never bore fruit and the bridge remains today, though largely without the advertising hoardings that adorned it throughout the twentieth century.

Long before the Loopline Bridge, and not without controversy either, there was the proposed Dublin Metropolitan Railway. In 1836, Charles Blacker Vignoles (the engineer responsible for Ireland's first railway, the Dublin and Kingstown) proposed a rail line running between Westland Row and Watling Street to link with a projected line to the south of Ireland, from what would become known as Heuston Station. Part of the projected line would run along the south quays on a raised colonnade in a style Vignoles' report called 'Grecian architecture of the Ionic order'.

The scheme called for bridges spanning D'Olier Street and Westmoreland Street, going through tunnels in south Dublin's buildings en route. The trains would: 'either be towed by horse or by ropes connected to stationary engines designed to consume their own smoke'. The report continued by saying that 'the number of houses to be actually taken down or materially injured is only thirty-seven and but few of these are of great value', and the works could 'be rendered not unsightly, but rather ornamental'. The proposal was dismissed.

However, it wasn't dismissed completely by engineer Frederick Barry, as he reinvigorated the idea in the early 1860s, alongside one to build a central train station and hotel near Eustace Street.

Negotiations for Barry's proposal were at an advanced stage and the Corporation went so far as to install a dummy bridge across Westmoreland Street purporting to show the effect a bridge would have on the area. A piece of timber is alleged to have fallen from the mock-up and killed a female pedestrian. The Dublin Metropolitan Railway was doomed and the bill shortly to be laid in front of the House of Lords in Westminster was summarily dismissed. A redoubled effort from Barry in a second bill, proposing tunnelled sections, was also dismissed.

The Civic Offices at Wood Quay need little introduction, their development having been the biggest act of cultural vandalism the city and arguably the country has ever seen. In terms of archaeological importance, the Viking site uncovered during the construction of the offices was priceless and practically unrivalled by anything found to date in Europe. An article in *History Ireland* would state: 'The remains were astonishing: complete foundations of wattle-and-daub houses; interior hearths and benches; workshops; timber pathways and boundary fences; and even latrines and rubbish pits filled with unique artefacts.'

What happened is a story every Irish person knows well. A petition that garnered 200,000 names and protest marches culminating in one 20,000 strong were ignored, and Sam Stephenson's bunker-like monstrosities stand on the site. Protests against development on the site went back as far as the 1950s, when a previous plan proposed in 1955 by Messrs. Jones and Kelly for the the new headquarters of Dublin Corporation was opposed. The disquiet regarding its construction was largely rooted in worry about the impact the building would have on one of the oldest parts of Dublin, and the effect it would have on the Christ Church vista.

The Liffey quays could have looked very different, from a railway running on a colonnade above them to a museum being built across them. Nothing compares though, to the plan to cover them altogether. On Monday 13 June 1960, a proposal from Cllr Frank Sherwin went before Dublin Corporation that was designed to alleviate the city's traffic and parking chaos. This included plans to culvert part of the Liffey and roof it in from Grattan Bridge to Butt Bridge, in order to provide space for parking for a thousand cars. This gained very little support, with both the city planning officer and the city engineer coming out against it on the grounds that it would increase the danger of flooding, and would cost more than a multi-storey car park. The planning officer is quoted in several press sources as saying that he

> felt that the river was one of the dominant charac-
> teristics of the city and, as for a proposal to extend
> platforms from quay walls supported by piles, this,
> he said, would convert the river into a sort of a canal,
> with dark gloomy recesses, festooned with seaweed.

Thankfully, in this instance, some sanity of some sort pre-vailed.

Interview with Paul Cleary
of The Blades

Sam McGrath

When I spoke to a healthy Philip Chevron (The Radiators/ The Pogues) in April 2012, I asked him about Paul Cleary and The Blades, and he replied with genuine warmth:

> I very much admired Paul Cleary. He appears to have retired from Irish music, which is a huge loss, but I don't blame him. I know how difficult it is. I have the utmost admiration for him and the band.

It's hard to believe that just over 18 months later, Philip lost his battle with cancer at the age of 56. And Paul emerged from perceived retirement to play with The Blades on stage for the first time in decades.

Philip invited Paul to play at his self-described 'testimonial' in the Olympia Theatre in August 2013. That night was summed up perfectly by musician and journalist Eamon Carr, when he wrote: 'The audience agreed on two things. One: the spirit of Philip Chevron would live forever. Two: Paul Cleary had stepped out of some ghost estate of the heart to save Ireland in a time of crisis.'

Illustration of Paul Cleary by artist Mice Hell
(riggerthumbs.wordpress.com).

Dubliners Paul and Phil had the rare ability to write
both fantastic love songs and hard-hitting political
anthems. Born just a couple of years apart, the explosion
of punk changed both their lives. Philip formed The

Radiators from Space at the dawn of punk in 1976, while Paul had to wait until 1977 to form The Blades. Both bands received widespread critical acclaim, but found little financial success.

Their song-writing styles were very different. Philip was strongly influenced by the theatre, the literature of James Joyce, and cabaret stars like Agnes Bernelle. Paul's Dublin was closer to that of James Plunkett and Sean O'Casey. It was kitchen-sink realism with a Dublin twist.

So Philip Chevron wrote 'Song of the Faithful Departed' (1979):

We'll even climb the Pillar like you always meant to,
Watch the sun rise over the Strand.
Close your eyes and we'll pretend,
It could somehow be the same again.
I'll bury you upright so the sun doesn't blind you.
You won't have to gaze at the rain and the stars.
Sleep and dream of chapels and bars,
And whiskey in the jar.

And Paul wrote of a city torn apart by unemployment and monotony in 'Downmarket' (1983):

On a rainy afternoon
On a gambling machine
Same old jukebox, same old tune:
It's hard to break this old routine
Everything's black and white and grey
Living from day to day to day
It's a fatal resignation, when there's nothing left to hope for

In a hopeless situation
I'm not waiting at an airport
I'm not waiting at a station
I'm standing at a bus stop

In November 2013, I spoke to Paul on a number of topics and this is an edited extract:

I heard you were quite a decent player in your younger days?
I played seriously until I was about 14 or 15. I was good enough to play for Dublin schoolboys. A scout from Man United came down to my parents and they were going to send me over for a trial but a few weeks before I was supposed to go over, I pulled a ligament in my ankle.

And you were a Shamrock Rovers fan from day one?
Yep, my dad used to bring me to Milltown as a kid. We'd walk up from Ringsend most times. Though sometimes we'd get the 'football' double-decker bus from town. We'd go home after the match and listen to Brendan O'Reilly reading the sports results. Then from around the age of 14 or so, I started going with a gang of mates.

Did music become your next passion after football or was there a bit of an overlap?
There was an overlap. My dad was really into music. He had a very eclectic taste. He was into classical, jazz, and pop. One day he went out to get a [Felix] Mendelssohn album, but came back with Bad Company's *Run With the Pack* [1976]. He also had all the Beatles albums plus Buddy Holly, Bill Haley and other rock 'n' roll stuff too.

Did you start buying your own records then at around that time?
Yeah, from the early 1970s onwards. Cat Stevens, Elton
John, Paul Simon, James Taylor. Maybe a bit of Slade and
T-Rex. It seems the opposite of punk, but this was all pre-
punk. Punk blew all that out of the window. I used to visit
a place on Tara Street called The Banba. Albums were £2.40
and singles were 50p!

Can you remember how you heard of the whole punk explosion?
It would have been through reading about it in *NME*, I suppose. Reviews of the Sex Pistols and the like. I remember
one reviewer said something along the lines of – 'This is not
rock 'n' Roll, it's more important than that.' It just sounded
great to me and I loved the name the Sex Pistols. Rock music
had become very stagnant and stale by that stage. All that
prog-rock rubbish.

Were you going to many gigs at this point?
Yeah, well then me and my brother started going out to see
bands. We had to see the Irish equivalent of what we'd been
reading about in *NME* and *Sounds*. We saw a few bands, and
I won't name them because that would be unfair, but they
weren't that good.
But then we saw The Vipers one Saturday afternoon in
McGonagle's on South Anne Street. The first thing that
struck me was that there was a queue outside the door. Now,
I'm not nationalistic at all, but I remember thinking 'this is a
queue of local people to see a local band and this can only be
a good thing'. They were very good. They wrote pop songs
with energy and they didn't look like middle-class tossers
in it for only a laugh. They looked like genuine people into
their music. I remember turning to my brother Lar and

saying, 'We can do this too.' At the time, The Vipers were the benchmark for us.

Were bands like The Boomtown Rats and The Radiators from Space in your orbit?
Not really, they'd moved to London about the time I started going to gigs. The other lads in the band went to see the Rats in Moran's Hotel at one of their last gigs before they left, but I didn't make it. They said they were a good rhythm-and-blues band.

Dr Feelgood-esque?
Yep, exactly. I really liked Dr Feelgood. In a way, they helped pave the way for the whole punk thing.

One of your first big gigs was supporting them and The Specials in the Olympic Ballroom in November 1979?
It would have been, yep. Wilko Johnson wasn't playing with them at that stage. I think The Specials were booked for that gig well in advance, before they had really broke. So when the gig came around, they were the bigger band. So in a way Dr Feelgood were relegated to second. The Specials blew me away that night. I learnt a lot from them at that gig. I remember watching The Specials and taking note of how they worked the crowd.

How did the legendary Magnet gigs come about?
We started playing The Magnet on Tuesday nights. It was mainly known as a cabaret venue at the time. Maybe Boppin' Billy was doing the rockabilly nights at that stage, but it definitely wasn't a place to see punk bands. It was only up the road from us anyway, so people starting associating The

Blades with The Magnet. It was a real small, sweaty place and I don't think we ever played a bad gig there.

In terms of your diehard mod and scooter-boys support, did you ever feel that that fan base could hold you back in terms of acquiring wider success?
I didn't mind it at all. Sometimes we may even have cultivated it a bit! I always liked the mod gear myself. I'm not stylish enough to be one myself, but I always loved Northern soul and Motown. I never shoehorned The Blades into a specific mod category, but I'm happy enough to be considered part of the wider mod family.

How did you first become politically aware?
It was just my background really. Seeing how life was unfair in terms of access to opportunities. How society and how politics was run in general. I would have started having political arguments when I was 15 or 16. All the bullshit from big business and the Fine Gaels and Fianna Fáils of the country. Even the PDs saying that they would be good for the general society when they were only really interested in helping their own kind of people – people they went to Clongowes with or whatever.

Have your politics shifted over time?
I probably wouldn't be as edgy or spiky as I was then, but I still hold most of those political ideals. I'd still be voting hard left.

It seems that your political songs are more relevant today than at any time since the early 1980s, has the irony been lost on you?
No, it hasn't at all. It's sad in many ways. We haven't really moved on that much, even if some people thought we had.

During the Celtic Tiger years, there was some who promoted the notion that 'We're all middle class now.' There was a lot of 'Pull the ladder up, we've made it here.' It was just an illusion though. It seems today that things are more anti-collective-bargaining, anti-trade-unionism etc. It's still a very right-wing country. That's the political culture we have here. Some of it has to do with the Catholic Church. Fianna Fáil and Fine Gael and other parties have been pulling the wool over our eyes for so long. We haven't built up that culture of left-wing politics yet. We have a culture of anti-imperialism, but that hasn't really translated into anything else.

Did republican politics ever interest you?
Not narrow-minded nationalism. I know Sinn Féin talk a lot about socialist issues, but to me they're still a nationalist party. For me, nationalism and socialism don't mix. Nationalism is all based on the bit of land you were born on. I don't believe somebody is any better if they were born in Dublin or in Manchester.

In 'Talk About Listening', you describe the warehouse worker toiling away all week for one night on the town on the weekend. Very few bands in Dublin in the early 1980s were writing about similar genuine day-to-day experiences.
The song is a bit arty in a way in its construct. There's very few lines, it's very minimal. Almost Beckettian without sounding pretentious. It indicates someone's state of mind in a job like that. As the song is based in a warehouse, it's bleak, so there's not six or seven verses. It's not the blue-collar stuff of Bruce Springsteen. It's not all doom and gloom, but working-class life can be very bleak. It lacks hope. It

lacks a future. They're the real things. There was a horrible politician in the 1980s who said that they could live on X amount a week out in Ballymun. Of course she could. She could do it for six months, but the fact is that once you know that you can step out of that environment, it's easy to do. The whole thing about being poor or not having a job is the feeling that it's always going to be like that. It's not that you can only afford a small pan loaf of bread. It's the fact that you can only afford a small pan loaf of bread every day for the rest of your life.

'Fortress Fownes' and the Story of the Hirschfeld Centre

Donal Fallon

On 6 May 1933, Adolf Hitler's Brownshirts made their way into the Institute for Sexual Studies in Berlin and seized thousands of books and publications they deemed immoral. At the same time, bookshops and lending libraries were raided across the city, denounced as 'literary bordellos' by ignorant thugs. Thankfully, the founder of the institute, Dr Magnus Hirschfeld, was on a speaking tour of the United States. A witness at the institute described how for three hours the raiders:

> emptied inkwells onto carpets and broke, or vandalised, framed paintings and prints ... They confiscated books, periodicals, photographs, anatomical models, a famous wall tapestry, and a bust of Hirschfeld. After music, speeches and songs outside at noon they departed but were succeeded at 3pm by SA men, who removed 10,000 books form the institute's library. A few days later they carried the bust of Hirschfeld on a pole in a torchlight parade before throwing it on the bonfire with the books from the institute.

Flikkers Disco

Fri./Sat.	10.30 p.m. to 2 a.m.
buddys night **Sun.**	9.30 p.m. to 1 a.m.
reduced rates **Wed.**	10.00 p.m. to 1 a.m.

Flikkers Disco Hirschfeld Centre
10 Fownes St.. Dublin 2. Tel. 710939
admission & membership reserved

From Brand New Retro exhibition at the Little Museum of Dublin.

A memorial plaque in Berlin's Tiergarten today remembers the raided institute.

Unsurprisingly, Hirschfeld would never return to Germany. A Jewish sexologist stood little chance in Nazi

Germany, and Hirschfeld lived out his final days in France. On 14 May 1935 he turned 67 and died of a heart attack in Nice. Once dubbed the 'Einstein of sex', he was just one of many intellectual leaders who suffered at the hands of fascism.

Hirschfeld came to be honoured by LGBT activists all over the world, including here in Dublin. At the Little Museum of Dublin, the bronze sign from the front of the Hirschfeld Centre in Temple Bar is today on display to the public. This institution, which opened its doors in March 1979, retains a special place in the gay history of Dublin. For many, seeing the sign in a museum context is a reminder of a different time entirely, both for Dublin and the Irish gay community.

Temple Bar in 1979

Writing in 1979, an English journalist said of the Irish capital: 'Suddenly, Dublin has become a shabby city – shabby because its centre is peppered with crude concrete structures, flashy mirror-glass facades and other inappropriate schemes which have no connection at all with the spirit of the place.'

There was a certain air of 'rip it down and start again', which was nowhere more evident than in Temple Bar. Once a district synonymous with manufacturing and production, the wheels of industry had largely ceased turning there by the late 1970s, and urban decay was setting in. In 1977, there was a massive proposal to develop a new central bus station in Temple Bar and link that with a tunnel under the River Liffey to a complementary development on Ormond Quay, and also to incorporate the Dart rail system into the project. This would have spelled the end of Temple Bar as Dubliners knew it.

The CIE bus company began buying up huge chunks of property in the area, planning eventually to demolish the structures that stood there, but in the meantime making them available on short-term leases. Geographer Paul Knox has written:

> Paradoxically, this triggered a process of revitalization. Activities which could afford only low rents on short leases moved into the district. These included artists' studios, galleries, recording and rehearsal studies, pubs and cafes, second-hand clothes shops, small boutiques, bookshops and record stores, as well as a number of voluntary organisations. Together with the district's architectural character, the youth culture attracted by the district's new commercial tenants brought a neo-bohemian atmosphere to Temple Bar.

Temple Bar was a district in transition, which it seemed was up for grabs. It was in this changing neighbourhood that the Hirschfield Centre was founded. When interviewed by James Redmond for his documentary on the early days of rave and dance music in Dublin, LGBT activist and archivist Tonie Walsh made the point that:

> It was on Fownes Street because it was so derelict. It made an ideal place for a gay community centre at a time when homophobia was endemic. It was important to get somewhere that wasn't too in the public eye, that was a little bit discreet. Because of course you had to run the gamut of gay bashers, or people wanting to torch the place. I mean there were grills on it. A

poet friend of mine from Finglas, John Grundy, used to refer to it as 'Fortress Fownes'. It looked like it was totally grilled. Barricaded.

A New Social Centre
The driving force behind the centre was the National Gay Federation, which is today the National LGBT Federation. The centre housed 'meeting spaces, a youth group, a café, a small cinema and film club and it ran discos at the weekend where gay men, lesbian women and transgender people socialised'.

In the years before this, it had become clear that such a premises was needed. In October 1975, more than 300 people had attended the opening night of the Phoenix Club, the headquarters of the Irish Gay Rights Movement (IGRM), at 46 Parnell Square, which proved the 'massive need for a dedicated queer social space in Dublin city.' Following on from the Phoenix, something bigger was needed.

The plaque on the new Temple Bar premises was unveiled by Dr Noel Browne, a TD who had bravely raised the issue of gay rights inside Leinster House in 1977, and who had clashed with conservatives forces in the past, most famously during the Mother and Child Scheme controversy. On the day of the unveiling of the plaque, a speech heralded the centre as 'living proof of gay people's newfound pride … testimony to the fact that [we] the gay citizens of Ireland need no longer fear to be openly ourselves'. The *Irish Times* reported that:

> The four-storey building was once a warehouse, but has been renovated and equipped with fire escapes

and firefighting equipment as well as with more 'fun' items like the massive disco speakers and imported record collection straight from New York's most up-to-date record shop, and the brown wood-slatted cafeteria selling Bewley's coffee. The cinema is already fully functioning.

It was reported that 'NGF members will be able to get pink plastic triangles from the centre to wear on their lapels as a sign of membership'. In explaining this, David Norris told the press that 'Gays were the first to be interned in Nazi camps and also the first to be medically experimented on. And though half a million gays perished in the camps, both German republics have consistently refused to compensate or even commemorate the fact.'

Norris invested heavily in the new centre. Indeed, the *Irish Times* reported that it had been 'very largely funded by David Norris ... with money from selling his home in Greystones, Co. Wicklow, and he is resigned to the fact that he may not get his investment back again'. Could anyone have predicted the immediate successes of the centre? In a country where homosexuality was still illegal, hundreds came through its doors on the first night alone. David Norris recalled that:

The first night the Hirschfeld Centre opened there were three or four hundred people in the place, and when I went to check downstairs I could hear the floorboards were bouncing. A member who was also a structural engineer approached to say it could be dangerous, so I had the music switched off. I addressed the throng and told them they could have a refund, or they could stay and chat to their friends and the coffee bar was free for the night, but there would be no more dancing that evening. I was booed and hissed at before one guy stood up and said 'Hold on a minute, isn't it just as well there is someone who does give a shit about our safety?' and the boos turned into cheers!

By the mid-1980s, there was a belief that Temple Bar had been rescued, and that life had been 'brought back due to cheap short-term leases for shops and cafes'. The Hirschfeld was seen by many as an important part of this transformation, and in particular its nightclub component Flikkers. The name was taken from Dutch slang for 'faggot'. To the *Times*, it was 'one of the liveliest and musically up-to-date [clubs] in town. Records are imported directly from London and, as a rule, are played months before they hit the radio and charts.' DJ Paul Webb remembered it being an entire new world:

> It was brilliant. How do you explain it? It was like being reborn – when you are going out clubbing and you don't want the same twenty clubs up on Leeson or Harcourt St all playing the same twenty songs … You could experiment there. I used to play 12-inch instrumentals of James Brown with people doing speeches or raps over it.

One journalist who was sent to investigate felt compelled to write that:

> Though homosexuals have a reputation for voracious sexual appetite, there is little evidence of it here. In seating to one side of the room, two men were kissing … It is a surprisingly young crowd, most of whom

appear to be in their early 20s. Most have business-men's haircuts and wear moderately casual clothes. A few conform to the traditional image of gays, floridly dressed, wearing necklaces and earrings and with their faces painted with lipstick and eye shadow.

Sinister forces worked against the centre. On a November night in 1985, Norris climbed onto the roof of the premises to discover 'the asphalt-coated felt was on fire, and there was a milk churn full of explosives sitting there, surrounded by firelighters and two barrels of petrol. It was as if the whole roof was a giant petrol bomb, just waiting to explode.'

Two years later, the premises was gutted by a fire that the National LGBT Federation history notes was 'presumed to be accidental', although others maintain it was arson. In the years that followed the fire, Norris and other campaigners sought National Lottery funding to reopen the Hirschfeld Centre, but were blocked time and again. Gay Health Action, Tel-A-Friend, Liberation for Irish Lesbians, and other organisations lost much with the destruction of the premises, though thankfully some important artefacts survived. The legendary decks of the Flikkers nightclub made it through the fire, and despite some damage, are still in working order.

In the true spirit of the man after whom it was named, the centre had begun the important task of correlating and collecting items relating to the history of the LGBT community in Ireland. Today, Tonie Walsh maintains the Irish Queer Archive, a treasure trove housed in the National Library of Ireland, which continues that work. While the original plaque is today in the Little Museum, perhaps it is time a plaque was added on Fownes Street, marking this important location in the history of Dublin and LGBT rights.

Daniel O'Connell's Last Duel

Ciarán Murray

It may come as a surprise to some, but Daniel O'Connell, who in his political life deplored the use of violence, took part in and won a duel in Bishopscourt, Co. Kildare, in 1815. His opponent was an experienced duellist by the name of John D'Esterre and it was widely expected that O'Connell would lose. D'Esterre, a former royal marine, was a crack shot: it was said he could snuff out a candle from nine yards with a pistol shot. It wasn't O'Connell's first potential duel, having challenged an opponent in court to a duel only two years previous, though on that occasion he backed down at the last minute and the duel did not take place.

The cause of the duel was a political speech made by O'Connell to the Catholic Board on 22 January 1815, in which he described the Ascendancy-managed Dublin Corporation as beggarly. D'Esterre, a member of the Corporation and at the time nearing bankruptcy, took this as a personal insult and sent O'Connell a letter demanding its withdrawal. When this letter went unanswered, he sent a second letter, to which O'Connell responded, asking D'Esterre why, if he wanted to challenge him, he hadn't yet done so. D'Esterre set out to provoke O'Connell into a challenge, and at one stage ventured out onto the streets of Dublin looking for him, horsewhip in hand, only to be forced into seeking refuge in a sympathetic home, such was the crowd that began to follow him around.

Days passed, the bubbling tension between the two became the talk of the town, finally D'Esterre laid down a challenge, and a letter sent to O'Connell's second. Jimmy Wren's *Crinan – Dublin: a History of 13 North Inner City Streets* names Sir Edward Stanley of 9 North Cumberland Street as D'Esterre's second, and an *Irish Press* article from 1965 names Major MacNamara, a Protestant from Clare, as O'Connell's.

The duel was to take place on Lord Ponsonby's demesne at Bishopscourt on the afternoon of the challenge, and the weapons of choice were pistols provided by a man named Dick Bennett. Both pistols had notches on their butts, denoting kills. The parties were limited to one shot each, leading Stanley to retort 'five and twenty shots will not suffice unless O'Connell apologises!' A light snow fell as a crowd gathered and the men took their places. D'Esterre shot first, but fired too low and missed. O'Connell returned fire, hitting D'Esterre in the groin, the bullet lodging in the base of his spine. D'Esterre fell, and the crowd roared. As much of a crack shot as D'Esterre was, O'Connell was a better one, having trained for such an eventuality.

As they made their way back to Dublin, the news spread before them and the route home was lined with blazing bonfires. Although O'Connell boasted that he could have placed his shot wherever he wanted, he did not intend to kill D'Esterre, and was shaken to find two days later that the man had bled to death. Bailiffs almost immediately moved in and seized everything of value from D'Esterre's home.

Saddened by the outcome, O'Connell offered half his income to D'Esterre's family, but the offer was all but refused. Only an allowance for his daughter was accepted, which was paid regularly until O'Connell's death more than thirty years later. He would never duel again and, while attending church or passing D'Esterre's widow's door, often wore a glove on, or wrapped a handkerchief around, the hand that had fired the fatal shot.

The Four Corners of Hell: a Junction with Four Pubs in the Liberties

Sam McGrath

The Four Corners of Hell was the colloquial name given to the junction where New Street, Patrick Street, Kevin Street and Dean Street meet in the Liberties, Dublin 8.

In the shadow of St Patrick's Cathedral, this crossroads was infamous for having a public house on each corner, and the immediate area, after closing time, was legendary for its rowdy crowds and punch ups. Revellers from rival neighbourhoods or families would pour out onto the streets when the pubs shut and would settle old scores and new disputes with their fists. Famed local cop Lugs Brannigan and his men, based out of nearby Kevin Street Garda station, would often have their work cut out for them. Its heyday was from the 1950s to the early 1980s.

The crossroads is almost unrecognisable today, due to the demolition and road-widening that occurred in the 1980s, but let us remember the four pubs: Kenny's, Quinn's, O'Beirne's, and Lowe's.

Liam Kenny's was on the corner of 49 Patrick Street and 9 Dean Street. In the 1920s, it was run by an F. Martin, and was known as Martin's Corner. In February 1921, he was robbed at gunpoint by a man who made off with £10.

Illustration of the so-called Four Corners of Hell, Dublin.

In August of 1948, late one night, two local men produced a pistol, forced themselves into the bar, asked for a dozen stouts and whiskeys and then shot and broke a bottle of wine and a mirror, according to the 12 January 1949 *Irish Times*.

Christopher Dunne (32) and Laurence Tierney (26), both of New Street, were found guilty of being in a possession of a firearm without a certificate. Dunne was sentenced to six months of hard labour, while Tierney was given a suspended sentence of nine months. (Dunne was the father of career criminal Christy 'Bronco' Dunne Jr, who, along with his brothers, played a key role in the flooding of heroin into Dublin in the late 1970s and the 1980s.)

Publican Joseph Cody took over the premises around 1950. He had previously run a pub on Braithwaite Street, in the nearby inner-city area of Pimlico. In October 1949, he'd been fined £12 for having opened his pub during prohibited hours on the previous 10 April (Good Friday); twelve men had been found on the premises by police. On 3 January 1951, by then living in Dean Street, Cody was fined £1 for allowing two women to drink in his bar after closing time.

On 21 November 1953, William Jackson (24) of Dowker's Lane, off Lower Clanbrassil Street, was sentenced to nine months' imprisonment for having stolen £7 from a cash box in Cody's pub. Two others, Patrick Dandy (24) of Oliver Bond House and Thomas Claffey of Cashel Avenue, Crumlin, were sentenced to 12 months' imprisonment each.

On 14 September 1954, John Kelly (40), with an address on Cork Street, was sentenced to four months' imprisonment for assaulting Joseph Cody. The publican was shoved down the stairs, kicked repeatedly, and received two black eyes in the attack.

It was reported in the *Irish Times* on 9 August 1955 that Mrs Breda Cody, landlord Joseph's wife, was brought before the district court to 'answer a complaint that she had taken a widow's pension order book in exchange … for intoxicating liquor … and had failed to return it'. She was bound to be of good behaviour for two years. Her husband was fined 10 shillings for opening his premises on the Good Friday on which the incident had occurred.

The family was going through a difficult patch, Mr Cody said:

> they were unable to make ends meet … [and] unable to pay a mortgage on the premises … They had not even

a home now and were allowed by the purchaser of the premises to leave their furniture temporarily in them.

Liam Kenny took over the premises around 1963, and it was known as Kenny's thereafter.

In the mid-1980s, a large area of Patrick Street and Dean Street was taken over and demolished by the corporation, using compulsory purchase order. Patrick Street was widened, and after years of stalled building work and planning objections, the seven-storey apartment block Dean Court, comprised of 200 apartments in eight blocks, was put on the market in 1994. The shopfront where Kenny's once stood was a Chartbusters video-rental shop, and is currently a 99 cent discount newsagent.

Quinn's was situated at the corner of 50 Patrick Street and 31/31a Upper Kevin Street. This pub had previously been known as P. Kenna's, Kiernan's (mid-1900s to 1920s), Cahill's (1930s), Brannigan's (mid-1940s), and Hamilton's (late 1940s). It was taken over by John Quinn and his brother James around 1950.

In December 1952, Thomas Lane (21) from Oliver Bond House was charged with breaking into the pub, stealing liquor and then assaulting a garda. He was sentenced to two months in jail. In the late 1950s, the Unemployed Protest Committee used 50 Patrick Street as its contact address.

It was reported in the *Irish Press* on 9 November 1960 that four young men had been charged with assaulting publican John Quinn and his brother James on the night of 23 September. They also smashed a plate-glass window. The four individuals, all from Crumlin, were William Travers (21), 306 Cashel Road; William Doran (22), 38 Durrow Road; William Kinselle (22), 39 Durrow Road and Henry

Hickey (18), 27 Windmill Park. The trouble started when the men tried to bring their bottles and glasses downstairs from the lounge. When Quinn tried to stop them, they set upon him.

John Quinn passed away in April 1965. The pub was later taken over by Patrick Nash. At some stage, the building was knocked down and a one-storey Nash's replaced it. I've heard from two sources that in 'Dublin wit', you could finish a relationship by telling your boy/girlfriend that you'd meet them upstairs at Nash's. As the story goes, the jilted lover would turn up to the one-storey pub and realise the game was up.

The premises was demolished and replaced by a modern bar (retaining the name Nash's) with apartments upstairs. Pat Stacey, reviewing the pub in the *Irish Independent* on 10 July 2001, described its decor as 'simple and comforting – a mixture of stone walls and wood furniture'. The clientele was made up of 'a bedrock of locals, drawn from the four corners of the junction ... [and] a light sprinkling of passers-by and tourists'. This reincarnation of Nash's closed down a couple of years ago, and the premises is still empty.

O'Beirne's was on the corner of 30 Upper Kevin Street and 1 New Street. At the turn of the twentieth century, the pub was owned by Alderman John Davin. From 1905 to 1935, it was known as the Premier House and was run by Daniel Lynch. Following a brief period when it was under the direction of Christopher Casey, the pub was managed by Francis Moran from the late 1930s until 1947. That year, Desmond 'Dessie' O'Beirne from Sandymount, Dublin 4, bought it for £8,000. The pub was demolished circa 1980, along with many parts of Upper Kevin Street/New Street, to make way for road-widening and the new crossroads.

Lowe's was at the corner of 7 Dean Street and 57 New Street. Previous owners had included James Vaughan (1897–1917), James Madigan (1917–23), and Joseph Dunne (1924–55). It was taken over by William Lowe in the mid-1950s, and it closed in 1989. It was demolished and replaced by apartments, while other houses on Dean Street, one of the city's smallest streets, remain standing.

*

Journalist Frank McDonald, disturbed about the plans for widespread destruction in the area, wrote in the *Irish Times* on 13 Nov 1979 that:

> Patrick Street will soon become a major highway as soon as all the buildings opposite St Patrick's Cathedral are knocked down. The corner of Patrick Street, Kevin Street and New Street will be transformed into a major traffic interchange, although the gents' toilets, surrounded by oak trees, is to be preserved because of its 'outstanding civic design character'. But there's doubts that it will look somewhat incongruous in its new surroundings.

On 13 May 1985, McDonald wrote in the *Irish Times* that the corporation's work in the mid-1980s was completely devastating Patrick Street:

> with the street left pock-marked for years by derelict sites, scrapyards and half-demolished buildings. But for the Iveagh Trust flats, St Patrick's Park and the cathedral, Patrick Street would have been lost. Three

local pubs which have long served as neighbourhood centres will go, never to be replaced. New Street and Clanbrassil Street will lose a total of five pubs.

While the Liberties is still a thriving, bustling and exciting neighborhood, the development of this particular crossroads, and the related destruction, had a huge negative impact on the area's community spirit. It turned a community intersection of pubs, shops and life into a soulless traffic junction.

John 'Spike' McCormack

Ciarán Murray

Within sight of O'Connell Street, on the wall of an innocuous red-brick house, there is a plaque that reads: 'A tribute to the champion boxers and the people of the Sean McDermott Lr. Gardiner Street area 1930–1940.' The house sits on the corner of the aptly named Champions Avenue, the street taking its name from the several boxing champions the area produced throughout the 1930s and 1940s. Gardiner Street and Sean McDermott Street spawned a good many talented fighters, Paddy Hughes, Peter Glennon, Mickey Gifford, and Mylie Doyle among them. But arguably the most famous was John 'Spike' McCormack.

Though Spike would become synonymous with the north inner city, he was born in Listowel, Co. Kerry, in 1919. The McCormack family moved to Dublin when he was 8, and Spike would take up boxing soon after that, fighting amateur by the early 1930s. In 1939, along with Peter Glennon and Mickey Gifford, he went to America with the Irish amateur boxing team to fight against the Chicago Golden Gloves amateur champions in Soldier Field. The trio returned home as victors, with the Irish team matching their hosts, claiming five fights apiece.

Either side of his trip to the US, Spike had enlisted in the British Army, and his strength and physical fitness led

Champions Avenue, named for the champion boxers and the people of the surrounding area, 1930-1940. (Photograph by Ciarán Murray)

Spike in a press image circulated at the height of his career. Spike's legacy is such that he is still spoken of in high regard by all who remember him.

him to become a commando. It was his sense of adventure that led him to join the British Army rather than the Irish one, his son John 'Young Spike' McCormack remembering him saying, 'Hitler took Poland by storm and Ireland by telephone.' Initially stationed in Scotland, he boxed there and was highly thought of, even receiving an offer from a promoter to buy him out of his service. Once, while there, according to friend Frank Hopkins, 'the night before St. Patrick's Day in Kilmarnock, he painted a statue of King Billy green to aggravate the town's Orangemen'.

In 1943 during his second spell with the army, an expeditionary raid down the French coast ended in a short but brutal clash, and Spike sustained an injury to his thigh from a grenade blast. He returned to Ireland and, while recuperating in the Mater Hospital, was approached to fight Jimmy Ingle in what was to be the latter's last amateur fight. Feeling the injury he was carrying, Spike went down in the third round, exhausted. Kevin Kearns' *Dublin Voices: an Oral Folk History* quotes Young Spike as saying:

> They took off his shorts and saw this big hole in his side and they said 'Jesus Christ, he shouldn't have been able to stand. So Jimmy Ingle turned professional but my father said 'I'll get him back when I'm good.' So my father turned professional – just to get back at Jimmy Ingle.

The fight sent Spike straight back to hospital and he underwent surgery the following day. Following an extended recovery, he undertook heavy training and it was after that that he turned professional. His first fight was a victory against Jack Sean Clancy, in a bout held in Dalymount Park. His second fight ended in a loss to Northern title holder Tommy Armour. His third fight gave him the opportunity to make good on his promise – he went the distance with Jimmy Ingle in a fiercely combative contest, and won on points.

The men would fight each other a further four times in the space of three years, twice for the Irish middleweight title. Spike would win both of these fights, before fighting to a draw in a bout in Dalymount in June 1946, and losing to Ingle in May 1947 in Tolka Park. A lack of opponents at middleweight eventually led McCormack to step up to light-heavyweight where, despite his stature – he was 5 foot 8 – he excelled, several times beating larger, heavier fighters.

Though greatly respected for his ability in the ring throughout his career (and long afterwards) his fame was not solely confined to it. For, as good a boxer as he was in the ring, his prowess as a brawler in the streets drew huge crowds whenever (and it was often) someone decided to chance their luck against him. He had an ongoing feud with the local Corbally family that went back to his and their parents' time, and pubs would empty to see him take on the sons of the family. He was easily provoked, especially when he was drinking whiskey (something he admitted), and this was a trait that was taken advantage of – sometimes due to sheer begrudgery, often for the entertainment of others in whatever bar he was drinking in (generally Killane's on Gardiner Street, where he would count Behan as one of his accomplices), and on occasion for more sinister reasons.

The local Gardiner Street 'Animal Gang' would count Spike as one of their number when muscle was required, and were known to rile him up and point him in the direction of trouble. He took part in what would become known as the 'Battle of Baldoyle', which took place on 14

May 1942 and was ostensibly sparked by a dispute between Northside and Southside bookmakers over the hedging of a bet. The bookmakers acquired the services of their respective gangs, and a large set-to occurred at Baldoyle Racecourse. An account in Kevin Kearns' *Dublin Tenement Life* speaks of Spike being the Gardiner Street gang's prime weapon in a melee that involved 'knives, walking sticks, bits of lead pipe, knuckle dusters, a French bayonet'. The fight saw two people stabbed and resulted in several people being jailed.

Despite frequently being on the wrong side of the law, Spike struck up an unlikely friendship with Garda Jim 'Lugs' Branigan. The men had great respect for one another, and Branigan when dealing with Spike's street fighting, would warn his colleagues to stay out of the way of his fists, and come at him from behind, in numbers. Those who ignored his advice would end up on their backs.

As well as being a champion boxer, Spike was a deep-sea sailor for almost twenty years – his family (six boys and eight girls) receiving a retainer from Irish Shipping when he was away at sea. And although the retainer guaranteed that money would come into the household when he was gone, his wages on his return did not. Young Spike, in *Dublin Voices*, would say:

> When my father used to come home he'd get all his money and bring it up to the fellas that was maybe laid off the ship and he'd buy them food for their children ... So consequently he became like a Robin Hood ... And when father got drink on him he'd go home at night and all the kids used to be around him and he'd take out handfuls of pennies and ha'pennies and throw them money ... And when he'd reach Sean McDermott Street he'd reach into his pocket and throw all the

money ... My mother used to say to me 'Go down and get the money, pick up as many crowns and half-crowns as you can and let him give the kids pennies.'

The same book also mentions an interesting episode involving Spike being sent onto a ship being brought out to sea by scab labour while the union was on strike. Spike, reluctant to board the ship because of his disdain for the scabs, was asked to do so by the union in an attempt to take it back. When the captain of the ship abandoned it to the scabs and locked himself in his room:

My father worked as a greaser in the engine room and he went up – and this is history – on the deck with a big fire hatchet and he says, 'There's no way you're taking over this ship, cause you're scabbies and I won't have that' ... Oh, he went amuck on the ship with the hatchet.

Spike's sons would follow him into the ring: Young Spike was British light-heavyweight champion 1967–69, and Pat was light-welterweight champion in 1974. Spike died in 1986, at the age of 66, in his own words 'an old gunfighter'. Young Spike said of his father's funeral:

They all said 'he was a great friend, your father' ... 'When your father walked into a room, he lit it up.' He had this Kerryman's way of lighting up a room and he knew everyone. Older people still say today, 'oh you're Spike's son' ... Young Spike. I loved my father.

While he made the streets of Dublin his own, it was said that Spike was the only man who could stand on Hill 16 and shout for Kerry. Who was going to try and stop him?

De Valera and the 'Indian Priest'

Donal Fallon

The Eucharistic Congress of 1932 brought hundreds of thousands of people onto the streets of Dublin, but one man certainly stood out from the pack. Father Philip B. Gordon, known as 'the Indian Priest', was only the second Native American Catholic priest ordained in the United States. Gordon was a champion for the rights of Native Americans, and clashed with the bigoted KKK on more than one occasion in the 1920s. Newspapers in Dublin described him as 'a full-blooded Indian priest of the Chippewa tribe who appeared in the regalia of his people in a procession of the Congress'.

His presence on the streets of Dublin was a reminder of a moving moment in 1919, when the Chippewa tribe made an important gesture towards Irish nationalists. In that year, Éamon de Valera visited the Chippewa reservation in Wisconsin, where he was honoured by community leaders. De Valera told the Native American people that 'You say you are not free. Neither are we free and I sympathise with you because we are making a similar fight. As a boy I read and understood of your slavery and longed to become one of you.'

From June 1919 until December 1920, de Valera traversed the United States as an elected representative of the 'Irish Republic', a revolutionary state which sought international recognition and allies. While he failed in securing recognition from President Woodrow Wilson, which was perhaps an overly ambitious goal, he did succeed in raising enormous sums of money for the cause, as well as in shining a light on the Irish question in the American media.

Interest in Ireland didn't come only from the predictable corners, such as the Irish Diaspora. Marcus Garvey, founder of the Universal Negro Improvement Association and African Communities League and a champion of pan-Africanism, had named the Harlem headquarters of his movement Liberty Hall in honour of the centre of trade unionism in Dublin. In one speech, made at a time when de Valera was in the United States, Garvey proclaimed that 'the time has come for the Negro race to offer up its martyrs upon the altar of liberty even as the Irish had given a long list, from Robert Emmet to Roger Casement'. Similarly, Puerto Rican nationalist Pedro Albizu Campos would express his admiration for the cause of Ireland and for de Valera, while making quite the impression on the visiting Irishman.

Joined by a team that included the Dubliner Harry Boland, de Valera's journey across America brought him to places of great symbolic importance. He laid a wreath on the grave of Benjamin Franklin, visited a memorial to George Washington, and even touched the famous Liberty Bell. Enthusiastic crowds mobbed him in cities including New York, and the cameras were never far away. Some in the American press compared him to Benjamin Franklin, and Harry Boland told one New York newspaper that 'in Ireland five men out of six are prepared to die for him'.

The visit of the Irish delegation to the Chippewa reservation created a lot of excitement in the American press, and the Irish certainly enjoyed themselves. Boland remembered that 'we had the pleasure of seeing the native games and dances, fed on venison and wild rice and other delightful Indian dishes'.

In the pages of the *Irish World and American Industrial Liberator* newspaper, it was reported that:

> Éamon de Valera, president of the Republic of Ireland, is a Chippewa Indian Chieftain. He was adopted today by the old Indian tribe on their reservation in Northern Wisconsin and was named 'Dressing Feather' or Nay Nay Ong Abe, after the famous Indian chief of that tribe who secured for the Chippewa their rights to the Wisconsin land under the treaty of 1854.
>
> The ceremony took place in an open field in the reservation in the presence of more than 3,000 Indians and white people and was interpolated by a weird series of Indian dances and speech-making.

The ceremony began with Chief Billy Boy greeting the Irish leader in Chippewa. The headsmen of the tribe then 'presented the Irish leader with a handsome beaded tobacco pouch and moccasins'. When de Valera began his speech, he spoke in the Irish language, before telling the gathered crowd of thousands:

> I speak to you in Gaelic ... because I want to show you that though I am white I am not of the English race. We, like you, are a people who have suffered and I feel for you with a sympathy that comes only from one who can understand as we Irishmen can.

Thirteen years after he was honoured by the Native American people, de Valera hosted the visiting Father Gordon during his time in Dublin, demonstrating that he hadn't forgotten the honour bestowed upon him by the Chippewa people.

Feuding Unions and Mills' Bombs

Ciarán Murray

'[To] organise the workers of Ireland for the attainment of full economic freedom'. So reads a section of the rules submitted to the registrar of friendly societies on 15 July 1924 by Peter Larkin for the creation of a new union, the Workers' Union of Ireland. The trades and occupations organised by the WUI were listed as 'dockers, coal carters, builders, bakeries, public services, distributive and productive and miscellaneous'.

The union was in part a product of a very public falling out between the leadership of the ITGWU (and, in particular, its general secretary, William O'Brien) and Jim Larkin on his return from the United States, where he had served three years of a five- to ten-year sentence meted out in the midst of the first 'red scare'. Larkin's return was well heralded, and he assumed that he would walk back into a leadership role in the union, which did not happen.

His refusal to adapt his anarchic oratory style and organisational methods did not endear him to the leadership of the ITGWU, but in a short time many of that union's members would leave en masse to join the new union, swayed by the personality cult around Larkin. Harry Pollitt, general secretary of the Communist Party of Great Britain, said of him around this time: 'Jim Larkin and his most immediate associates can think of nothing else but Jim Larkin. It is difficult to argue or venture any opinion that does not coincide with his own, and yet the man is undoubtedly a leader.'

A bitter pay dispute between the Shipping Federation and the ITGWU added to the conflict, with the latter suspecting (correctly) Larkin's influence on a number of workers who were unwilling to accept a compromise the ITGWU had won on their behalf. A third factor was a dispute between the union and one of its members, who on being promoted, and so expected to relinquish ITGWU membership, refused to do so. Strike action was approved at branch level in support of his case, but William O'Brien refused to sanction strike pay. Larkin was (correctly) assumed to be the instigator, putting the final nail in the coffin. This incident led to an occupation of Liberty Hall by a group of men including Larkin, which ended only after the new Free State army, with truck-mounted guns, surrounded the hall. The men were arrested and charged with trespass.

Following on from this incident, and with Jim Larkin having left Dublin on 27 May 1924 to attend a meeting of the Comintern in Russia, his brother Peter announced the foundation of the new union – arguably despite instructions not to. Regardless, Jim would join the union as general secretary on his return from Moscow on 25 August 1924. Membership of the ITGWU temporarily hemorrhaged, with upwards of 40,000 workers moving to the new WUI, the latter known colloquially as 'Larkin's union', its members proudly identifying as 'Larkin's men'.

There was to be nothing but acrimony between the two unions, whose members would not work peacefully alongside each other. In July 1925, the Coal Merchants' Association, fed up with the constant conflicts between members of the two unions, temporarily locked out both sets of workers and refused to readmit them until they could work amicably together. The ITGWU would break, with scabbing members returning to work under no little intimidation from WUI members. Newspaper reports tell of ITGWU men and their families suffering harassment at the hands of their WUI counterparts, with fights a regular occurrence, and a near riot breaking out at Alexandra Basin where coal was being unloaded. In a letter, William O'Brien told leader of the Labour Party, Thomas Johnson:

> Things have gone fairly smoothly with us here, especially in the coal dispute where we are getting stronger every day that passes. We have now a very large number of men engaged and are putting on extra men practically every day. There have been a considerable number of attacks on our men, but the position is not as bad as we expected. A bomb was thrown last Saturday into the Custom House docks, where a number of our men are housed, but no damage was done.

The feud culminated in the incident O'Brien mentioned in his letter, when a Mills bomb (a type of hand grenade) was thrown into an ITGWU-manned dockyard near Connolly Station. It did not cause much damage, but it could have been a lot worse. The blast, which rang out across the north inner city, occurred near a shed in which the union men, all but permanently stationed at the site, were resting. A 28 September *Irish Times* article sub-headed 'Supposed Attempt at Intimidation' reported:

> The eight coal workers were in their hut, just thirty yards from the office and close to the high wall and

the 'up' platform of the station. It appears that only one piece of the bomb struck the hut. It pierced the iron side and buried itself in the bed of one of the men, who was on the point of falling asleep at the time. He had a wonderful escape, for the hole made by the bomb splinter was about two inches from his head.

The report also spoke of the 'professionalism' of the attack, suggesting that the distance and accuracy of the throw indicated that the bomb was lobbed by someone who knew what they were doing. (This was perhaps unsurprising since the country wasn't long out of the horrors of the Civil War.)

In an attempt to gain the upper hand in the feud, Larkin struck a deal with a Welsh pit owner, and imported hundreds of tonnes of coal, which he sold to WUI members and Dublin's poor at cost price, killing two birds with one stone: the deal provided affordable fuel – dubbed 'unity coal' – to Dublin's needy, and it partially funded his strike in the process. Larkin would claim that provision of affordable coal to the poor of Dublin taught the employers of the city that the old spirit of militant unionism was not dead in the country. With Larkin's Union owing £12,000 to the pit owner, supply was threatened. In reply, Larkin argued that if the strike should fall, there would be no money to pay for the coal – an argument he would win, though it's probable no payment actually changed hands.

The lockout eventually ended, but not amicably. The workers returned to the yards, but bitterness between the two unions was to remain for decades.

Arthur Horner: the Welsh Refusenik of the Irish Citizen Army

Donal Fallon

Arthur Horner (1894–1968) was a miner, a communist, a conscientious objector to the First World War, and a trade unionist. Born in Merthr Tydfil, South Wales, he was politicised in the early twentieth century by the rise of the Scottish socialist leader Keir Hardie, the first Labour member of the House of Commons in Westminster, and by the rise of militant trade unionism in Wales.

He offers one of the most unusual stories of the Irish revolutionary period.

Inspired by the Dublin Lockout and the Easter Rising, among other events in Ireland, and ignoring his call-up papers for military service during the First World War, Horner arrived in Dublin in 1917, aligning himself with the recently re-formed Irish Citizen Army. To Horner, it was an important act of solidarity. In his memoir *Incorrigible Rebel*, he wrote that 'the Citizen Army, which Connolly created, represented to me the only possible struggle –a movement of the working class aimed at economic as well as political freedom'.

Avoiding military service for the empire during the seemingly never-ending war had created great difficulty

The Irish Citizen Army at Liberty Hall, 1917. Notice the
damage to the building from Easter Week.
(Image: Irish Military Archives)

for Horner and young men like him, when he was back in
Wales. He recalled that:

> Sometimes I used to sneak home at weekends. The
> military police used to swoop on the house from time
> to time, but never when I was there. It was a frustrat-
> ing life. I could not take any serious part in political
> activities.

He remembered going along to a meeting in the Miners' Hall
at Yunshir, 'on the struggle of the Irish people, with particular
reference to Jim Connolly'. These meetings had a profound
impact on the young man. Horner recalled that 'some of the

miners offered to help me to get away to join the struggle in Ireland. By this time, the police were on the track.' Horner claims that it was 'sympathisers with the Irish cause' who got him on a boat to Dublin. His partner was four months pregnant at the time, and 'she sent me away with a brave smile'.

Horner's sympathies with Ireland were based not only on class, but also nationality:

As a small nationality ourselves, we had watched with sympathy the Irish people's fight for independence long before the war broke out. When war came we were told the fighting in France was for the rights of small nations. But we recalled that Lord Carson and F.E Smith (later Lord Birkenhead) had threatened civil war rather than accept the Home Rule Act … So it is easy to understand how we, who had seen the viciousness of the coal owners, regarded what was happening in Ireland as the real struggle for the rights of small nations in a war-torn world.

Arriving in Dublin, Horner 'was sent to a house in Redmond Hill. There I enlisted in the Citizen Army and joined the Irish Transport Union. Everything was well organised.' He adopted name Jack O'Brien, and 'to cover my Welsh accent I said I had mixed with Welsh immigrants in America, and was unable to return to America because of the war. It sounded a bit thin to me, but I got away with it.' Horner 'found a congenial niche with a firm of druggists in Westmoreland Street, and trained in the Dublin hills with the remnant of the Citizen Army … Horner's daughter was born while he was in Dublin', according to an April 1966 *Irish Independent* article.

Before working in the druggists, he had briefly worked as a window cleaner, but he didn't feel that it was a profession for him. Horner joked that 'I don't mind being killed for Ireland's freedom, but I'm not having someone write home to the Welsh miners telling them Arthur Horner was killed cleaning windows at sixpence a time!'

The Irish Citizen Army in the Aftermath of the Easter Rising
The Irish Citizen Army was never a particularly large body, and it lost much in the Easter Rising. Not only were some of its leading figures killed, such as Captain Seán Connolly and the executed leaders Mallin and Connolly, but the organisation had to contend with the growing lure of the IRA in the years that followed.

A new leadership, led by Commandant James O'Neill, attempted to put some shape on the organisation. A committed trade unionist, O'Neill, of St Catherine's Park, Leixlip, had 'led the Lucan and Leixlip contingents of the recently formed Irish Citizen Army on the march to Dublin' during the Lockout of 1913. He had also been a very significant figure in the Easter Rising. With experience as a bomb maker, he found himself serving as quartermaster general in the GPO.

By trade, O'Neill worked in construction, and he took charge of the restoration of Liberty Hall, which had endured structural damage during the Easter Rising, having been shelled by the *Helga* from the River Liffey. Under O'Neill's command, the Citizen Army would play a peripheral but still very important role in the War of Independence that lay ahead.

The myth that the Irish Citizen Army ceased to exist in 1916 with the Easter Rising is slowly fading away, thanks to the emergence of more archival materials, in particular from the Bureau of Military History collections. The ICA did important work in the field of intelligence, secured weaponry for the republican movement through sympathetic men in the British armed forces and members working in the docks, and was also centrally involved in the enforcement of the Belfast Boycott. ICA Captain Joseph Connolly, a serving member of the Dublin Fire Brigade, was central to the successful burning of the Custom House in 1921, and the ICA fought as a unit in the Battle of Dublin during the Civil War.

In 1917 however, the focus of the ICA was on restructuring itself. Some in the organised labour movement were hostile to the workers' militia, and even retaining a presence in Liberty Hall proved difficult at times. O'Neill remembered that there was a desire to keep the ICA as a body distinct from the larger IRA:

> After 1916, I met Cathal Brugha (a senior figure in the IRA). We discussed the thing, as to how it could be reconciled to the Volunteers, or vice versa. We found it was not possible. We were not prepared to fuse. Then, it was decided the two peoples should exist as independent units, and work in close co-operation with each other.

Horner's time in Dublin seems to have primarily been spent on work typical of the ICA in this period: gathering intelligence and hiding wanted men. His account gives a sense of just how much the attitude towards republicans had changed among the populace, but also how the entire national struggle had become synonymous with two words:

Sinn Féin. According to Horner, 'in the middle of Dublin, if you rushed into a house and shouted "Sinn Féin", every door shut behind you to keep out your pursuers'.

The No Conscription Fellowship and Avoiding the War
Horner biographer Nina Fishman has noted that 'Horner's flight from conscription was hardly unique', and as the First World War progressed it was increasingly clear 'that being drafted for active service meant terrible hardship and suffering at the very least. High casualty rates had produced pervasive, collective war weariness.' She points towards the existence of a clandestine network, mainly operated by the No Conscription Fellowship, which assisted young British men in fleeing to Ireland.

For most, the primary objective was to get false Irish papers, giving them an Irish identity. 'They could then go back to Britain, and find work, typically in a London war factory, where anonymity was easy to preserve. Geography made it comparatively easy for Welsh refuseniks to get to Ireland,' Fishman writes. For Horner, the imperative to return home to Wales came with the news of the birth of his daughter. He wrote to his partner requesting that she be named Vol, in honour of Voltairine de Cleyre, an American socialist and feminist who had died in 1912. His next daughter would take the name Rosa, in honour of the murdered socialist leader Rosa Luxemburg.

Though it was remarkably dangerous, he boarded a ferry at Dún Laoghaire in the summer of 1918, complete with a suitcase containing left-wing propaganda from Ireland. Fishman notes that he was arrested when the ferry docked at Holyhead in North Wales 'along with two other South Walian miners, Frank and George Phibben, brothers from an

ILP [Independent Labour Party] family in Pentre, Rhondda. The brothers had fled to Ireland with two friends and made contact with the No Conscription Fellowship.'

The Phibben brothers were returning to Wales with newly acquired false papers. Horner and the Phibben brothers were sentenced to six months of hard labour, serving their sentences at Wormwood Scrubs in West London. Defiantly, Horner had told the court that:

> I live alone to destroy the system, the cause of so much sorrow and misery to my class, and wait for the awakening of the workers of the world to a true understanding of their interests ... Therefore gentlemen it should be clear to you that my conscience of these things has erected an insuperable barrier to the exclusion of any plans which have for its aim the transforming of me into a soldier in any capitalist army.

This was a time before the outbreak of the War of Independence in Ireland, the twilight period between the Easter insurrection and what was to come. That members of the Citizen Army assisted this Welsh refusenik in Dublin was quite remarkable. As Fishman has noted, 'having no urgent need of men, their acceptance and sponsorship of political refugees from Britain was an act of solidarity, without immediate practical benefit to the Irish cause'.

Horner would in 1921 become a founding member of the Communist Party of Great Britain (CPGB), and he was in 1946 elected general secretary of the influential National Union of Miners (NUM). He died in September 1968. In his own words, he remained an 'incorrigible rebel' to the end.

Before Monto, There Was Grafton Street

Donal Fallon

Any discussion of prostitution in earlier times in Dublin will inevitably focus on the so-called 'Monto' district of the north inner city, the area around Montgomery Street, which became notorious enough to warrant a mention in the *Encyclopedia Britannica* of 1903: 'Dublin furnishes an exception to the usual practice in the UK. In that city the police permit "open houses" confined to one street; but carried on more publicly than even in the south of Europe or in Algeria.'

While Monto emerged in the late nineteenth century, there was nothing new about prostitution in the city. Indeed, all that tended to change with time was where prostitution was to be found. In earlier decades, and in particular the 1860s and 1870s, the Grafton Street area was regarded as a centre of prostitution in the city. This infuriated sections of Dublin society, who complained repeatedly in the letters pages of newspapers that the street had become 'impassable to virtuous women'. In the words of one writer to the *Freeman's Journal* in 1870:

Let some half-dozen men of the G Division [Dublin's intelligence police] parade Grafton Street at the hours of four to six. This was found very successful in Sackville Street during last summer, and I have no doubt we shall soon be free of these social pests, and can again escort our wives and daughters through one of our finest streets.

An earlier letter writer to the same paper described how the street 'literally swarmed with women of loose character'. It is worth considering whether the emergence of the Monto district was tolerated to a degree because it removed the sight of women working in the Grafton Street area, something that clearly troubled some.

While the above letter calling for the G Division to be deployed against prostitutes bore little sympathy for the women themselves, others avoided such loaded and vindictive terms as 'social pests'. A letter writer who signed a piece of correspondence as 'Strike at the Root' instead referred to the women as 'poor unfortunates', and insisted that it was not 'motives of avarice or sensuality' that drove most women to the streets.

Certainly, there were two very different versions of Grafton Street. While some, like our letter writers above, believed the street was in decline, guidebooks to the city throughout the 1860s and 1870s praised it, with one insisting that:

> the elite of Dublin ... will be found in Grafton Street ... This street is the brightest, cheeriest street in Dublin. It is the fashionable shopping street. Equipages in the very perfection of good taste may be seen in long lines at both sides of the street in front of the principal shops.

This was at odds with how a priest saw the street in 1877:

> Dozens upon dozens of females belonging to that class truly designated unfortunate, the majority of them not eighteen years of age ... passed me, using language and openly flaunting a shame the very mention of which is enough to bring a blush to the cheek of virtue.

The sheer number of women working in Dublin in this period as prostitutes was quite remarkable. It wasn't that numbers in Dublin were proportionately higher than the numbers in cities like London and Manchester – they were *actually* higher. Take the figures from Joseph V. O'Brien's study of Dublin at the turn of the century, for example: in 1870, London witnessed 2,183 arrests for prostitution, Manchester 1,617, and Dublin 3,255.

The city clearly lacked any kind of industrial employment options for women (not least when compared to Belfast), with about 40 percent of all female workers in the 1901 census described themselves as 'domestic labourers'. To historian Pádraig Yeates, prostitution in Dublin 'was caused by chronic unemployment, aggravated in this instance by the presence of a sizeable military garrison'. Some nationalists developed a tendency to blame the presence of the military garrison in Dublin entirely for the presence of prostitution in Ireland, and as Maria Luddy has written, 'the issue of venereal disease was much used by advanced Irish nationalists to denigrate the British soldier in Ireland and the returning soldier from the front'.

Montgomery Street, across the Liffey and out of sight, was a world away from the fashionable Grafton Street. By the 1870s, the police had the powers they needed to close the brothels there, but the authorities instead allowed the district to function as a red-light district. While the emergence of Monto certainly brought about a decline in prostitution on Grafton Street, Sackville Street, and the like, there were still women dragged before the Southern Police Courts in Dublin for working in the Grafton Street area. In October 1889, a DMP man in court described 'girls loitering in Grafton Street, opposite the Provost's house, and loitering for improper purposes'. It would be more than thirty years before the beginning of the end for Monto, raided at last in 1925.

Max Levitas: Jewish Dubliner and Working-Class Hero

Sam McGrath

When he turned 100 in July 2015, Max Levitas celebrated with family friends in Whitechapel, East London. At the end of the festivities, he called for the crowd to offer up a collection for the *Morning Star* newspaper. This symbolised Max's absolute generosity and unbroken commitment to progressive, left-wing politics going back over 80 years.

Max's parents, Harry Levitas from the Lithuanian shtetl of Akmeyan and Leah Rick from the Latvian capital, Riga, separately fled the anti-Semitism of tsarist Russia in 1913 to join relatives in Dublin. The couple met in Dublin and married in the synagogue at 52 Lower Camden Street. Three of their Dublin-born children would later participate in the 1936 Battle of Cable Street in London's East End: Max (1915–), Maurice (1917–2001), and Sol (1919–2015). Also born in Dublin were the late Celia and Isaac, the infant boy dying as a result of a tragic domestic accident in their Warren Street home. A sixth child, Toby, was born following the emigration of the family to Glasgow.

Max and his brothers attended St Peter's Church of Ireland National School on New Bride Street, beside the Meath Hospital. His father struggled to earn a living, sometimes

Max Levitas outside his old home at 13 St Kevins Parade, Portobello where he lived from 1925-27. (Photograph by Luke O'Riordan)

Sam and Ciaran of CHTM! with Max Levitas holding copy of the first book (September 2015). (Photograph by Luke O'Riordan)

dealing in scrap metal, but more often working as a tailor's presser. He became an active member of the International Tailors', Pressers', and Machinists' Trade Union, known to Dubliners as 'the Jewish Union'. The Levitas family lived in a series of houses in Portobello, which was known then as 'Little Jerusalem': 15 Longwood Avenue (1915), 8 Warren Street (1916–25), and 13 St Kevin's Parade (1925–27).

Then the family left for Glasgow. In a 2011 interview with *Spitalfieldslife.com*, Max recalled:

> My father was a tailor and a trade unionist. He formed an Irish/Jewish trade union and then employers blacklisted him, making sure he could never get a job. The only option was to leave Dublin and we lived in Glasgow from 1927 until 1930, but my father had two sisters in London, so we came here to Durward Street in Whitechapel in 1931 and stayed ever since.

Arriving in London in the early 1930s, the teenage Max and his brother Maurice soon became active in left-wing politics. In 1934, at the age of 19, Max was appointed secretary of the Mile End Young Communist League. That same year he became an East End hero when he was arrested for writing anti-Fascist slogans on Nelson's Column in Trafalgar Square. He told *Spitalfieldslife.com*:

> There were two of us, we did it at midnight and we wrote 'All out on September 9th to fight Fascism', 'Down with Fascism', and 'Fight Fascism', on Nelson's Column in whitewash. And afterwards we went to Lyons Corner House to have something to eat and wash our hands, but when we had finished our tea we

decided to go back to see how good it looked, and we got arrested – the police saw the paint on our shoes.

Max was name-checked by Oswald Mosley around this time, who, according to the book *Britishness Since 1870*, sarcastically told a fascist audience:

> Ragotski, Schaffer, Max Levitas, Fenebloom, Hyam Aarons, Sapasnick. Old English names: thirty-two of them out of sixty-four convicted since last June for attacks on fascists. Thirty-two names of that character. Spontaneous rising of the British people against fascism!

Two years later, he took part in the Battle of Cable Street, when tens of thousands of anti-fascists (including many Jews and Irish) prevented Mosely and his Blackshirts from marching through the East End. Max remembers:

> I was working as a tailor's presser in a small work-shop in Commercial St at the time. Mosley wanted to march through Whitechapel … and I knew the only way to stop him was to have unity of the people. I approached a number of unions, Jewish organisations and the Communist League to band together against the Fascists but although they agreed what I was doing was right, they wouldn't support me.
>
> But I give credit to the huge number of members of the Jewish and Irish communities and others who turned out that day … There were thousands that came together in Aldgate, and when we heard that Mosley's intention was to march along Cable St from Tower Hill into Whitechapel, large numbers of

people went to Cable St and barricades were set up. The police attempted to clear Cable St with horses, so that the march could go ahead, but the people of Cable St fought back and the police had to give in.

In 1937, Max's brother Maurice 'Morry' Levitas joined the British battalion of the XV (International) Brigade to fight against Franco in Spain. He saw action at Teruel, Belchite and Aragon, and then was captured and spent 11 months in jail, where he was subject to violent interrogations, arbitrary beatings, and mock executions. He was among sixty-seven republicans released in a prisoner exchange in 1939. He later served in India and Burma with the Royal Army Medical Corps, and then worked as a plumber, teacher, and lecturer. He died in 2001.

In 1939, Max was the convenor of a successful twenty-one week rent strike while living in Brady Mansions in Whitechapel. He explained in a 1999 interview how such strikes 'could also demonstrate another aspect of class unity':

> We were fighting the Jewish landlords the same way as we'd fight any landlord that increases rents, doesn't care if he repairs flats, so forth and so on: these are the enemies of the people and must be fought – if they are a Jew, black or white. And this helped to develop a much more broader understanding and [to unite] the struggle against Mosley and the fascists.

Preventing the growth of fascism in Britain was a political as well as personal undertaking for Max and so many others. Members of the extended Levitas family who had remained behind in Eastern Europe suffered the fate of many Jews during the Second World War. Max's paternal aunt, Sara, and all her family were burned to death, along with fellow villagers, in the synagogue of Akmeyan. Their maternal aunt, Rachel, and most of her family, were massacred by the Nazis in Riga. A paternal uncle who thought he had emigrated far enough westwards by moving to Paris was murdered on his own doorstep by a Gestapo officer.

Elected as a Communist Party councillor for the borough of Stepney in the East End in 1945, Max retained his seat for 17 years. He continued to be politically active throughout the succeeding decades. He outlived both his wife Sadie and his son Stephen (who passed away in 2014). In 2011, he helped deliver leaflets promoting a march to oppose the English Defence League in his local Tower Hamlets area, and spoke eloquently to the anti-fascist crowd on the day. In 2015, the council demanded that he pay £25,000 for repairs to the ex-council flat in which he has lived for more than five decades. Max, being Max, decided to fight back, and Channel 4 news featured the campaign.

Weekend in Dublin

On Friday 25 October 2015, Max was the guest of the Lord Mayor Críona Ní Dhálaigh of Sinn Féin and Deputy Lord Mayor Cieran Perry, an independent republican socialist councillor, in Dublin's Mansion House. On Saturday, he attended the wonderful main concert of the Frank Harte Festival in the Teacher's Club on Parnell Square, which *Come Here to Me!* friends and favourites Lynched headlined. On Sunday, Max visited Portobello, where he was born and spent his early years.

Myself and Ciarán Murray were delighted to meet Max and talk politics and football over dinner on the following Monday in the O'Riordan family home. We gave him a signed copy of our first book, *Come Here To Me!* as a small gesture. *Salud* Max! *L'chayim*!

The Christmas Monster 'Kohoutek' and the Children of God

Ciarán Murray

'What will the Christmas Monster bring? Geological cata-clysms? Political Catastrophe? Economic Chaos? New World Order? Great Confusion? Energy Crisis? Atomic War? End of the World?' So read the rear of an eight-page pamphlet distributed outside the GPO in late 1973 by a group calling themselves the 'Children of God', heralding the arrival of the comet Kohoutek and the group's belief in the impend-ing apocalypse. The comet had been discovered on 7 March of that year, and astronomers predicted that it would be the brightest 'naked-eye' comet since Halley's passed in 1910. Dubbed the 'comet of the century' by the media, it fell well short of expectations. The *Wall Street Journal* declared it 'a disappointment to sky-watchers, if not a fizzle'.

The Children of God were a fundamentalist Christian sect founded in 1968 in California by David Brandt Berg. 'Moses David', as he was known within the group, declared himself to be 'God's prophet', and his organisation had an estimated 165 'colonies' in late 1973, from London to Paris, Dallas to Liverpool – and, in Ireland, Dublin, Cork, and Belfast. Followers were expected to live a communal existence, obey communiques (known as 'Mo letters') from

Front page of a pamphlet distributed by the 'Children of God'
outside the GPO, late 1973. (Image: Harry Warren)

their leader, adopt biblical names, and refuse to accept secular
employment. Marriage among members was encouraged,
but couples were not monogamous. Rumours of child abuse
in the organisation were rife.

According to a 16 September 1973 Des Hickey article in the *Sunday Independent*, a Children of God colony was active in Dublin and based themselves out of a two-storey house in Rialto. There were ten members of the organisation living in the house, including a 22-year-old named Zibeon, his American wife Aphia, 20-year-old Parable, and his English wife Magdala. Both Zibeon and Parable were Irish, Zibeon having attended Blackrock College before going to the North for university, though both men spoke with 'indeterminate American accents'.

The month after the article was written, a yellow bus belonging to the group, and featuring its name in big red writing, caught fire while parked on Nutley Lane in Donnybrook. 'Gardaí at the time could not tell if the fire was malicious or not,' the *Irish Independent* reported on 17 October 1973. The group was looked upon suspiciously by established churches. Several religious organisations spoke out against it, with the 'Presbyterian Church Notes' column in the *Irish Times* commenting on their 'eccentricities and questionable characteristics'. A public meeting held by the Church in Malahide in 1984 proclaimed that young people were at grave risk from cults operating in Ireland, and included the Children of God (alongside the Mormons and Opus Dei) on a watch list.

In the 1970s, the organisation in Ireland grew to approximately one hundred members. At one point there were 27 members living in a in a three-storey derelict house opposite the Bull Wall wooden bridge in Clontarf. Their main work consisted of selling literature, 'rehabilitating' drug addicts and alcoholics, and 'converting' them, a process that involved signing over everything they owned to the organisation.

Judging from the fact that the address given on the 1973 pamphlet was a post-office box in Fairview, it's possible that they were living there that year. The organisation also based itself in other locations around the city, including Rathmines, Portmarnock, and Milltown, according to the 3 December 1978 edition of the *Sunday Independent*. Moses David never paid the Dublin colony a visit, but he did, according to the same report, issue them with upwards of 500 edicts, 'with instructions ranging from how to brush their teeth to what music they should listen to'.

The pamphlet handed out at the GPO largely contained gibberish – proclamations and counter proclamations of impending doom or salvation, warnings that the apocalypse would happen either in forty or eighty days, or actually sometime in 1986. Here are some of the more 'interesting' passages:

> According to our own calculations, 1986 should be about the time of the final takeover of One World Government by a world dictator known as the 'Anti-Christ' and the beginning of his reign of terror!
>
> For the heat of the comet shall be sevenfold, and men shall gnaw their tongues for pain for the travail that shall come upon them when the Lord shall arise to shake terribly the Earth! Thank You for the words Thou hast given their father! In Jesus' name, Amen.'

The pamphlet also included two pages of useful survival tactics, along with instructions to 'pray and stay close to the Lord!' The opening paragraph of these pages ends with the following line:

Are you even ready for the riots, the sabotage, the wrecking of utilities, the blowing up of your bank, the cutting off of your electricity and water, the problems of sewage and garbage disposal and food and gasoline rationing and shortages of all kinds in a state of emergency, and the brutality of martial law under the reign of terror of a military dictatorship of a dying nation that has forgotten God? What will YOU do?

The main focus for the group seems to have surrounded Kohoutek, and reports about the organisation died down after it passed, the Children of God's trail in Ireland more or less going cold around 1978. At the beginning of the 1980s, there was apparently a small community in Mountjoy Square, but they fled the country to Argentina in 1981, afraid of another impending apocalypse proclaimed by Moses David. A couple of newspaper reports appeared in 1993 of a Dublin man taking his wife to court for custody of their daughter, whom she had taken without his knowledge to live with the Buenos Aires branch, now known as 'The Family'.

The Rabble and the Custom House

Donal Fallon

The architect James Gandon (1743–1823) is today truly synonymous with Dublin. While he worked in other cities, and
was born in London's New Bond Street, his most celebrated
buildings are to be found here. From the Four Courts to
parts of the historic Parliament building on College Green,
and from King's Inns to the Rotunda Assembly Rooms, his
work is a reminder of the style and vision of the Georgian
period that transformed Dublin.

Gandon's first project in Dublin was undoubtedly his
most controversial. While the Custom House is today
recognised as a Dublin landmark, at the time, the very
prospect of its construction infuriated Dubliners, who
believed it would shift the entire axis of the city and
negatively impact on their own incomes. So controversial
was the development that Dublin workers (dismissed in
contemporary accounts as 'rabble') would force their way
onto the site of the development to halt construction, led by
the firebrand 'populist patriot' James Napper Tandy.

Moving the Custom House
Before Gandon's Custom House, an earlier one could be
found at Essex Quay, more or less at the site of Clarence
Hotel. Constructed in 1707, it was plagued by numerous

1811 illustration of James Gandon's Custom House.
(Image: The British Library, Creative Commons)

problems, including the fact that large vessels had difficulty reaching it thanks to the presence of a large reef in the Liffey known as 'Standfast Dick'. So, as Maurice Curtis discusses in his recent history of Temple Bar, they often had to use smaller craft , known as 'lighters', to unload cargo. Also, the building itself was problematic, with its upper floors discovered to be structurally unsound in the early 1770s.

By 1773, plans were afoot to address these problems, with the powerful Revenue Commissioner John Beresford leading the campaign for a new Custom House to be constructed further east down the river, nearer to the sea. As Joseph Robins notes in his history of the Custom House:

the proposal was opposed by a variety of individuals who feared their interests would be damaged by any shift in the location of commercial activity. Petitions against the project were presented by the merchants, brewers, and manufacturers of Dublin, and by the city corporation, but the government decided in 1774 to go ahead with the move.

James Gandon Arrives in Dublin

The architect selected for this development was the Londoner James Gandon, grandson of French Huguenot refugees who had fled religious persecution. Gandon had already been awarded the gold medal for architecture by the Royal Academy in London, and was in considerable demand beyond these shores; the Romanov family had attempted to lure him to St Petersburg around the same time as the Custom House controversy in Dublin.

When Gandon arrived in Dublin, he was kept a virtual prisoner by Beresford. His biographer Hugo Duffy has written of the fear that gripped Beresford, writing that Gandon's suspicion of the whole project 'must have been heightened when he realised the opposition was so violent as to keep Beresford in a state of anxiety lest it became known that the architect had arrived'.

The primary figure that stood between Gandon and the new Custom House was James Napper Tandy, one of the great characters of the Dublin of his day. An ironmonger by trade, Tandy was elected to the City Assembly in 1777 and was a champion of Dublin's poor, not to mention a vocal campaigner against corruption in local politics. Later a founding member of the United Irishmen, many were unkind towards his appearance, with one observer of a political meeting he addressed remembering: 'He was the ugliest man I ever gazed on. He had a dark, yellow, truculent-looking countenance, a long drooping nose, rather sharpened at the point, and the muscles of his face formed two cords at each side of it.'

The poor regarded Tandy as a hero, not least when he denounced the police of the day as 'a ruffianly and licentious rabble', or when he campaigned for rights for the Catholic majority. His life would take some remarkable turns, and indeed he arguably came to owe it to Napoleon Bonaparte, who intervened vigorously on his behalf after the disastrous 1798 rebellion and his capture. At the time of Gandon's arrival, however, '98 was still far away, and Tandy's aim was to ensure that the unhappiness of the Dublin merchants and workers he represented was clear to Gandon and Beresford. Gandon was warned that labourers in Dublin were 'frequently turbulent, and in the habit of combining together for increase of wages, when works required quickness of execution'. Certainly, Tandy contributed to that.

The 'Rabble' Storming the Site

Gandon was well aware of the unpopularity of the project. As Robins notes, he received threatening letters on more than one occasion and even carried a cane sword, 'which he believed he could still wield to some purpose if forced to defend himself.'.

On a September day in 1781, the protestors arrived on site. Gandon had been warned that Tandy and his followers constituted 'the most desperate of the mob' opposed to the project, and the press delighted in reporting his arrival on the construction site, 'followed by numerous rabble with adzes, saws, shovels, etc.'. Tandy's men 'came in a body onto the grounds and levelled that portion of the fence, which had been thrown up, adjoining the North Wall and River Liffey'.

Beresford would encourage Gandon in the aftermath of this to 'laugh at the extreme folly of the people', but certainly Tandy had made his point. Tandy has been described as a 'real force in the municipal and street politics of the capital', and this was not the first or the last time he would infuriate the authorities.

Gandon's masterpiece was eventually completed, though the project took a decade in total and cost what was at the time an extraordinary sum of money, with the bills running to a sum in excess of £200,000. Napper Tandy wouldn't be the last radical to storm the site: on 25 May 1921, the men of the Dublin Brigade of the IRA, assisted in their task by sympathetic members of the Dublin Fire Brigade, ensured that the building burnt. The centre of local government administration in British-occupied Ireland, the building's interior was gutted. Despite drastic changes inside, the building's magnificent exterior today reminds us of the fine talents of James Gandon, who is buried in Drumcondra, having died on Christmas Eve, 1823.

Remembering Paweł Edmund Strzelecki

Donal Fallon

The sudden closure of Clerys department store in June 2015 took everyone in the city by surprise, not least the people who worked there. By December of the following year, the historic bronze signage bearing the company's name disappeared without trace from its exterior, presumably stolen.

Thankfully, still affixed to the building is a plaque in honour of Paweł Edmund Strzelecki (1798–1873). An explorer and geologist of considerable fame abroad, Strzelcki's contribution to the distribution of famine relief in the west of Ireland during the Great Hunger is remembered on the plaque in English, Polish, and As Gaeilge. It is a beautiful tribute, unveiled in March 2015 at a ceremony that was attended by members of the Polish community in Ireland and representatives from the city of Poznan.

There are many stories of international assistance being provided to Ireland during the Great Hunger. Some are well-remembered and commemorated. This includes the story of the help provided by the Choctaw Nation of Native Americans, and the story of French chef Alexis Soyer, who established a temporary soup kitchen at the site of what is now the Croppies Acre memorial in 1847,

feeding thousands. Dublin historian Frank Hopkins has noted that:

> The poor were admitted to the hall in shifts of 100 at a time by the ringing of a bell. When they had finished the soup, they were handed a piece of bread and left by the second door. The bowls were then cleaned and the next batch of people was summoned, again by bell.

Strzelecki's story is much less widely known than those of Soyer or the Native Americans, but was brought to prominence in recent years by the efforts of the Polish community in Ireland.

Born in Głuszyna (near Poznan) in 1797, Strzelecki lived a remarkable life. He served in the Prussian army, but only briefly – he was instead destined for exploration. Denis Gregory, author of *Australia's Great Explorers,* has noted that travelling around Europe, Strzelecki developed 'an interest in science, agriculture and meteorology. History notes that he had a look around the mines in Saxony and Mount Vesuvius in Italy.' (Such travel and intellectual curiosity was the preserve of only a small wealthy elite, of course.) Strzelecki also travelled widely in North America and South America, and made it to New Zealand in the early months of 1839.

As an explorer, he is best remembered for his time in Australia. On the invitation of the governor of New South Wales, Strzelecki conducted a mineralogical and geological survey of the Gippsland region, where he discovered gold in 1839. His find was suppressed by the governor, who 'feared the social disruption that a gold rush would inevitably cause in what was still demographically a convict colony'. Strzelecki would chronicle some of the most remote parts of Australia, and an impressive monument in his honour stands today in Jindabyne, New South Wales.

The failures of the British state in relation to the suffering of the Irish peasantry throughout the years of the Great Hunger are well documented. Sir Charles Trevelyan believed that:

> The judgement of God sent the calamity the teach the Irish a lesson, that calamity must not be too much mitigated … The real evil with which we have to con-tend is not the physical evil of the Famine, but the moral evil of the selfish, perverse and turbulent char-acter of the people.

Such beliefs were not those of some hack, but rather a politi-cal administrator who could directly impact on the lives of the suffering masses. As historian Melissa Fegan has noted, Trevelyan and many of those around him were 'convinced that the Famine was providential in nature, and even if political economy had not forbidden a radical intervention in the markets, who could challenge the hand of God?'

Despite such abhorrent views from some in authority, huge sums of money were raised in Britain for the purpose of famine relief. This came from migrant Irish workers, Quakers, sympathetic businessmen, and a wide cross section of society. The most significant body to operate in Ireland during this period was the British Relief Association, described by historian Christine Kinealy as the body that provided 'the greatest amount of relief' in Ireland. It was for this body that Strzelecki laboured over a period of eighteen months, overseeing the distributing of relief in the west of Ireland, which was worst affected by the failure of the potato crop.

Strzelecki was one of only twelve agents working on behalf of the British Relief Association in Ireland. At first, he had responsibilities for Mayo, Donegal and Sligo. As Enda Delaney has observed, 'his confidential reports to the committee in London chronicled the descent of this region into complete starvation'. He wrote that:

> The population seems as if paralysed, and helpless, more ragged and squalid; here fearfully dejected ... stoically resigned to death; then, again, as if conscious of some greater forthcoming evil, they are deserting their hearths and families. The examination of some individual cases of distress showed most heart-breaking instances of human misery, and of the degree to which that misery can be brought.

In Dublin, things were miserable too. The *Freeman's Journal* reported in May 1847 on a woman named Eliza Holmes, arrested by the police while begging on Sackville Street with her dead infant in her arms. Refugees from the countryside flooded into the urban centres. Many were destined to leave the island via the port in the capital. As David Dickson has written, this was in many ways to the benefit of the city, as 'if access to either Britain or North American ports had been denied to Famine refugees during the late 1840s, Dublin would have been catastrophically overwhelmed by those seeking institutional protection'. One man exposed to the horrors of 1840s Dublin was Frederick Douglass, the famed American abolitionist, who was so disturbed by the city that he wrote, 'I spent nearly six weeks in Dublin, and the scenes I there witnessed were such as to make me blush, and hang my head to think myself a man.'

Strzelecki lived and worked in Dublin during some of his time in Ireland, basing himself in the Reynold's Hotel in Upper Sackville Street. For a time, he was incapacitated by 'famine fever', but he continued to carry out important administrative work.

For his troubles, the Polish explorer was made a Knight Commander of the Honour of Bath in 1848 (remarkably, so was Trevelyan). Strzelecki sought and received no payment for his work in Ireland during the Great Hunger. One early historian of the period would later note that 'the name of this benevolent stranger was then, and for long afterwards, a familiar one if not a household word in the homes of the suffering poor'.

Strzelecki died in October 1873, and was buried in London's Kensal Green Cemetery. In 1997, his remains were returned to Poland. It is fitting that he is remembered on the streets of Dublin today.

18 Aungier Street: from Neighbourhood Local to Cocktail Bar

Sam McGrath

It is a brisk 20-minute walk from Portobello Bridge to the bottom of South Great George's Street, but on your way into town you pass nearly thirty pubs.

There's something for nearly everyone on this stretch, locals and tourists alike. For the LGBT community (The George), for those looking for one of the best pints of Guinness in the city (The Long Hall), for people seeking cheap cocktails (Capitol Lounge), for blues fans (J.J. Smyth's), for DIT students (The Karma Stone), for fans of craft beer (Against the Grain), for techno and house lovers (Opium Rooms), for country folk (Flannery's), for true music heads (Anseo), for the pizza-loving hipster crowd (The Bernard Shaw), and so on and so on.

However, in late 2015, a small pub called Delaney's and its next-door off-licence at number 17–18 Aungier Street shut their doors without much of a fuss. There's a strong argument to be made that Delaney's was one of the last remaining genuine working-class 'local' pubs left in this part of the south inner city.

Only a stone's throw away from the glitz of Fade Street and the shopping district surrounding Grafton Street, Delaney's

Delaney's pub on Aungier Street in c. 2015 before it was bought over and reopened as a cocktail bar. (Photograph by Jar.ie)

was an anachronistic institution for this part of town. It was a pub that did not attempt to compete for the business of tourists or anyone else. By no means was it an unwelcoming bar, but it was certainly a local bar for local people, with a sizeable number of patrons coming from the nearby York Street flats.

It was a pub that offered cheap pints, a Lotto draw for the local football club on Mondays, karaoke on Tuesdays, and bingo on Wednesdays. DJs with names like DJ Gaz and DJ Bubbles played on the weekend. There was a darts table and a poker table. The pub had no website, but it had an active Facebook personal account. If you're standing with your back to the former Central Bank headquarters on Dame Street, where would be the nearest pub that would match such a description south of the Liffey? By my reckoning, you'd have to go all the way to Townsend Street or Pearse Street in one direction, and all the way to Thomas Street in the other.

In just a few months, the pub was closed, renovated and reopened as an up-market cocktail bar called Bow Lane. Now you can get a Pompelmo (grapefruit vodka cocktail) for €11 or a bottle of Gagliardo Serre Barolo red wine (2007) for €105. Online news articles about the opening of the new business are quite interesting – particularly the kind of language they used.

A piece on the *Daily Edge* described Delaney's as a 'closed-down pub … an unassuming place you've probably been walking past for years'. Delaney's wasn't a long-term derelict pub. It was only shut for a very short time before the redevelopment.

FFT.ie talked about the 'extensive refurbishment' of an 'old rundown unit, adding to the ongoing transformation of one of Dublin's oldest streetscapes'. It may not have been sleek, but it was certainly wasn't an 'old rundown unit'.

Lovin Dublin revealed that patrons of the new venue could expect an 'authentic inner-city pub experience', whatever the hell that means, before declaring that 'oxtail ragú lasagnette, roasted squash fettuccine and slow-cooked rabbit pie' would be on offer.

The new pub's own blurb was a nauseous bit of PR nonsense:

> Bow Lane is an authentic, late-night cocktail bar that appeals to a cross-section of Dublin society, from the gritty underclass of sophisticates to creatives and the party set. Bow Lane has areas that satisfy a want for exclusivity and other areas that create a space for typical Dublin social intercourse.

*

No. 18 Aungier Street is a terraced, three-bay, four-storey building that has been a licensed premises since at least the mid-nineteenth century. From 1852 to 1890, the lease-holder of the business was John Hoyne, a wine merchant and grocer. The *Irish Times* on 13 June 1890 described the premises as:

> old-established, well and favourably known. A retail seven-day, licensed grocery, tea, wine, spirit, and malt drink concerns, unexceptionally situated on one of the greatest and still rising main line streets in Dublin. The establishment has very fine frontage. The exterior and interior are in splendid condition. A depth of 150 feet gives ample room for present genuine trade and further extension as may in future require for increased business.

In 1892 it was owned by a Joseph C. Reynolds, but by 1901 it was the hands of Patrick Coughlan from Kilkenny, according to the census. The business was put up for sale in 1924 and then again in 1930, when it was described in the *Irish Times* on 7 June as a 'spacious' premises with 'bar fitting, cash desk and show cases … in richly-carved Domingo wood; there is good yard space with beer and bottling stores and excellent lavatory arrangements'.

It went through a slew of names in the twentieth century – Patrick Brady's The Central Bar (1930s), The Central Bar (early 1970s), and The Millhouse Inn (late 1970s). In the 1970s, it was home to the Dublin Welsh Choir. Members included Irish republicans Roy Johnston, Deasún Breathnach, and long-term *Come Here to Me!* contributor known as PhotoPol. From about 1980 to 1997, it was known as Gleeson's. In late 1980s, it was sold for £200,000 to German businessman Hans Heiss, who moved to Ireland with his Irish wife. In the early 2000s, the pub was known again as The Central Bar, before finally setting on Delaney's.

This was not an extraordinary pub that could boast the best pint of Guinness in the city, or a remarkable Victorian interior, but it was a genuine neighborhood bar in a part of town that has very few left. Its closure and redevelopment (almost) overnight into an expensive cocktail bar should not go unnoticed.

The Proclamation and William Henry West

Ciarán Murray

Read aloud by Pádraig Pearse from the steps of the GPO on Easter Monday, the Irish Proclamation is synonymous with Easter Week and the birth of the modern Irish State. Widely accepted to have been composed by Pearse himself, there remain very few physical copies in existence, largely down to the fact that the paper upon which they were printed was of such poor quality. (Even fewer copies exist of a facsimile of the Proclamation issued by the Irish Citizen Army for the first anniversary of the Rising – there is believed to be only one surviving.)

In 1916, it is likely that fewer than 1,000 of an intended 2,500 copies of the Proclamation were printed in Liberty Hall for distribution around the country. These were entrusted to Helena Moloney for transport to the GPO. Seán T. O'Kelly, who would be the second president of Ireland, remembered collecting them from there, and posting them around the north and south inner city.

Responsibility for printing the document lay with two Volunteers – Michael Molloy and Liam O'Brien – and Christopher Brady, who had until then overseen the printing of the ITGWU's weekly *Worker's Republic*. Compositors and printers by trade, these men were approached by James Connolly in the run-up to Easter Week and asked to forego the planned parading of Volunteers in St Anne's Park on Easter Sunday morning, and instead to meet him in Liberty Hall for a task he had prepared for them. Upon arrival, Connolly and Thomas MacDonagh handed them a sheet of paper with the Proclamation inscribed upon it and remarked, 'Do if you wish to, and if not we won't be the worse friends.' The three accepted the job.

As they launched into their work, it became obvious that they would not have the necessary tools to finish the job. The machine upon which they were to perform their task, an old Wharfedale Double Crown upon which the *Irish Worker* was printed, was wholly inadequate for the task at hand, the paper of an inferior quality, and type for the machine severely lacking. Different fonts had to be used (the wrong letter 'e' is used more than twenty times), and many letters had to be fashioned out of others (in several cases, a capital 'E' was made by adding wax to a capital 'F'). Eventually, the men realised they would not have enough type and would simply have to borrow some more.

The type was borrowed from an Englishman named William Henry West, a printer whose premises were located on Stafford Street. Following the tradition of Wolfe Tone, the Protestant revolutionary for whom Stafford Street would eventually be renamed, West appears to have been sympathetic towards the cause of Irish freedom. Census returns for 1911 list West as 41 years of age, with an address at Brigid's Road Upper, Drumcondra. His job title is 'letterpress printer' and his religion is given as 'Cooneyite'. Cooneyism was an offshoot of a home-based church movement known as the 'Two by Twos', which gained some traction in Ireland in the late nineteenth and early twentieth centuries in Ireland. It was known as an 'itinerant' religion, and its lay people were called 'tramp preachers' due to the homeless and destitute nature of their calling.

West was the printer of choice for the ITGWU for a time, and had appeared twice in the courts alongside Jim Larkin. In January 1913, he appeared as a co-defendant with Larkin in a case in which a Mr William Richardson was claiming a sum of £500 after allegedly having been libelled in the *Irish Worker*. In September of that year, he appeared in a bankruptcy case involving himself, with the creditor bringing the case against him and the same Mr William Richardson, still looking to eke out punishment for his alleged libelling. In examination of his firm's accounts, West had listed the ITGWU's debt as a 'bad debt', or one which he deemed unrecoverable. West's examination by the prosecution is below:

Mr. Larkin owes you £227 for the printing *The Worker* – isn't Mr. Larkin the proprietor of *The Worker*?
He is, and he owes me £227.
Have you put that down as a bad debt?
Yes, because it is a bad debt.
Why?
Because I cannot get it.
Can you not recover it from Mr. Larkin?
I wish you could show me how. (laughter)
Has Mr. Larkin refused to pay the amount?
Well, he cannot pay.
He refused to pay?
No.
Did you ask him for it?

Of course, often. But he can't pay what he hasn't got.

You know that Mr. Larkin is Secretary of the ITGWU?

Yes, I have heard so.

And can you not recover this amount by suing him for it?

Do you think I would do that, when he's my best customer? (laughter)

The case also refers to debt owed by other organisations, including the Labour Party and a drama class at Liberty Hall. West was asked whether he could not sue for payment, to which he replied 'I don't believe in suing, I've never sued anybody in my life', again to laughter.

The Bureau of Military History witness statement of Commandant Liam O'Brien states that on Easter Sunday, upon realising their shortage of type, Michael Molloy was ordered by Connolly to West's printers along with a messenger and Citizen Army man employed by the *Worker's Republic* who was known to him by the name 'Dazzler'. West provided the type, with the understanding that it would be returned to him intact, or he would be compensated if it was lost – it was his livelihood, after all. Of course, this wasn't to be, as Liberty Hall was first pounded by shells from the *Helga*, and then gutted by fire. When British soldiers entered the building after the fighting had died down, they found the second half of the type still on the machine.

It is unclear what happened to West after Easter Week, but his is another story of the many from the Rising: the English Protestant printer who supplied the type for the Irish Proclamation.

Antonin Artaud, the Staff of Saint Patrick, and a Trip to Mountjoy Prison

Donal Fallon

One of the most puzzling little stories of 1930s Ireland has to be Antonin Artaud's arrival here in 1937. The French poet, dramatist and theatre director is remembered as one of the major figures of the Avant-garde art movement of his time, but to the people of the Aran Islands, and to the confused gardaí of Milltown in south Dublin, he was a total mystery.

Arriving in the country in August, a troubled Artaud was convinced he carried with him the staff of Saint Patrick, which he felt he had to return to its rightful home. To him, this was a spiritual mission of sorts, and the staff possessed magical qualities. He also carried a letter of introduction from the Irish legation in Paris, who were unaware of the nature of his pilgrimage. He would end up in Mountjoy Prison for his troubles, before being deported as a 'destitute and undesirable alien'.

Born in Marseilles in September 1896, Artaud endured both physical and psychological illness in his youth. At the age of only 4 he was diagnosed with spinal meningitis, and he would spend most of his life 'beset with ill-health, pain and nervous depression'. He developed addictions

Antonin Artaud in 1926. (Image: Bibliothèque nationale de France)

to pain-reducing and hallucinatory drugs from a young age, something that would come to shape the course of his life.

He was inducted into the French armed forces in 1916 when war was raging in the country, but was quickly dismissed on health grounds. It was in 1920, following the end of the horror show that was the First World War, that a young Artaud arrived in Paris, at a time when the city was redefining culture in its own unique ways. Ian Buchanan maintains in his *Dictionary of Critical Theory* that Artaud 'never had a proper career. He lurched from one thing to another seemingly at random, but apparently with the constant aim of challenging the perception of reality.' In Paris, he studied under Charles Dullin, theatre manager and bold director, and appeared in a number of French cinematic productions, including *La Passion de Jeanne d'Arc*, a beautifully shot 1928 silent film in which he played the role of Jean Massieu, the Dean of Rouen.

For a period, Artaud was a core part of the surrealist art movement in Paris, contributing to and editing publications that explored this new approach. Surrealist art was colourful, playful, and often very political. Salvador Dalí said that 'Surrealism is destructive, but it destroys only what it considers to be shackles limiting our vision.' In time, Artaud drifted from the surrealists, in part owing to the political direction of the art movement, but he still made important cultural contributions in France.

One such contribution was the so-called Theatre of Cruelty, his desire to 'reject form and inject chaos' into theatre. He wanted a new approach, with lights, noise, and setting all playing new roles. As Lee Jamieson has put it in his study of Artaud, 'by turning theatre into a place where the spectator is exposed rather than protected, Artaud was committing an act of cruelty upon them'.

Artaud and Ireland
So, what brought this puzzling artist to Ireland? In 1997, the sociologist Peter Collier wrote a fascinating article, entitled

'Artaud on Aran', which tried to understand the thought process of Artaud at the time. In short, he had become convinced that a walking stick he had acquired from a friend was the staff of Saint Patrick, and reading texts like the *Confessions of St Patrick* and parts of the *Annals of the Four Masters* only further increased this belief.

This was a mentally unsound individual, convinced he had the so-called Bachal Isu (or 'Staff of Jesus') in his possession. This staff had once been kept at Christ Church Cathedral in Dublin, but was destroyed in 1538 in Skinners Row, following the Protestant Reformation, on the basis that it was a 'superstitious relic'. Yet Artaud believed he had it, and was obliged to return it.

A curious file in the National Archives, held in the collections of the Department for External Affairs, explains more. It opens with a short note from Artaud to the Irish legation in Paris, explaining to them his reasoning for wishing to travel to Ireland. He outlined that his visit to Ireland was concerned with research, but that 'this isn't a literary project, nor that of an academic or museum curator … It is vital that I reach the land where John Millington Synge lived.' In return, he received a letter of introduction from Art O'Briain, the Irish minister plenipotentiary in Paris:

This letter will make known to you Monsieur Antonin Artaud from Paris.

M. Artaud is about to leave for Ireland in search of information concerning ancient Gaelic customs and other matters relating to ancient Ireland, her history and so forth.

He himself would be very grateful for any help that you can give him.

In addition to this letter of introduction, Artaud was provided with a list of individuals to whom he might appeal to help him in researching ancient Irish traditions. Susan Sontag, editor of some of Artaud's writing, has noted that he was 'in an extremely agitated state before his departure for Ireland'. The Frenchman would arrive in Cobh clutching this letter of introduction, but without a visa. It proved enough.

Travelling across Ireland

Artaud spent slightly more than six weeks on the island of Ireland, passing through the Aran Islands and Galway city before arriving in Dublin with almost nothing to sustain himself. From Ireland, he sent numerous postcards and letters home to France, writing to friends and former collaborators. In one, he made his feelings clear:

> The cane I possess is the very same one of Jesus Christ and, knowing I am not crazy, you will believe me when I tell you that Jesus Christ speaks to me every day, reveals all that is going to happen and arranges for me to do what I am going to do. Therefore, I came to Ireland to obey the exact orders of God, the Son, incarnated in Jesus Christ.

His biographer, David A. Shafer, has described the letters he sent from Ireland as 'a bizarre admixture of spiritual prophecies and political rantings'. The French, Artaud wrote, 'whether identifying with the right or left, are all idiots and capitalists'. He also poured scorn on the Spanish Republic, Jews, and just about everyone else.

On Inishmore, locals seemed more confused than anything by Artaud's arrival there. Bridget O'Toole, 20 at the time of his arrival, recalled later:

There was something in the stick. I was always play acting to get it off him. My mother would shout after him – 'Stop chasing with that one as she's only married' … but I was not afraid of him. The only thing was to keep away from the stick but I suppose I was a divil, like himself.

He left the islands, owing locals a significant sum of money for lodgings, and departed for Galway city. He would lodge in the Imperial Hotel, sending confused postcards (depicting Eyre Square) home, and again departed owing money.

Artaud arrived in Dublin on 8 September, a man with little English struggling to communicate with anyone he encountered. In the capital, he would spend a night at the Saint Vincent de Paul shelter for homeless men at Back Lane, while also seeking out some of the people who he had been pointed towards in Paris. He introduced himself to the publisher Richard Foley, who later beautifully described meeting him: 'Máire Ní Daboinean, my assistant editor, knows French very well and spent a good while in France. We came to the conclusion that our visitor was travelling light in the upper storey.'

Artaud would later arrive at the grounds of the Jesuit College in Milltown, convinced of the need to speak to the Jesuits, but gardaí were called to have him removed from the grounds. Seán Murphy, assistant secretary of the Department of External Affairs, would write to the Irish legation in Paris about this:

Since his arrival in this country Artaud has failed to pay his hotel bill in Galway and has had to be removed from the grounds of Milltown Park, where he called to interview some of the members of the [Jesuit] community. On being informed that the priests were on retreat and that he could not be granted an interview, he refused to leave the grounds. The Gardaí had to be called by the Milltown Park authorities to have him removed. As he is destitute he has had to be confined in Mountjoy Prison awaiting the order for his deportation.

For a man in his mental state, Mountjoy must have been traumatic. To compound confusion, his walking stick was lost in the fracas with gardaí, and never recovered. Deportation came on 29 September, when the SS *Washington* set sail from Cobh. Murphy noted that:

On arrival at Le Havre, Artaud was sent to the Havre General Hospital in a strait-jacket. He was later transferred from that hospital to the Departmental Insane Asylum at Rouen. It is understood from the latest information available that this man is not in a fit condition to be questioned.

Artaud's journey to Ireland has caught the imagination of many. Aidan Mathews dramatised the story for RTÉ radio, and *Artaud in Ireland* was performed at the Samuel Beckett Theatre in 1999. Artaud would die alone in a psychiatric clinic on 4 March 1948, having spent the final phase of his life in numerous asylums.

Before Panti, There Was Mr Pussy

Donal Fallon

It says something about modern Ireland that one of the most recognisable faces in the country today is that of a drag queen: the much-loved alter ego of Rory O'Neill, known as Panti Bliss. In May 2015, images of a smiling Panti on stage at Dublin Castle (alongside Gerry Adams and Miriam O'Callaghan) were beamed into homes across the world, as Ireland voted overwhelmingly in favour of legalising gay marriage.

Before Panti, there were drag acts in Irish society, and none as important to the story as Mr Pussy, who drew huge crowds in the 1970s, and who baffled some in the Irish media, who couldn't quite get their heads around the idea of a drag queen in Dublin. 'If this is what female impersonation is about, the sooner it's buried the better!' declared one writer in 1970. Others saw things differently, though. 'If anybody has helped to lure Irish audience into a broad-minded era', the *Sunday Independent* said a few short years later, it was Mr Pussy.

In reality, Mr Pussy was (and is) Alan Amsby, a Londoner by birth. In one of the earliest feature pieces on Mr Pussy, Donall Corvin wrote in the June 1970 edition of the *New Spotlight* that 'Pussy's act is slick. He/she gets full marks for professionalism. But I'm surprised there hasn't been an

Mr Pussy's first Irish publicity shot (with thanks to Alan Amsby).

outcry from indignant bishops and moderators.' Amsby, it was noted, had arrived in Belfast three months earlier, and 'he was to do six shows. Now he has done more than fifty appearances and has become the most successful cabaret act ever to visit Ireland.'

Paul O'Grady, a popular broadcaster and a friend of Amsby's, recounted in his memoirs that Mr Pussy became 'Ireland's foremost and, at the time, only drag queen. During the sixties he'd been working on the flourishing drag scene in London as part of an established act called Pussy and Bow.' When that act broke up, Amsby came to Ireland. O'Grady wrote that 'drag queens were rare as hen's teeth in Holy Ireland. He caused a sensation and never came back.' Of the London days, Amsby remembered in 1987 that 'all the other acts were doing the glamour bit, but we were in the miniskirts and the modern look. Everyone came to see us – Judy Garland, Ringo Starr.'

In his entertaining memoir, *Mr Pussy: Before I Forget to Remember*, Ambsy recalled his initial take on Dublin:

> It was only fifty years since the War of Independence, and many parts of the city seemed to be stuck in a time warp, with the old colonial areas falling into decay. Georgian Dublin was being bulldozed and allowed to fall into ruin. I think many politicians associated it with the old regime and wanted to modernise the city. That's why so many ugly new buildings were going up, like the appalling Bank of Ireland HQ on Baggot Street.

Journalists rushed to interview Amsby, almost all commenting on his male appearance and youth. At the time of Donall Corvin's feature in *New Spotlight*, Amsby was a mere 22 years old. Ginnie Kennealy informed *Irish Press* readers in January 1972 that he was a 'slight figure, startlingly young ... with shoulder-length fair hair'. To her, he was 'neither effeminate nor pointedly masculine. Instead he has very much the uni-sex look of the seventies.'

No doubt the Ireland of the 1970s was in many ways a socially conservative place. Amsby recalled that 'Ireland was a homophobic country, with cruel and outdated laws, and an attitude to gays that was dismissive, derisive and fearful.' Yet beyond the very occasional condemnation in the press, it seemed drag was well-received here in the early 1970s. A glance at the entertainment page of one Irish newspaper from 1973 shows Mr Pussy bringing in crowds not only in Dublin but across the island. Looking over the page, it's surreal to see the name alongside those of Planxty, the Wolfe Tones, the Women's Lib Carnival Dance and Gerry Walsh and the Cowboys.

Being a drag artist in the Dublin of the 1970s could bring you to some interesting places. In her women's interest section of the *Irish Press* in February 1971, Mary Kenny recounted sharing the floor with Mr Pussy during a debate in Trinity's College Historical Society, known as 'the Hist'. It was a time of great change in Trinity; the Hist had 'only opened its historic portals to the female sex some two years ago'. In attendance for the discussion was 'poor Father Heffernan, the chairman, and incidentally the first Catholic chaplain to be appointed to TCD'. Kenny remembered that 'Pussy certainly added a note of gaiety to the whole debate'.

In the early days in Dublin, Mr Pussy primarily performed in the legendary Baggot Inn on Baggot Street, which will forever be remembered for hosting some great gigs in the 1970s and 80s. Christy Moore recalled that 'the Baggot hosted all sorts of gigs, from Mr Pussy to Paddy Reilly'. Of Pussy's time in the venue, the *Sunday Independent* wrote that 'at first, he was playing to just a handful of people', but that within a short period 'he was filling the Inn six nights a week and doing private parties before or after his show'.

Having seen Mr Pussy there in July 1970, an *Irish Press* journalist wrote that:

It was absolutely packed. Frightfully hetero audience, as someone had warned me, but still they appreciated Mr Pussy like mad. Mr Pussy is a gorgeous-looking dame, the spitting image of Sandie Shaw. He sings appallingly and has the bluest line of patter I have ever heard. He is screamingly funny but frankly I couldn't reproduce a single one of his jokes here.

Mr Pussy quickly made the leap from pub stage to theatre stage, with *Little Red Riding-Would* at the Eblana Theatre early in 1972, which one reviewer described as 'off-beat, way out by traditional panto standards'. In his memoir, Ambsy joked that the Eblana was once referred to as 'the only public toilet with its own theatre', saying that 'It was very small and cosy and had no wings, but it was a great place to work.' Ambsy shared the stage of the venue with Dermot Morgan, and remembered how the Eblana 'had a reputation for breaking new material in the days before the Project or Andrew's Lane'.

When interviewed in 1994, Amsby stated that 'the boy who came to Ireland 25 years ago with his act, Mr Pussy, for one week's booking only, is still here because I love it here'. His story continued into subsequent decades, and to the younger generation of drag performers Mr Pussy became a legend, proving that even conservative Ireland could let its hair down. While Dublin may be home to a significant number of drag queens now, it all began in the Baggot Inn.

Historic Dublin Pub the White Horse is Now a Starbucks

Sam McGrath

What links Captain William Bligh of *Mutiny on the Bounty* fame, Brendan Behan, Green Day, and early morning techno gigs? One address: 1 George's Quay, Dublin 2. On the Southside between the Rosie Hackett Bridge and the Butt Bridge, this well-known and well-loved early house pub closed in July 2016 and reopened less than a month later as a Starbucks.

As The White Horse, it was a popular haunt from the 1950s to the 1970s for the city's journalists and literary set, due mainly to its close proximity to the *Irish Press* building. In the 1980s and 1990s its upstairs venue, The Attic, played an important role in Dublin's rock scene. A relatively unknown Californian punk band called Green Day played there in December 1991, at a gig organised by the pioneering Hope Collective.

Most people would probably say that the pub lost its true charm after a massive refurbishment in 1998. However, up until recently as The Dark Horse, it played host to an array of techno, reggae, and other 'underground' gigs. Its closure reduced the number of early houses in the city to eleven.

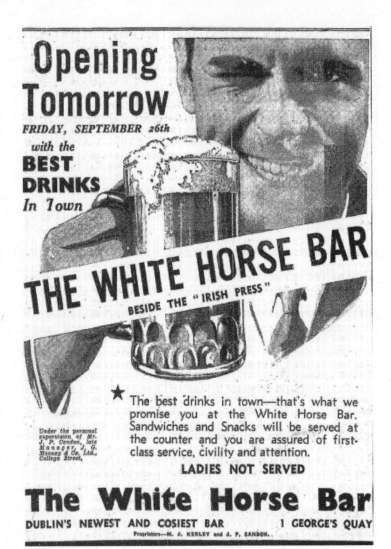

Advertisement announcing the opening of the White Horse Bar from the *Irish Press*, 25 September 1941.

Nineteenth-Century History

Captain William Bligh, who was in command of the HMS *Bounty* in 1789, when its crew famously rebelled, arrived in Dublin in September 1800 and stayed for about a year. A number of accounts have him staying in lodgings above the tavern at 1 George's Quay. There was apparently a plaque outside the pub confirming this historical claim, but it has long since disappeared. During his time here, he conducted a survey of Dublin Bay and recommended the construction of the Bull Wall.

In the 1820s, 1 George's Quay was the business premises of White's Spirits Stores, owned by Philip White. By the 1840s, it was in possession of a vintner named Eliza Fagan. *Thom's Dublin Street Directory* of 1862 listed its owner as a 'wine and spirit dealer' called William Bergin. Denis Bergin, presumably his son, sold the pub in 1880.

An *Irish Times* article on 29 June 1880 described the premises as an 'old-established wine and spirit concern' situated in this 'great leading thoroughfare and commercial district, close by Corn Exchange, and the immediate shipping traffic, which … always leaves it one of the most desirable houses of its kind in the city'. The public house had 'recently undergone a complete change, having been taken down and rebuilt in its present modern form at an outlay of several thousand pounds'.

Twentieth-Century History

The 1901 census shows that James Ennis (50), a 'tea and spirit merchant' from County Meath, lived in the building with his sister Ellen (35). They employed two commercial assistants from County Carlow – William Byrne (30) and John Byrne (23). A servant, Mary Monaghan (50) from Meath, also worked for the Ennis siblings. All five individuals in the house were Roman Catholic and unmarried.

James Ennis died in 1905, and the pub was taken over by businessman John McGrath.

In the 1911 census, John McGrath (33), listed as a licensed vintner from County Monaghan, lived at the premises with his wife Mary (23), from Dunishal, County Wicklow, and their two Dublin-born daughters Lizzie (3) and Mary (11 months). They employed two shop/pub assistants: James Fitzpatrick (18), from Ferns, County Wexford, and Robert Leggett (21), from Dublin. A domestic servant, Kate Kavanagh (17) from Thurles, County Tipperary, also worked in the house.

After the 1916 Rising, John McGrath made two successful claims to the Property Losses (Ireland) Committee (PLIC). This body was established in June 1916 to assess claims for damages to buildings and property as a result of the destruction caused by the Rising. His first claim was for £7 11*s.* 7*d.* of stock, including sugar, biscuits and cigarettes, taken by crown forces at his pub. A payment of £6 6*s.* 7*d.* was recommended by the PLIC. The second was for £3 1*s.* for damages to the building, including broken bedroom windows; full payment was recommended by the PLIC.

John McGrath emigrated to the Bronx, New York with his family in the late 1920s and died there in 1937.

The Irish Press Connection
The Tivoli cinema building beside the pub was originally known as the Conciliation Hall and was built as a meeting place for Daniel O'Connell's Loyal National Repeal Association in 1841. After his death six years later, the building was used as a grain store before reopening as the Grand Lyric Hall in 1897. After a period of staging variety shows, it was relaunched in 1901 as the Tivoli cinema. Closing in

1928, the imposing building was bought by the *Irish Press* and converted into the newspaper's headquarters.

The White Horse's Heyday

The pub was known as Galvin's for a period in the 1930s, before being bought by James P. Candon from Boyle, County Roscommon, and J. Kerley and reopened as The White Horse in September 1941.

An *Irish Press* advertisement published on the day before it opened offered potential customers 'the best drinks in town ... sandwiches and snacks ... first-class service, civility and attention'. At 'Dublin's newest and cosiest bar', the owners were clear from the outset that men were welcome but the rule was – 'ladies not served'.

In June 1948, Candon sold his stake in The White Horse. A strong union man, he later went on to become president and then secretary of the Irish National Union of Vintners and Allied Trade Assistants. He passed away in 1969 at the age of 51.

Candon sold his stake in the pub for £15,000 to Michael 'Mick' O'Connell, a farmer turned publican from Croom in County Limerick. It was during O'Connell's stewardship that The White Horse became the favoured watering hole for journalists and authors. He was known fondly as 'the Boss' O'Connell.

It was related by Bill Kelly's book *Me Darlin' Dublin's Dead and Gone* that writer Benedict Kiely often told the story about the time that fourteen different people invited him for a drink as he walked between O'Connell Bridge and The White Horse, a distance of less than 75 yards.

Brendan Behan was a regular during the 1950s and 1960s in The White Horse, along with The Pearl, The Palace, and other nearby spots. As were Brian O'Nolan (aka Flann O'Brien and Myles na gCopaleen), Seamus de Faoite and many others.

While Behan's drinking days have become more and more celebrated as time has passed, they were often a very depressing affair. This was illustrated by Tim Pat Coogan in his 2008 memoir, in which he wrote about his last time drinking in Behan's company:

> [It was] about a year before his death in 1964 … in The White Horse beside the *Press* building. I was acting as Terry O'Sullivan's stand-in on 'Dublin's Diary', and intended procuring a few Behanisms to enliven the column.
>
> Instead I found myself consoling Beatrice, his wife, as she gazed miserably but helplessly at Brendan standing at the bar with two well-known Dublin soaks. Every so often he would tell the barman to give him a ten-shilling note from the till. Then he would roll up the note, suck it for a while like a lollipop, and then spit it out. There was a ring of ten-shilling notes around the trio's feet.
>
> I offered to get the barman to stop, but Beatrice told me it was useless. All he would do was go to another pub and indulge in some similar caper, accompanied by the soaks, and probably there'd be more like them at the next venue.

Another regular patron was the late, great sports journalist Con Houlihan. In conversation with Keith Duggan in the *Irish Times* on 25 October 2003, Houlihan spoke about the importance of The White Horse and the surrounding area:

geographically, Burgh Quay was the focal point of Dublin. It was an intimate community with certain pubs for certain people. I suppose the Dublin I knew was bound by Mulligan's pub and you had perhaps 10 more around it. All great meeting places.

First and foremost, you had The White Horse. It would open around half six in the morning if you wanted an early drink. It was unique in that [Brendan] Behan could drink there as long as he stayed in a certain corner and didn't go around bothering people too much. And you found all kinds of humanity there. Bowes on Fleet Street was another.

The Swan on Burgh Quay, or the Mucky Duck as we called it … and The Pearl Bar was frequented by a coterie from the *Irish Times*, all good people but a niche group. It was like a village and I loved it. You felt safe at night. Change can come like a dam [bursting], and in Dublin it burst overnight. And there is a great sense of loss about that now.

Owner Michael O'Connell, then living at 68 Offington Park in Sutton, passed away at the age of 69 in March 1970. After his death, Pádraig Puirséal wrote about him affectionately in the *Irish Press* on 13 March 1970:

The 'Boss' O'Connell, God rest him, was a big, patient, understanding man, who could cope with any emergency in the White Horse, from an unexpected newspaper strike to Brendan Behan (and God rest him too) suddenly deciding to burst into 'ar thaobh na greine Sliabh na mBan' … he always seemed a man of the open air as, on the too few occasions we had time for private chatter, he talked of his youthful days around Croom, of horse and points-to-points, of running dogs and hurling men.

Mick O'Connell's son William (Bill) took over the reins of The White Horse.

In the 1970s, the bar was a meeting spot for an array of organisations, including the Irish Boxers' Mutual Benefit Society. A newspaper advertisement in the *Irish Press* on 29 October 1970 looking for a new barman specified that the individual must be a 'union member'. Different times.

Former *Irish Press* journalist Hugh McFadden, in a 9 August 2016 email to me, recalled his memories of The White Horse of the 1970s:

> It was an 'early house', of course, meaning that it opened about 7:30 a.m. in the morning, as it had a special licence to serve the dockers and shift workers on the quays.
>
> The shift workers included staff of the adjacent *Irish Press*, especially those who worked on the *Evening Press* … The downstairs bar would usually be quite busy around 8 a.m.–9 a.m. in the morning.
>
> The pub did have its literary associations, not alone the connection with the *Press*. The novelist and broadcaster Ben Kiely … drank there, and so did the Kerry short-story writer Seamus de Faoite, among others. The novelists and *Irish Times* columnist Brian O'Nolan often drank there in the 1950s and 1960s. Several of the *Irish Times* 'Cruiskeen Lawn' columns

are set in the White Horse, especially ones about the early opening hours.

Des Derwin remembers that the Socialist Workers Movement and New Liberty, a rank-and-file group in the ITGWU, met in the top room of the pub for a while around 1981. After the H Block riot on Merrion Street on 18 July 1981, Alan MacSimon says:

> Groups of Gardai had chased protesters back to the city centre and were using their batons on anyone they thought might have been [at] the march earlier. A few fleeing protesters arrived into the bar and told their possibly exaggerated, stories. Staff decided to lock the doors. A few minutes later Gardai turned up, demanding to be let in. But the doors stayed closed for about an hour, until the Gardai had moved on.

In March 1984, the bar was put up for sale but the offer was withdrawn after it received no bids. It was eventually sold in July 1987 to husband and wife Len and Ger Allen.

From the late 1980s, the upstairs part of the bar became a gig spot known as The Attic. Music promoter Andrew Bass was originally brought in to book bands. Robbie Foy, former manager of Light a Big Fire, later took over. Stephen Rennicks in a blog post about 1980s Dublin band The Idiots described The Attic as a:

> cheap to rent and very small venue [that] was an incredibly important place for certain bands of this generation to come together and share their music

… The Idiots were practically the house band at this time. They had a rehearsal room upstairs, drank and socialized downstairs and played live often at this midpoint between these two worlds. Their manager, Sinead, was also the house sound person for all the bands who played there as well.

Many people recall the floorboards that felt like they were going to give way at any second.

In a 10 August 2016 email to me, Niall McGuirk of the Hope Collective recalled that:

Andrew Bass asked if I was interested in getting bands to play in the Attic. For £30 we'd get the room and a sound engineer. It sounded interesting to me, but I didn't want to become a local promoter. It has always puzzled me as to why music is so inaccessible to people who aren't old enough to drink in pubs. Most folk start off in bands when they are under 18 but there is nowhere for them, legally, to play.

Back in the late 80s, Ireland's bar owners had a strange interpretation of the licensing laws. They would allow 'minors' (under 18s) on their premises until 6:30, but only if accompanied by a legal guardian and, obviously, without serving them alcohol. The police turned a blind eye if minors were on the premises before that time. That 'law' has since been rubbished, but in 1990 the only way to have no age restrictions at a gig was to play it in the afternoon. So I asked if it could happen! The Attic's manager, Lenny, agreed to try out Sunday gigs with no age restrictions, starting at 4 p.m.

Niall and his Hope Collective put on a host of cult Irish bands at The Attic, including Therapy? and Whipping Boy, in December 1990.

On a wintry Sunday afternoon in December 1991, the up-and-coming American punk band Green Day played in The Attic to about 40 people. Support came from Dog Day. The cover charge was £2, and the organisers lost £50 on the night. Niall recalled in his 2004 book *Please Feed Me: a Punk Vegan Cookbook* that singer Billy Joe Armstrong and the rest of the band didn't hang around in Dublin that evening:

> Dublin wasn't really the party city and Green Day left for Belfast straight after the gig, but not before getting some directions and food. They had enjoyed themselves so much in Belfast the previous night that they wanted to get back as quickly as possible.

Football and Redevelopment

The White Horse was a popular pub for football fans during this time as well. An array of soccer scarves from around the world was displayed in the bar downstairs. Shay Ryan, drummer with mid-1980s Dublin soul legends The Commotion, remembers the great atmosphere in the pub watching the Euro 1988 championship, especially the England game.

Booker Robbie Foy was a diehard Shamrock Rovers fan, as were owner Len Allen and barman Buzz O'Neill. Allen had played junior football as a goalkeeper for Baldoyle United and Oulton FC. As such, it became a favoured spot for Rovers fans during this period, particularly when the club played at the RDS from 1990 to 1996.

Sadly, signalling the end of an era, the *Irish Press* closed its doors in May 1995, with a loss of over 600 jobs. The White Horse, in its current incarnation, soon followed.

No doubt spurred on by the growth of the so-called Celtic Tiger and the popularity of 'modernizing' pubs, it was announced in the *Irish Independent* on 7 May 1997 that the Allen family had lodged planning permission to 'demolish and rebuild the well-known early house and traditional music venue'. The plan was to reconstruct the premises to include a pub on the ground floor and apartments overhead. This refurbishment cost well over £600,000.

The author of that article noted that the knocking down of the 250-year-old building marked the loss 'of yet another olde worlde pub in the capital'. The pub reopened around 1998 as a sleek, new modern bar, and it was certainly noticed. An unnamed journalist in the *Irish Independent* on 27 April 1999 didn't hold back on their opinions of the redeveloped pub:

Has any pub in history ever undergone as complete a transformation as the White Horse? It's doubtful.

Short of turning into some sort of Episcopalian church it is hard to see how it could have moved further from what it used to be.

The old White Horse was described in terms such as, er, basic while the new version looks like it has sprung from the pages of a Habitat brochure.

[It used to be] dank and dingy, full of bibulous hacks from the doomed *Irish Press* – many of whom took advantage of the fact that it was an early house and started boozing at 7 a.m. – and housed upstairs a creaking venue for rock bands who couldn't get a gig anywhere else.

The new incarnation is completely unrecognisable. It's spacious and airy, full of immaculately polished wooden tables and shiny metal trimmings; above all, it's suffused with light, pouring through from every angle of its largely glazed exterior.

Back then, the White Horse had atmosphere. Can you say the same for the new place? The jury is out.

New decor, new clientele. Gone are the old men, the plastered journalists and the spotty, long-haired teenagers. In their place are smart folk, dressed in suits and designer leather jackets. Yuppies, though not of the strident variety.

Recent History

It changed hands briefly in the early 2000s and was known as P. McCormack & Sons for a time. Len Allen sadly passed away from cancer in 2007, with the band Therapy? leading the tributes, but the Allen family took back control of the pub, and renamed it The Dark Horse around 2011. Len and Ger's son Con Allen, a DJ, and daughter Lyn Allen, a fashion designer, put their own mark on it.

The pub was one of the very rare early houses that encouraged partying and DJs. Promoter Bernard Kennedy started running early morning dance gigs there around 2004. From 2011 to 2015, Con Allen took up the mantle and ran an early morning techno and house club called the Breakfast Club every Saturday. Doors would open at 7 a.m. and a mix of all-night ravers and early risers would come to dance to talented local and international DJs.

Entrance was €10 and two bouncers on the door prevented any trouble. All the windows were covered with black curtains to provide punters with an artificial feeling that it was still Friday night. Sweaty clubbers were kicked out into the disconcerting sunshine and reality at 2 p.m. Some went home, while the more wired would go around the corner to Ned Scanlon's on Townsend Street.

From September 2011 to August 2012, Freda Hughes and her Poster Fish Promotions ran the Saturday night slot at the Dark Horse Inn. Some of the most memorable nights included DJ Mek of legendary Irish hip-hop crew Scary Éire, Captain Moonlight, DJ Welfare, and reggae MC Cian Finn.

Starbucks

The Dark Horse's last post on their Facebook page was in March 2016, and the pub closed its doors in July of that year. It reopened a few weeks later as a Starbucks coffee shop.

There are now forty-plus Starbucks in Dublin, including more than twenty in the city centre. They only make up a tiny percentage of the 23,768 stores the company had worldwide in 2016, but twenty is a lot for a central part of the city that only stretches in each direction for a couple of kilometres. Is there really a need for two opposite each other on Westmoreland Street?

Starbucks has moved into an array of premises, including the old Bewley's café on Westmoreland Street, the clothing shop Counter Propaganda on Liffey Street, Sawers fishmongers (established in 1959) on Chatham Row off Grafton Street, the clothing store and coffee shop Raglan on Drury Street, Marco Pierre's White Steakhouse and Grill on Dawson Street, Coopers Restaurant on Leeson Street and the Bia Cafe on O'Connell Street.

It would be disingenuous to simply portray this as a big, bad American multinational ripping apart a historic pub and putting in a cloned version of their coffee shop. The historic heart of The White Horse was almost totally torn out during the demolition and expansion work in the late 1990s.

But I'm sure I'm not the only one who feels unsettled by the sheer number of chain coffee shops, souvenir shops, clothing stores and fast-food restaurants that are proliferating in the city, often at the expense of independent establishments. Especially if it means another space like The Dark Horse – which was available for people who wanted to put on a reggae dub night or tech-house morning session – is taken out of circulation.

Dublin is fighting an uphill battle to preserve its independence and identity. Temple Bar, once known as an independent area with cheap rents in the 1980s, and then a tourist magnet from the 1990s, seems to have completely lost that battle. It now has a McDonald's, a Starbucks and a Costa Coffee, while its arts space Exchange Dublin, the bike shop Square Wheel Cycleworks and record shops like Borderline and Cosmic have closed their doors in the last few years.

Promoting progress while safeguarding heritage is a complex responsibility. You have to tread carefully. Nobody wants to sound like a clichéd Sean Dempsey in the song 'Dublin in the Rare Old Times', who I'm guessing would be that loud old drunk man who likes to remind people how Parnell Street and Moore Street are unrecognisable from his youth. But I also think it's perfectly fine to be alarmed by the rapid spread of a coffeehouse company like Starbucks, which is regularly criticised for violating labour laws, opening stores without planning permission and tax avoidance.

So goodbye to The White Horse and to The Dark Horse. Cheers for the memories.

'Severity for Suffragettes', Dublin 1912

Ciarán Murray

On 7 August 1912, four women – Gladys Evans, Mary Leigh, Jennie Baines (nom de guerre: Lizzie Baker) and Mabel Capper – were sentenced at Dublin's Green Street Special Criminal Court for 'having committed serious outrages at the time of the visit of the British Prime Minister Herbert Asquith'. The trial had lasted several days, during which police were criticised for initially refusing to allow admittance to women; under steady and mounting pressure, this ban was removed.

Asquith's visit to Dublin in July of that year had been met with defiance from militant suffragettes, some of whom – including the four above – had followed him over from England. On 19 July, a hatchet was thrown at his moving carriage as it passed over O'Connell Bridge. Around it was wrapped a text reading 'This symbol of the extinction of the Liberal Party for evermore.' The hatchet missed Asquith but struck John Redmond, who was travelling in the same carriage, on the arm.

There was also a failed attempt at setting fire to the Theatre Royal the following day, just as Asquith was due to talk on Home Rule. A burning chair was thrown from a balcony into the orchestra pit, and flammable liquid was spread

The harsh sentences handed down to the four women were met with widespread outrage. (Image: 'Votes For Women', August 1912)

around the cinematograph (projector) box and an attempt was made to set it alight. It caught fire, and exploded once, but was quickly extinguished. The *Irish Times* reported the attempt, which, in any case, was foiled by Sergeant Durban Cooper of the Connaught Rangers, who was in attendance:

> At this moment, Sergeant Cooper saw a young woman standing near. She was lighting matches. Opening the door of the cinematograph box, she threw in a lighted match, and then tried to escape. But she was caught by Sergeant Cooper and held by him. She is stated to

have then said, 'There will be a few more explosions in the second house. This is only the start of it.'

The four women mentioned above were accused and charged over both actions. The then attorney general for Ireland, C.A. O'Connor, conducted the prosecution, and Judge Madden presided over the case. It seems that the authorities were at great pains to quell the burgeoning suffragette movement, and so they set out to brand the women as highly dangerous provocateurs. O'Connor spoke of the horrors the fire in the theatre could have caused, and Judge Madden, upon passing sentence on the women, rendered it his 'imperative duty to pronounce a sentence that is calculated to have a deterrent effect'. Large crowds had gathered inside and outside the court for the sentencing, in response to which applause rang out around the largely hostile room.

Gladys Evans, daughter of a London stockbroker, was accused of trying to set the cinematograph box alight and found guilty on the charges of conspiring to do bodily harm and damage property. She was sentenced along with Mary Leigh to five years' penal servitude. This was the first time a sentence of penal servitude was handed down to a suffragette, and the sentence was met with dismay and indignation in Britain. The Women's Social and Political Union, of which the women were members, issued a statement calling the sentences 'an outrage which is not devised as a punishment to fit the offences, but to terrorize other women'. A petition was raised against the sentencing, stating that the 'purity and honesty of the motives of the accused were questioned by no one' during the case, and arguing that the sentences were 'far in excess of those that were ever passed down in the United Kingdom'.

Evans went on hunger strike upon her arrival at Mountjoy Prison and was force-fed for fifty-eight days until her release on 23 October 1912 due to ill-health. This was another dubious first: she was, along with Mary Leigh, the first suffragette in Ireland to be force-fed, as no Irish suffragette had been. Per a niece of Gladys' in a post on a genealogy website, Gladys eventually went on to drive a supply truck in World War I, and then went as a chauffeur to a relief mission in Château de Blérancourt, in France, near the Belgian border.

Mary Leigh, born Mary Brown in 1885, was a school teacher until her marriage. A long-serving activist within the movement, she is credited with being responsible for the first act of physical militancy by a suffragette when she was arrested for throwing stones at the windows of 10 Downing Street after witnessing acts of police brutality at a suffragette march. She was also responsible for throwing the hatchet at Asquith, missing and hitting Redmond.

Leigh had initially evaded arrest, but she had been caught along with Evans and the others in the incident at the Theatre Royal. She faced the same charges as Evans, having thrown the burning chair into the orchestra pit. She represented herself in court, and spoke so well that she elicited doubt as to whether she could be held responsible for the fire in the theatre. She was however, found guilty of throwing the hatchet, and was sentenced to five years' penal servitude.

Upon her imprisonment, she went on hunger strike and was force-fed for forty-six days until her release on 21 September 1912. She was re-arrested shortly after her release, and a retrial was attempted. This was ultimately thrown out, with several references in the court report to her 'fiery nature'. Putting her services forward upon the outbreak of World War I, she was turned down for being a 'troublemaker'. She reverted to her maiden name, and on reapplying was successful, going on to train as an ambulance driver.

Jennie Baines ('Lizzie Baker') was another long-time suffragette, and a volunteer in the Salvation Army. An early member of the Women's Social and Political Union, she was a powerful speaker, and well respected in the movement for placing an emphasis on action over words. She had not been seen near the theatre, and so blame for the fire could not be directly assigned to her. She had, along with Mabel Capper, come over with the other two, and lodged with them in a room on Mount Street, in which was found flammable liquid and rubber gloves. She pleaded guilty to the minor offence of causing damage to property, and was given seven months of hard labour. Like the others, she went on hunger strike, but in her case, the prison doctor feared that force-feeding may have serious implications for her health. As such, she was freed after a matter of days. In later life, she moved to Melbourne, and became a children's court magistrate there.

Mabel Capper had been born into a house driven by political activity. Her father was the secretary of the Manchester branch of the Men's League for Women's Suffrage, and her mother was an active member of the Women's Social and Political Union. Capper was imprisoned more than half a dozen times for activities relating to the suffragette movement. Although she was accused of being Gladys Evans' accomplice, the charges were withdrawn due to lack of evidence. Like the others, she adhered to Christabel Pankhurst's call for the WSPU to abandon its campaign in order to support Britain in WWI, and joined the Volunteer Aid Detachment.

On the case, and its outcome, the 16 August 1912 issue of *Votes for Women*, the voice of the WSPU, said that:

> by meting out punishment of such appalling severity, the government have created a situation which they themselves know cannot last. Even they realise that women cannot be sent for years to convict prisons as the alternative to giving them the vote.

On sentencing, Mary Leigh announced: '[I]t is a frightful sentence; but it will have no deterring effect on us'.

Konrad Peterson: Latvian Revolutionary and Pioneering Civil Engineer

Sam McGrath

Konrad Peterson (1888–1981) never wrote a memoir or gave a detailed interview, but we've been able to piece together his life with what is available. Born in Latvia, which was then part of the Russian Empire, at the age of 17, he took part in the Russian revolution of 1905. Following a daring prison raid, he was forced to flee, and having escaped with his life, ended up with relatives in Ireland. He became active in socialist and Irish republican politics in Dublin, becoming friendly with many famous names of the time, and allegedly played a minor role in the 1916 Rising.

In 1919, he returned home to Latvia, which had recently declared independence. There he would be a witness to both the Nazi and Russian invasions of his home city of Riga during World War II. And through a chance encounter, he would return to Ireland to work with Bord na Móna and live in County Kildare until his death.

Although, Sandra Bondarevska of the Latvian community and local Athy historian Frank Taaffe have done much to help ensure that Peterson hasn't been totally forgotten, there is still much about him that we don't know.

Konrad Peterson in Dublin, ca. late 1910s.
(Image: Brady Collection via Sandra Bondarevska)

What we do know is that Peterson was born in Riga in 1888. He became involved in the Latvian revolutionary movement from a young age, and during the 1905 Russian revolution, he participated in the 10,000-strong workers' demonstration in protest of the Bloody Sunday massacre.

Three days earlier in St Petersburg, Russia, over 1,000 unarmed demonstrators were shot dead by soldiers of the Imperial Guard as they marched towards the Winter Palace to present a petition to Tsar Nicholas II of Russia.

John Langins, a history of science professor at the University of Toronto, met Peterson in later life, and retold in his memoirs how Peterson was involved:

> in the bloody demonstration in January [1905]. Jumping over the wall, one Cossack tried to spear him ... but [the] spear [went through his] thick coat [and] out the back ... [He] later was an active combatant in Riga and in the countryside. These revolutionary instincts remained with Conrad [sic] [his whole] life-time.

In September 1905, Peterson was involved in a daring rescue of two imprisoned comrades. In the wake of the brutal repression following the revolution, Peterson was smuggled out of Riga. According to Langins' memoirs, Peterson:

> hid [in a] ship that traveled to Scotland with a few comrades. Some were concealed [among] potatoes and some within [flax bales]. Those [in] potatoes [were] found, and right there on the ship [were] shot, but those who were in the [flax bales] was [sic] moved to one [friendly] small cabin, where they spent several days and nights in meetings, motion-less on one bed ... When [they] jumped down from the board in Scotland, they almost could not walk and was [sic] accepted as heroes of the English trade unions.

Arriving in Dublin about 1906, he moved in with his uncle Charles Peterson (of the well-known pipe firm Kapp & Peterson), who lived in Leinster Road in Rathmines. Their home was just a few minutes' walk from Constance Markievicz's Surrey House in Leinster Road, and she later became good friends with the family.

Peterson enrolled at Patrick Pearse's school St Enda's for the year 1908–9 and was listed as being a pupil in Fourth Class, Division II. While Peterson would have been about 20 years of age in 1908, as he had only been in Ireland for two years with presumably little or no English, it makes sense that he would be in a class for much younger children.

At the time of the 1911 census Konrad, aged 21, was listed as a scholar. For his religion, he put down 'Free Thinker', as did his uncles Charles (60) and John (45), both pipe-makers. Around this time, Konrad enrolled as an engineering student at the Royal College of Science for Ireland (RCScI). He remained active with the Socialist Party of Ireland, and in 1911 offered advice to Irish republicans who were organising protests against the visit of King George V and Queen Mary.

In her Bureau of Military History witness statement (No. 909), Sidney Czira (aka John Brennan) recalled:

> It was suggested to us by Conrad [sic] Peterson, who was a student in the College of Science and who had some experience of shock tactics in czarist Russia – he was from Riga – that we should adopt the methods used by demonstrators in Russia i.e. fold all the leaflets in two and catching them by the corner, fling them into air if we saw the police approaching. They would fan about the crowd and be picked up.

Czira (née Gifford) was an officer of Cumann na mBan in Dublin, and sister of Grace Gifford, whose husband Joseph Plunkett would be executed after the Rising.

Peterson was active in labour politics in Dublin in 1913, but it is not known to what extent he participated in the turbulent events of the Lockout. A wonderful picture from around 1913, published in Fearghal McGarry's book *The Abbey Rebels of 1916: a Lost Revolution*, shows Peterson, Constance Markievicz, Helena Molony, Michael O'Gorman, and George Doran in fancy dress.

In his book *Man of No Property*, C.S. Andrews wrote that during this time Peterson: 'formed close links with many of the literary and theatrical figures of Dublin … including, in particular, the famous Daisy Bannard and the man who she afterwards married, the republican journalist Fred Cogley'.

Peterson graduated in 1913 with an engineering degree from the College of Science. On 4 May 1915, he was granted naturalisation by the British government. He was listed as 'Konrad Peterson, from Russia. Resident in Rathmines, Co. Dublin.' Around this time he also married Helen Yeates from Dublin.

Peterson was in Dublin during the 1916 Rising and was friends with many of its leading personalities, including Connolly and Markievicz. The *Irish Press* on 24 May 1951 said Peterson 'helped in the organisation of communications for the Rising', but there is no more reliable source to back up this claim.

In February 1918, he was present at a large meeting that took place at the Mansion House to celebrate the first anniversary of the 1917 Russian revolution. 'The Red Flag' was sung and red and republican flags were waved. The *Irish*

Independent on 5 Feb 1918 wrote that 'Mr Conrad Peterson, who announced himself as a Russian social democrat spoke strongly in support of "the great struggle for peace, liberty and bread".' Those present also included Cathal O'Shannon, Dr Kathleen Lynn, Countess Markievicz and Maud Gonne MacBride.

In 1919, Konrad and his wife returned to Latvia, and it was in Riga in 1923 that Helen gave birth to their only child, Izeult Pamela Peterson. Konrad Peterson visited Ireland that same year, and journalist Patrick Smyth (aka 'Quidnunc') wrote in the *Irish Times* on 19 June:

> I happened to meet during the week a visitor to Dublin whose name will be remembered by many of his old associates in the College of Science – Mr Konrad Peterson, who is now director of public works under the government of Latvia.

The piece mentioned that Peterson was 'for several years associated with labour politics in this city'. Smyth obviously thought very highly of him, as he remarked that his 'cheerful and vigorous personality has had much to do with the extraordinary progress' of the Latvian economy!

Peterson was hugely interested in the Shannon hydroelectric scheme, as a similar project was under consideration for the River Dwina in Latvia. He also lauded the progress made in 'the construction of roads in the Irish Free State'. By now a high-ranking official in the Latvian government, he visited Dublin again in 1937. According to the *Irish Times*, Peterson had a special interest in Ireland's peat industry, and was in charge of the Latvian state peat works at Liepaja.

After the end of the Second World War, he and his family moved to Sweden.

Meanwhile, in Ireland, IRA volunteer turned civil servant C.S. Andrews had been put in charge of turf development when Fianna Fáil came to power in 1932. A few years later, he became managing director of the newly established Bord na Móna, and in 1945 was sent on a delegation to Sweden to learn more about the peat industry there. He takes up the story in *A Man of No Property*:

> We were in the office of one of these peat moss factories when the discussion was interrupted by the arrival of a heavily built, middle-aged man who addressed us in a loud, cheerful voice speaking thickly accented English 'Are you boys from Dublin? Do you know Daddy Orr and the College of Science?' We were astonished at this apparition. Daddy Orr was a legendary and eccentric professor of mathematics in the College of Science, who was alleged to have believed himself to be the square root of minus one. It was surprising, to say the least, that his fame has spread to an obscure peat moss factory in a remote corner of Sweden.

Andrews had by chance bumped into Konrad Peterson. The Irish delegation took him and his wife to dinner in Malmö, 'and to say that his life story kept us entranced until the small hours would be an understatement', recalled Andrews.

During this time, Bord na Móna was developing a bog at Kilberry, near Athy, for peat moss production. As this was a new project, in which Ireland had as yet no experience, Andrews asked Peterson if he would be willing to take charge of it.

Peterson readily accepted the offer, and returned to Dublin circa 1946, where the family moved in at first with his cousin Isolde on Winton Avenue in Rathgar, Dublin. Isolde was later to become a founding member of Amnesty International, along with Sean MacBride, Helmut Clissmann, Sybil Le Brocquy and others.

In 1948, Peterson spoke at the inaugural meeting of the Dublin University Fabian Society, which was focused on the current political landscape in Eastern Europe. Described as a 'Latvian refugee' in the *Irish Times* on 2 November 1948, he told the audience that:

> '[I]n the police state there was no freedom of speech
> … There was one party – the Communist Party – and
> God help anyone who tries to put up an opposition.'
> He described the regimes in Eastern Europe as 'new
> slavery', not 'new democracies'.

Peterson was obviously hostile to Stalin and the Soviet Union. A report in 'The Irishman's Diary' the following day referred to Peterson being a member of a 'left-wing party that was not communist' in Latvia.

In the decades that followed, he became well-established as manager of Bord na Móna's peat moss factory at Kilberry, County Kildare, finishing his career in Bord na Móna's experimental research station.

His wife Helen died in 1959, and following his retirement Konrad moved to Canada with his daughter Pamela and son-in-law Dr Dermot Murphy, where he remained for a short time, before returning to Athy. He died there in the local St Vincent's Hospital on 16 January 1981, aged 93.

No obituaries followed his death in any English-speaking newspapers that I could find. It is bitterly disappointing that he was never interviewed by any journalists or historians about his long life and the extraordinary world events to which he was a witness.

He had no grandchildren. Soon, his grave in St Michael's cemetery, Athy, became neglected. However, in March 2013, a group of Latvians living in Ireland, including ambassador Peteris Elferts, restored Peterson's gravestone, which by then was illegible.

From a daring young Latvian revolutionary to managing Bord na Móna's peat moss factory in Athy – Konrad Peterson's was a truly remarkable life.

The Shooting of Thomas Farrelly in the Markets

Sam McGrath

Twenty-year-old Thomas Farrelly of 30 Mary's Lane was shot and killed by the British Army in the north inner city in August 1920. A neighbour, 19-year-old Thomas Clarke of 16 Green Street was seriously wounded in the attack.

It occurred during a turbulent month within a turbulent year. On 7 August, an IRA flying column ambushed a six-man RIC foot patrol near Kildorrery, County Cork. Two days later, the Restoration of Order in Ireland Act received royal assent, giving Dublin Castle the authority to replace the criminal courts with courts martial, and to replace coroners' inquests with military courts of inquiry. On 12 August, Cork's lord mayor, Terence MacSwiney, was arrested for possession of seditious articles and documents, and he was sentenced after four days to two years' in Brixton Prison. He began his fatal hunger strike a few days later.

Planned Visit of Archbishop Mannix
During the summer of 1920 the outspoken Cork-born Dr Daniel Mannix (1864–1963), archbishop of Melbourne, was undergoing a speaking tour of the United States. He shared a platform with Éamon de Valera at Madison Square

SCENE OF THE LATEST CITY TRAGEDY

The street, with banner of welcome to Dr. Mannix, in which a young man was shot dead and another wounded in Dublin by military yesterday morning.   "Evening Herald" Photo.

Crowds with tricolour on Greek Street to celebrate the planned
visit of Archbishop Mannix to Dublin on the night
Thomas Farrelly was shot dead by British Army soldiers.
(*Evening Herald*, 11 August 1920)

Gardens in New York, telling the audience of 15,000 people that Ireland should be given the 'same status in postwar
planning as the other small nations of Europe'. He openly
expressed his support of the 1916 Rising proclaiming: 'I
am going to Ireland soon and I am going to kneel on the
graves of those men who in Easter Week gave their lives for
Ireland.'

On 31 July 1920, Mannix boarded the transatlantic liner
Baltic at New York for his long journey to Queenstown
(Cobh) in his home county of Cork. The ship had made it
so close to the Irish coast by 8 August that Mannix could
see the lights of Cobh and the flames of huge bonfires of
welcome on the hilltops. But then the ship was intercepted
by the Royal Navy.

Mannix was denied entry to Ireland, arrested and brought to Penzance, Cornwall. Padraig Yeates, in his brilliant 2012 book *A City in Turmoil*, wrote that Mannix was prohibited from addressing any public meetings in any part of England with large Irish immigrant populations. Mannix remarked with characteristic irony: 'Not since the Battle of Jutland had the British Navy scored a victory comparable with the capture of the archbishop of Melbourne without the loss of a single British sailor.'

A Summer's Night in Dublin

Bonfires to welcome Archbishop Mannix to Ireland had also been lit across Dublin city, including one on Greek Street in the Markets area of the north inner city. A large Irish tricolour with the words 'Welcome Dr Mannix' was draped across the street by supportive locals.

Late on 10 August, a group of about ten young men were sitting around the dying embers of a bonfire at the corner of Greek Street, Mary's Lane, and Beresford Street. Newspaper articles reported that they were singing Irish nationalist songs. During 'The West's Awake', a truck full of British Army soldiers from the Lancashire Fusiliers pulled up. At the time, Dublin was under a strict military curfew, and people without the necessary permits could not be outdoors from 12 a.m. to 5 a.m.

At the following inquest, local witness Joseph Eccles of Church Street said: 'No challenge was given and nothing was said by the military' before they opened fire.

Thomas Farrelly ran in the direction of his home and was about twenty yards from the front door when he was hit by a volley of bullets. He was carried into his mother's house and laid on the kitchen floor. According to the *Sunday*

Independent on 15 August 1920, Farrelly exclaimed 'Oh mother! Oh mother!' and soon died in her arms.

Another young local man, Thomas Clarke, was shot and wounded in the knee. He limped into the same house, where he collapsed on the floor. Luckily, he would recover from his injuries.

Funeral

Mannix sent a telegraph to the lord mayor of Dublin, according to the *Irish Times* on 13 August 1920:

> Just now I can only use this means of thanking you and all my friends in Ireland for their welcome to Irish waters. Kindly convey my heartfelt sympathy to the relatives of the murdered man Farrell [*sic*]. God rest his soul and comfort those who mourn him.

Thousands attended Farrelly's public funeral, which took place on Friday 13 August 1920. The *Evening Herald* reported that 'all shops for a large area around were closed, and blinds in private houses reverently drawn'. The Irish tricolour flag with the message 'Welcome Dr Mannix' was draped over his coffin. Farrelly had helped to make this flag, which was hung near where the shooting took place.

The hearse was drawn by four black horses from Halston Street Church to Glasnevin Cemetery. Thousands lined the route, which ran from North King Street through Church Street, Mary's Lane, Little Mary Street, Capel Street, Parliament Street, Dame Street, College Green and Westmoreland Street to Parnell Square.

The *Evening Herald* stated that the scene from Dame Street to the cemetery was 'particularly impressive as the long line of Volunteers, members of the Citizen Army and numerous trade unions marched four deep behind the hearse'. A slow death march was played by the bands of the United Labourers' Union and the Irish National Foresters.

A number of clergy visiting the city from America and Australia, who had planned to meet Archbishop Mannix, joined the procession. Several hundred casual dockers employed on ships docked at the port also left work to take part in the funeral. A significant number of politicians attended, including TDs W.T. Cosgrave, J.J. Walsh, Phil Shanahan, and Richard Mulcahy.

The prayers at the church and graveside were recited by the Very Reverend Canon Grimley. Two friends of Farrelly – Christopher Reilly and John Deane – who were with him on the night he was killed, led the procession carrying a large Irish tricolour with a black cross in its centre. This was made by John Farrelly, an uncle of the deceased.

A lorry was needed to carry all the wreaths and flowers that were donated by friends and neighbours of the Farrelly family. Thomas Farrelly worked as a van driver for a local firm in the Corporation Market, and this was reflected in the sympathy messages. A selection of the inscriptions included:

To the one who gave his life for his faith and country from two friends
With deepest sympathy from the friends of Brunswick Street
With deepest sympathy from Miss Daly, South City Markets
From his comrade, John Tyrrell
From Mrs and Miss Lilly Corry, 87 North King Street

From his friends Mrs Kelly, Mrs Gibney and Miss
Mooney
With deepest sympathy from the neighbours of
Church Avenue
In loving memory from his friends on Stafford Street
In loving memory from his pals of Smith Street
With deepest sympathy from the Stafford Celtic
A.F.C.
With deepest sympathy from Daisy Market, per Mrs
Byrne and Mrs Quigley
With deepest sympathy from Kathleen Curran and
his friends of the Corporation Market
From Patrick Fagan, in loving memory of Thomas
Farrelly who died for his faith and for his country

Aftermath

In the weeks following his death, collections were made
in the area to help financially support Thomas Farrelly's
grieving mother. Due to some reprehensible characters
collecting money unofficially, Michael J. Nolan of the
Corporation Market had to write to the newspapers to
inform all sympathisers that they should only donate
directly to himself, another worker in the market or two
local priests.

The City Coroner Louis A. Byrne presided over an inquest
at the city morgue into the shooting. Two armoured cars
were stationed on the opposite side of the street, their guns
trained on the morgue. After local witnesses and members of
the military gave evidence, the jury, after an absence of only
fifteen minutes, returned the following verdict, according to
the 21 August 1920 *Irish Times*:

We find that the said Thomas Farrell [*sic*] died on the 10 August 1920 from shock and haemorrhage caused by the bullets fired by guns from the military without justification, and we strongly condemn the action of the military in empowering youths to endanger the lives of the citizens. We desire to place on record our deepest sympathy with the relatives of the deceased.

Thomas Farrelly was one of 270 non-combatant men, women, and children killed by the British Army in Ireland in a fourteen-month period from 1 January 1920 to 28 February 1921. He should be not be forgotten in the Dublin streets where he grew up.

Bull-Baiting in Eighteenth-Century Dublin

Donal Fallon

Bull-baiting was stupid, and it was also undeniably danger-ous. Given this, it's perhaps not surprising that it was hugely popular in Dublin and other urban centres once upon a time. It consisted of:

> a bull being tied to a stake with a rope between 10 and 15 feet long. It was then baited – bitten, scratched and savaged – by dogs, usually bulldogs or mastiffs especially bred for the sport ... Its appeal lay not only in its violence but also in the opportunities it presented for gambling on the performance of both the bull and the dogs.

As Paul Rouse has noted in his history of sport in Ireland, not everyone regarded bull-baiting as a form of sporting entertainment. A letter to *the Freeman's Journal* in 1764 called it and cockfighting 'inhumane', and Rouse wrote that 'in the early years of the nineteenth century, such views gained much greater currency', as reformers sought to ban such 'blood sports'. Still, for a time bull-baiting packed in the crowds to sometimes makeshift arenas in Dublin and other Irish cities.

One source tells us that 'the place for bull-baiting in Dublin was in the Cornmarket, where there was an iron ring, to which the butchers fastened the animals they baited', but it appears to have happened in other areas too. Rouse points towards Smithfield as a popular location for those gathering to bet on the spectacle, noting that 'not even the threat of public whipping and imprisonment of its devotees could deter those who engaged in it'.

References to the stealing of bulls can be found in the oral history of the city, in songs and poetry. These words come from the popular 'Lord Altham's Bull', written in the 1770s, telling the story of stealing a bull (or a 'mosey') for the purposes of bull-baiting:

> We drove de bull tro many a gap,
> And kep him going many a mile,
> But when we came to Kilmainham lands,
> We let de mosey rest a while

A writer named John Edward Walsh wrote a very enter-taining and colourful book entitled *Ireland Sixty Years Ago* in the mid-nineteenth century, which cast an eye back on some of the problems of Irish cities in decades gone by, including 'bucks, bullies, rapparees, duelling, drunkenness, bull-baiting, idleness, abduction clubs and a thousand other degrading peculiarities which marked the higher as well as the lower classes'. Walsh took a particularly dim view of those who engaged in the sport, writing that:

> The custom of seizing bulls on their way to market, for the purpose of baiting, became so grievous an evil in Dublin in 1779 that it was the subject of a special

enactment, making it a peculiar offence to take a bull from the drivers for such a purpose, on its way to or from market.

On more than one occasion, violence erupted among crowds who had gathered to observe bull-baiting. Dead bodies were left on the street when soldiers opened fire on a crowd that had gathered in 1789 for a bull-bait. On St Stephen's Day,

> a day devoted by the lower classes to relaxation and amusement, some of the tradesmen had purchased a bull, and brought him into a field, in the vicinity of the city, which was enclosed with a very high stone wall, and a gate which was kept shut. Some humane persons, who considered bull-baiting as a cruel amusement, went to the sheriff and required him to call out a military guard to put a stop to the proceeding. Vance, the sheriff, complied.
>
> His interference produced a riot. Oyster shells and pebbles were thrown by the mob, and the soldiers retaliated by firing on the people. Many were wounded, four were killed.

James Mahassey, Patrick Keegan, Ferral Reddy and an unnamed man lost their lives that day. In the aftermath of this sad affair, the families of those killed found an unlikely champion in the form of Archibald Hamilton Rowan, who was destined to become an influential member of the United Irishmen. The subject of a recent biography by historian Fergus Whelan, Rowan was something of a champion of the poor and marginalised in Dublin, and he regarded the killings as an abuse of power on the part of the sheriff and the authorities against the poor of the city. Sheriff Vance was tried for the killing of Ferral Reddy, and in court Rowan made it clear that he was personally 'confirmed in the opinion of its being a most diabolical exercise of power'. The case was dismissed.

Sometimes it wasn't the bull-baiting itself that was condemned, but the drunkenness and violence surrounding the event. The *Freeman's Journal* bemoaned a 'terrible riot' in December 1787, when men converged on Finglas for the purpose of bull-baiting, but, unable to locate a bull, they 'proceeded, after having drunk to intoxication, to insult the town of people and quarrel among themselves, and in the course of their rioting, it is reported, three were killed'.

As in Ireland, there was a perception elsewhere that bull-baiting was a sport for the so-called lower orders of society. Douglas A. Reid notes in his study of bull-baiting in England that aficionados of the sport were described in English newspapers as being 'our labouring classes', the 'operative classes', and of the 'working population'. In the House of Commons in 1825, it was asked 'why were the sports of the poor to be put down, and those of the rich to be left unmolested?'

The eventual decline of bull-baiting was driven by many things, including political factors but also changing moral attitudes to blood sports. Rouse points to 'cruelty to animal' reformers as playing an important part in the story of the end of bull-baiting on the streets of British cities.

From McDaid's to the Summer of Love: the Mysterious Emmett Grogan

Donal Fallon

Emmett Grogan was a lot of things. One of the leading figures of the hippy movement that exploded in the United States in the 1960s, he was an Irish-American wild child from Brooklyn who rejected any kind of conformity. He was centrally involved in setting up a free-spirited political society known as the Diggers, who were at the heart of the San Francisco scene. Grogan sang on Bob Dylan's 'Mr Tambourine Man' and knocked around with bands like The Grateful Dead, and he never let the facts get in the way of a good story. There are more questions than answers about his life, even now. His memoir, *Ringolevio*, includes some fascinating insights on the Dublin of the 1960s, though if they should be believed is another matter entirely.

Writing about Emmett Grogan, Ian McGillis noted that 'in 1978, when Bob Dylan dedicated his *Street Legal* album to the late Emmett Grogan, it was more than just a salute from a counterculture icon to a far less famous fellow traveller. It was one master of self-reinvention recognizing another.' Given his clear influence on Dylan and others, it is remarkable just how little is known about Grogan's origins.

The cover of Emmet Grogan's *Ringolevio*.

He was born Eugene Grogan in November 1942, and his contemporary Peter Coyote remembered that 'as the son of a clerk who served wealthy clients, Emmett felt consigned to an obscure future, to viewing wealth and power from the wrong side of the counter'. By a young age he was dabbling in drugs on the streets of New York, and also dabbling in a spot of crime to feed his addictions.

Grogan's memoir is in many ways the tale of a young man who refuses a conventional existence. He would insist that the book was true, but that 'names, places and some dates … have been changed to protect the innocent'. Travelling Europe, Grogan chronicled Paris, Amsterdam, London, Rome, and other great cities that had long attracted American backpackers. From Italy, he made for Ireland, writing that he withdrew his last $500 from the bank, packed one bag full of clothes and another full of books, and then 'boarded a plane for Dublin, Ireland, to see if he could get himself straight into the Auld Sod of his forefathers'.

In 1964, he arrived and lodged at the Abbotsford Hotel on Harcourt Street, remembering it was 'an elegant Georgian house in a row of handsome Georgian houses', though 'it looked and smelled like a bishop's rectory. It was too prim and clean and polite and had the air of a British townhouse.' Grogan thought little of Neary's public house, believing it to be full of 'neatly dressed middle-class people, talking about the theatre'. Instead, he felt much more at home in the nearby McDaid's, remembering how:

> He liked the saloon with its high ceiling, scattered tables and solid wooden bar. It was a big, funky room and the only decor was the people in it. They were very hearty and whether they were laughing or argu-ing, discussing or pontificating, they were enjoying

themselves and each other. They weren't dressed up to impress anybody.

Grogan claims to have encountered IRA activists who took him under their wings in the city, and 'invited him to be a man of action as well as letters, and to go North with them'. The young American claims to have taken part in a frantic border raid, which 'blew the wall out of a tiny post on the border of Armagh near a place called Forkill late one Saturday night, and they were back in Dublin when the pubs opened for the Sunday afternoon session'. Grogan says he lodged at the Brazen Head, the oldest pub in the city, and mingled there among men he described as 'short-changed by de Valera and his pack of cronies … condemned to bitterness, a meagre pension and a glass of booze or two at places like the Brazen Head'.

After a few months, Grogan left Dublin because 'he had enough goofs and … he was sick of eating fish and chips all the time and taking wages for a living. Besides, he hadn't been laid since he'd been in Dublin, because women weren't allowed in the rooms at the Brazen Head and he didn't like to pay hookers for the clap.' He eventually found sex in Dublin too, something he took the time to vividly recall.

There are problems with Emmett Grogan's account of Dublin. He claims that he was 'posted on the corner of North Earl and Marlborough Street where he stopped pedestrians and traffic from entering O'Connell Street' on the night Nelson's Pillar was destroyed. The explosion 'severed the Lord's head clean from its body and dropped it neatly below to O'Connell Street in one piece'. At the time Grogan left the city, Admiral Nelson was still gazing down happy over the metropolis, his demise coming two years later.

Ringolevio is important as the story of a young backpacker travelling Europe, but it could be argued the story of Grogan was only beginning as he left the continent. Back in America, and still in his 20s, he became the driving force behind the Diggers movement in San Francisco, right there during the 'Summer of Love'. They were all about freedom – keeping things free and staying free. From free food the focus turned to clothes, education, and even recreational drugs. Grogan and the Diggers refused cash donations, and he sometimes burnt cash to make the point. In the words of *Vanity Fair*, Grogan and his people 'created the poverty-is-sexy ideology for young panhandlers'. This all sounds like madness (because it *was* madness), but in the San Francisco of the 1960s it was perfectly normal.

'Freedom means everything free!' was Grogan's rallying cry. Abbie Hoffman remembered that 'Emmett Grogan was the hippie warrior par excellence. He was also a junkie, a maniac, a gifted actor and a rebel hero.' Grogan died in April 1978, his body discovered on a New York subway train. One contemporary said that when 'Emmett Grogan died of a heroin overdose, the dreams of the '60s were starting to fade'. Yet while the folklore of Emmett's death suggests an overdose, his death certificate points towards heart failure.

How much of his Dublin memoir was true? We'll probably never know.

Edward Smyth's Moving Heads

Ciarán Murray

There's not much left by the way of pre-boom buildings on Sir John Rogerson's Quay. Row upon row of mismatched shining steel-and-glass structures tower over the few remaining Victorian warehouses and engine houses, relics of an era when Dublin's docks bustled with industry. One warehouse that has managed to survive, a double-gabled red-brick building that sits where the Samuel Beckett bridge meets the Southside, boasts two unusual features.

The warehouse at 30–32 Sir John Rogerson's Quay was built in the 1890s, and was once home to the Dublin Tropical Fruit Company, which occupied it for decades. It has played a part in plenty of drama in its lifetime. In the mid-1930s, a young teenager fell to his death from the roof.

On 16 April 1950, the *Abraham Lincoln* arrived into Dublin bearing tonnes of bananas bound for the warehouse. When the ship made port, it was discovered that its cargo of fruit was already too ripe for sale, leading the company to refuse it, and the ship's crew to dump tonnes of black-skinned bananas overboard. Alexandra Basin was lined with scores of people waiting for the chance to grab any that might float ashore, while rowboats set out from Ringsend with the aim of getting to the booty first. Gardaí struggled to maintain order as hundreds of children tried to force entry into the basin.

In the 1960s there was a long-running strike on the premises, and the 1980s saw a fire come close to gutting the building. The building later housed offices belonging to U2, and is now home to a software company.

Over the doors of the building hang two recognisable figures – granite keystones representing Anna Livia and the Atlantic. Originally sculpted by the eminent (though self-effacing, some records state) Edward Smyth, they once adorned the archways of Carlisle Bridge, which predated what we now know as O'Connell Bridge. Carlisle Bridge had three arches, with a hump rising high above the water. It was remodelled in the late 1870s, and the granite keystones were removed. The new bridge had arches that sat much lower over the water, and Anna Livia and the Atlantic were deemed too large to fit. So they somehow ended up on the facade of the warehouse on Sir John Rogerson's Quay.

Smyth (1749–1812) was a sculptor and modeler who served an apprenticeship under Simon Vierpyl, the clerk of works for the Casino building in Marino, and later worked for a Dublin stonecutter named Henry Darley. His work was mainly ornamental, according to the *Dictionary of Irish Architects* – that is, until Darley recommended him to one of the leading architects working in Ireland in the early 1780s, none other than James Gandon. Smyth rose to prominence under Gandon's patronage, and went on to sculpt some of the most recognisable features on some of Dublin's most famous buildings. From humble beginnings, he was to become a wealthy man.

Looking out over College Green from the roof of the old Parliament stand his figures Justice, Wisdom, and

Liberty. His works are dotted around the Custom House: the fourteen keystones representing Irish rivers on the building are his, along with the Arms of Ireland – a lion and a unicorn standing on either side of the Irish harp. He was also responsible for work on a number of churches throughout Dublin; ornaments, statues, and coats of arms at King's Inns; and the anthropomorphic figures playing billiards and other parlour games on the windows of the Kildare Street Club.

In her 'This Ireland' column in the *Irish Times* in March 1975, Elgy Gillespie noted that it wasn't until the 1950s that the discovery of Smyth's keystones on the building at Sir Rogerson's Quay was made, quoting Harold Leask (an architect who was in part responsible for the reconstruction of the GPO) in the *Royal Society of Antiquaries Journal* on their discovery. That column unfortunately neglects to mention how the heads managed to make their way from Carlisle Bridge onto the facade of a building on Sir John Rogerson's Quay.

Lesser-Known Dublin
Jewish Radicals

Sam McGrath

A number of prominent Dublin Jews involved in radical politics have been rightly included in the *Dictionary of Irish Biography*. These include fascinating republican activists such as lawyer Michael Noyk, IRA gunrunner Robert Briscoe, and Cumann na mBan's Estella Solomons, as well as left-wing socialists like writer Leslie Daiken, artist Harry Kernoff, and International Brigade veteran Maurice Levitas. However, there are other Jewish Dubliners who did not make it into the dictionary, but made an impact on the political landscape. Individuals like Philip Sayers, Jacob Elyan, Dr Edward 'Eddie' Lipman, and Hermann Good all played their own small parts in Irish politics.

Philip Sayers (1876–1964), from Lithuania, was described as an 'early Sinn Féiner'. In 1909, Yiddish-speaking trade unionists in Dublin formed the International Tailors', Pressers', and Machinists' Union. Their first strike was organised against Jewish employers. Sayers, an active community member, helped to successfully negotiate a settlement.

During the 1917 South Longford by-election, it was Sayers who drove Arthur Guinness, legal advisor Michael Noyk, and

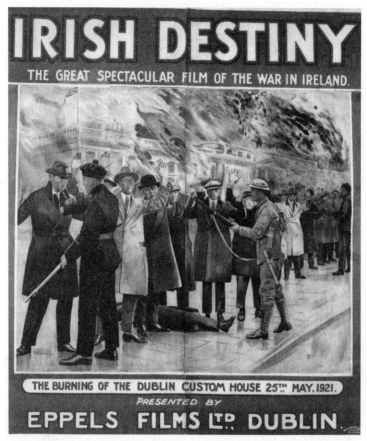

The poster for the film *Irish Destiny* (1926) which was financed, written and produced by Jewish GP and pharmacist Isaac Eppel.

Katherine McGuinness to Longford. Katherine's husband Joseph McGuinness, an Easter Rising veteran, was serving time in Lewes Gaol in England when he was elected an MP in the by-election. When he passed away at the age of 88 in 1964, Sayers' short obituary in the *Irish Times* on 15 May 1964 made known that he had 'took part in the Sinn Féin movement and was a lifelong sympathiser with the national movement'.

Sayers' Dublin-born son Michael was a well-known, celebrated poet and writer with strong political sympathies, who married Mentana Galleani, daughter of the militant Italian anarchist Luigi Galleani. When he passed away in 2010, it was noted in the *Independent* on 21 July 2010 that Michael had 'vivid childhood memories of [IRA] fugitives being hidden in the house and of police raids'.

Jacob Elyan (1878–1937) was a founding member of the Judaeo-Irish Home Rule Association, which was launched on 10 September 1908 at a meeting in the Mansion House that attracted around sixty Jews and three Irish Parliamentary Party MPs. The group was formed by Elyan and Joseph Edelstein, and was believed to have included about two dozen core supporters. MPs John Redmond and John Dillon sent their best wishes to the organisation, and the names of Daniel O'Connell and Michael Davitt were recalled at the meeting as great friends of the Jewish people.

An Irish Jew with unionist sympathies was ejected from the meeting after trying to disrupt proceedings, and a fight broke out among at least a dozen people towards the end. The *Irish Times* on 11 September 1908 reported that:

It appears that some of the Jews who were not in sympathy with the object of the meeting proclaimed their views rather loudly, with the result that they were rather roughly treated at the hands of their co-religionists, who were supported by a number of United Irish Leaguers.

The Judaeo-Irish Home Rule Association seemingly only lasted a few months, and didn't receive any media coverage except for of its inaugural meeting. Elyan is the only known original member who continued to be active in Irish republican politics, joining the United Irish League and becoming a member of its Dublin executive. He was later invited by John Redmond to stand for election, but declined due to ill-health. For the same reason, he was unable to take a seat in the Free State Senate of 1923.

Dr Edward 'Eddie' Lipman (1887–1965) was close friends with Countess Markievicz, Arthur Griffith, James Stephens and other figures in the world of Irish politics and the arts. He took up medical practice in London in the early 1920s, where he and his Mayo wife Dr Eva Kavanagh Lipman 'ministered generously, both in matters of health and in personal affairs, to Cockney proletarians and working-class Irish migrants and their families', the *Irish Times* noted on 7 January 1965.

During the Anglo-Irish Treaty negotiations in London in 1921, Arthur Griffith used to frequently call on Eddie Lipman for a 'talk and walk through the streets of the English capital'. Lipman worked in the East End until retirement, when he returned home to his native Dublin. He died there after a short illness in June 1965.

Herman Good (1906–81) was a Dublin-born solicitor active with the James Connolly Workers' Club in the late 1920s and the IRA-led Irish Labour Defence League in the early 1930s.

Qualifying as a solicitor in 1929, he served in the legal profession for over fifty years, rising to the post of justice of the district court. He was well-known for providing legal representation to the unemployed, strikers, and individuals injured in the workplace.

In November 1929, he defended a former soldier charged with 'riotous assembly' at a demonstration of the unemployed outside Leinster House, and the following month he defended two young men charged with breaking windows in St Stephen's Green after a protest march of the unemployed. In March of the following year, he appeared in court on behalf of the Irish Labour Defence League and appealed that the judge free several men, including Christopher Ferguson (secretary of the National Unemployed Movement) and John Fox (secretary of the Irish Labour Defence League) after their arrest at a demonstration.

In March 1931, he defended the five leaders of a strike at the Greenmount and Boyne Linen Company mill in Aungier Street who were charged with the assault of a man. Good described the charges as a 'frame up' to 'defeat the strike'. In May two years later, he defended former IRA volunteer Sean Murray and Sean Nolan (both members of the Revolutionary Workers Group), who were inside Connolly House on North Strand Street when it was attacked by a large anti-Communist mob. The following month, he represented ninety-six families of the Municipal Tenants Association in a case against Dublin Corporation, which was trying to evict them.

In July 1934, he defended four striking workers from the Samuel Oliver and McCabe shirt factory on South Great George's Street, who were charged with 'wrongfully and without legal authority watching and besetting' the factory. A year before the outbreak of the Second World War, he defended Austrian Koppel Roeffler, who escaped from the Nazis and was living in Dublin but who the state wanted to deport. During the war, Good became an officer in the Local Defence Force and helped Jews in Ireland who had successfully escaped Nazi Germany.

Good described himself as the first Jewish member of the Labour Party and ran for the party in the June 1933 municipal elections in Dublin's District No. 4. In the May 1944 general election, he stood in the Dublin Townships constituency and won 2,104 first-preference votes, keeping his deposit. This was a respectable result when you take into account that he was up against the mighty giants Sean MacEntee of Fianna Fáil and John A. Costello of Fine Gael.

Throughout his fifty-year legal career, Good defended a huge number of young shoplifters, joyriders, smugglers, and individuals injured in various bus, car, tram, and workplace accidents. He was an outspoken opponent of both corporal and capital punishment, and believed that the Swedish model of rehabilitation and re-education for offenders was the way forward. Never wavering from his republican views, he told Eileen O'Brien in an *Irish Times* interview published on 10 July 1976 that 'there will never be peace in Ireland until Ireland is united'. He passed away in 1981.

Other individuals and stories of Irish-Jewish radical history also deserve mention.

Abraham Volkes and an individual by the name of Barnet, Jewish workers living in Pleasant Street, Dublin 8, were active in the Irish Socialist Republican Party, according to that organisation's minute book of 23 July 1901 – a fact first publicised by Manus O'Riordan in a 1988 *Saothar* article. O'Riordan also informed us that the pair had previously been involved with the Social-Democratic Federation (SDF) in Salford. This was the organisation that James Connolly spoke for during his two public-speaking trips (1901 and 1902) to the city.

Leon Spiro, who moved to Dublin from Lithuania at the age of 2, became manager of the Pearl Printing Company in Drury Street. Spiro printed the IRA newspaper *An t-Oglach* during the early 1920s, and he employed Oscar Traynor

– commanding officer of the Dublin IRA – as a compositor. Natalie Wynn, in her 2012 essay 'Jews, Antisemitism and Irish Politics: a Tale of Two Narratives', suggests that the paper was indeed printed by Leon Spiro, but only after he had been 'forcibly detained' in his office. This information was gleaned from an unpublished memoir written by Leon's daughter Jessie Spiro Bloom.

A Jewish man by the name of Max Cohen lived in a house that was being used an arms dump at 3 Swifts Row beside Ormond Quay. George White, a member of C Company of the 3rd Battalion of the IRA's Dublin Brigade from 1917, recalled in his Bureau of Military History witness statement (no. 956) that Cohen 'knew all about the dump but said nothing about it' to the authorities. His brother Abraham, who ran an antique shop at 20 Ormond Quay, told White and another IRA member that they could use his shop anytime 'as a means of escape'.

In the witness statement (no. 723) of Dr Alice Barry, a close friend of many IRA leaders, she mentions that Dan Breen was taken in by a Jewish person while on the run in Fernside, Drumcondra, North Dublin. In October 1920, Breen, who had badly cut his legs while escaping from the Black and Tans, 'wandered round looking for refuge' until he eventually found it in the home of an unnamed Jewish person who also 'provided him with dry clothing'. (Unfortunately, and somewhat ironically, Breen took a very strong pro-Axis stance, and had a portrait of Adolf Hitler hanging in his study until as late as 1948.)

Mrs Sean Beaumont, a member of the executive of Cumann na mBan, recalled in her witness statement (no. 385) that trained nurses within the organisation set up a bureau at 6 Harcourt Street in October 1918 to help the general public during the flu pandemic. Among those nursed 'were many' Jewish families, who showed their gratitude by providing financial support for the republican movement and voting for Sinn Féin candidates in the years ahead.

The groundbreaking full-length silent film *Irish Destiny* (1926) was financed, written, and produced by Isaac Eppel (1892–1942), a Jewish doctor who ran a pharmacy on Mary Street. It was the first fiction film to deal with the War of Independence and had former members of the IRA among its cast, including Kit O'Malley, former adjutant of the Dublin Brigade, who acted as military advisor to the production.

Set between mid-1920, at the height of the War of Independence, and the truce of 1921, the film traces the love affair of IRA volunteer Denis O'Hara (Paddy Dunne Cullinan) and his fiancée, Moira Barry (Frances MacNamara). It was firmly populist and pro-republican, no doubt reflecting Eppel's own political views. The film interweaved actual newsreel footage of the Black and Tans, the burning of Cork, and the burning of the Custom House in Dublin, with dramatised scenes that were filmed in Enniskerry, London, and Dublin.

For more than five decades, *Irish Destiny* was believed lost, until the IFI Irish Film Archive found a print in the US Library of Congress in 1991, and restored it to its original tinted and toned glory. It was Eppel's first and only film. The production had cost him his marriage and bankrupted him. He gave up his medical career and took over the Palace (later the Academy) cinema on Pearse Street. He later emigrated to England and died in obscurity.

In 1939, a Dublin IRA member by the name of Harry Goldberg was sentenced to three weeks in Strangeways Prison for refusing to divulge the names of fellow Irish republicans in Liverpool. It is more than likely that he was Jewish. The *Irish Independent* on 25 Feb 1939 revealed that he worked as a mattress maker and lived on Auburn Street in Liverpool. He had moved over from Dublin in 1937. Goldberg admitted to attending two IRA meetings in the city, one being at a house in Edge Lane. In court, he was questioned but 'refused to mention names'. (For the full story of the IRA's bombing campaign in Liverpool, read Bryce Evans' excellent 2012 article 'Fear and Loathing in Liverpool: the IRA's 1939 Bombing Campaign on Merseyside'.)

These individuals and stories offer up another fascinating layer of Irish-Jewish history.

Herbert Simms and the 1930s War on Slumdom

Donal Fallon

More than twenty years after the birth of the Free State, a writer in the journal *Studies* complained that slumdom remained, and that the city was still home to 'conditions which are often quite unsuitable for cattle, much less human beings'. To Professor T.W.T Dillon, things were dire and not getting better:

> The pattern of dirt, decay and discomfort is everywhere the same. The filthy yard with the unspeakable closet often choked, always foul-smelling, serving the needs of all the families in the house; the single tap, often situated in the basement or even in the foul-smelling yard; the cracked and crumbling walls and ceiling covered with scabrous peeling paper or blistered paint; the leaking roofs and rat-infested floors. There are differences in detail, but in general a drab and disgusting uniformity is unrelieved by any sign of human dignity.

Yet while there was much work still to do in 1945, the previous decade had witnessed some significant changes and improvements, which we can still see in the urban landscape today.

Memorial plaque to Herbert Simms at Chancery House.
(Image: Paul Reynolds)

The year 2016 marked the eightieth anniversary of the opening of the Oliver Bond House scheme at Usher Street and Cook Street. Just like the beautiful Chancery Park complex across the Liffey, it serves as a reminder of the remarkable architect Herbert Simms, who was to be 'responsible for the design and erection of some 17,000 new homes' in his time as Dublin Corporation's Housing Architect from 1932 to 1948. In recent years, there has been a great resurgence of interest in Simms and his work, and public housing in Dublin more broadly speaking.

'Bread for the People': the Coming to Power of Fianna Fáil and the Issue of Slumdom.
The 1932 election is primarily remembered for the cynical 'red-scare' tactics of the outgoing Cumann na nGaedheal

government. Front-page newspaper advertisements from the party warned that 'The gunmen are voting for Fianna Fáil. The Communists are voting for Fianna Fáil.' One government publication warned that if de Valera's party took control, 'the extremist minority, as in Spain, as in Mexico, as in Russia, will get the upper hand'.

Fianna Fáil attempted to make the slums an election issue, promising increased public spending on housing. This was one contributing factor in Labour supporting the first Fianna Fáil government, with party leader Willie Norton declaring that:

> so far as the slum-dwellers are concerned, they need have no regret at the change of government, and the old-age pensioners have reason to be glad that the rich man's government of the past ten years was not in office at the present time to further reduce them.

Cumann na nGaedheal had, in truth, delivered some advances in public housing in Dublin. The Free State's first attempt at public housing was in Marino, taking the form of a 'garden city', a kind of public housing that was first envisioned by planner Ebeneezer Howard in 1898. As historian Rhona McCord has noted:

> Howard saw the city slum as morally and physically corrupting and hoped to replace them with out-of-town suburbs, surrounded by parkland and connected to the city centre by public transport. His vision would have a considerable influence on early public housing initiatives in Ireland.

The new state did look abroad for ideas on occasion. As architectural historian Ellen Rowley has noted, 'a collective of Dublin officials took a study tour to Amsterdam and Rotterdam in 1925 so as to examine the Dutch Expressionist housing by Michel de Klerk and Piet Kramer'.

On political platforms and stages, the slums became an issue. One Fianna Fáil candidate, Eamonn Cooney, declared at a 1932 election rally that 'in the slum dwellings there would arise a new hope' if the party were elected to power. In Smithfield, a Cumann na nGaedheal candidate was heckled by Fianna Fáil supporters about the condition in local slums, attempting to deflect criticism by asking if people were prepared to see 'the red flag flying' in Dublin.

Fianna Fáil's policies undoubtedly owed more to populism than socialism, but as historian Brian Hanley has noted, the party did evoke the promise of the revolutionary period:

> It talked about putting into practice the 'ideas embodied in the Democratic Programme of the First Dáil' while de Valera claimed James Connolly as his major inspiration and promised to make 'the resources and wealth of Ireland ... subservient to the needs and welfare of the people'. Furthermore, there would be more than simply political independence; Ireland would be 'self-supporting economically'. Much mocked now, Fianna Fáil's commitment to protectionism and native industrial development was fresh and radical in a state whose government

seemed content to maintain itself as a giant beef ranch for the British market.

When Seán MacEntee read the first Fianna Fáil budget before the Dáil, he emphasised that this was a new approach to ruling. Now, there would be 'bread for the people'. The poor were promised dignity, and that meant pulling down the slums.

Throughout the decade, the slums of Dublin were spoken of as hotbeds of vice and crime. To *The Irish Times*, the slums were 'Dublin's deepest shame and gravest peril', and it was 'almost a miracle that hitherto communism has not flourished aggressively in that hideous soil'. In 1936, an Archdeacon Kelleher was reported as saying:

> Slums could be called the breeding grounds of potential communists. The fact that they are not producing the natural destructive effects of typical communism is to be attributed, in my mind, to the fundamental Christian virtues of faith, charity, and humility.

Horace O'Neill, the City Architect, went as far as to tell a 1935 meeting of the Old Dublin Society that 'slums are barbarous. If I were born and lived in a slum and unemployed, I would be a revolutionist.'

Enter Herbert George Simms

The Londoner Herbert Simms entered the service of Dublin Corporation at the age of only 27, a veteran of the First World War who had served with the Royal Field Artillery. A scholarship received in the aftermath of the war had allowed him to study architecture at Liverpool University, and he was appointed temporary architect to Dublin Corporation in February 1925. Seven years later, and after a brief spell working as a planner in India, he was appointed to the position of Housing Architect for the Corporation. There was much work to do. Simms told one 1936 tribunal that 'they were now trying to do in one generation what should have been done by the last four or five generations.'

The early 1930s witnessed real change in the approach of the Corporation to housing. Until 1932, the construction of new social housing had been the job of the City Architect, but the creation of a specific office for a housing-focused architect meant there was a new focus on home construction. Praise was heaped onto new developments in the years that followed. The Greek Street flats were described in the press as being of 'the most modern type… they recall photographs of municipal flat schemes from Berlin, Moscow or Vienna'.

Christine Casey, a leading authority on Dublin's architectural heritage, has written about the distinctive nature of much of Simms' output, noting how:

> Simms developed a formulae for inner-city blocks of flats, which derived ultimately from Dutch housing design, but probably more directly from contemporary British models. They are generally composed of three- or four-storey perimeter walk-up blocks with galleried rear elevations and stair towers facing large inner courtyards.

Simms' work is instantly recognisable in Dublin today, his Art Deco housing schemes dotted across the city on both sides of the Liffey. Particularly popular is the Chancery Park scheme, completed by June 1935. Though comprising just twenty-seven flats, it is considered a masterful example of public housing, and boasts a beautiful small garden. Simms told a housing inquiry that he firmly believed the homes he was constructing would outlast the slum dwellings they were replacing. To him, 'flats should last at least 200 years … providing they were properly maintained'.

Simms is primarily remembered today for his work in the city, but he was also responsible for the erection of new dwellings in the suburbs, including in Cabra and Crumlin. Of course, rehousing people beyond the city in new suburbs brought its own challenges. Speaking in 1935, Simms outlined his belief that 'you cannot rehouse a population of 15,000 people, as in the Crumlin scheme, without providing for the other necessities and amenities of life'. Subsequent decades would prove this true.

In September 1948 Simms took his own life, throwing himself in front of a train near Coal Quay Bridge. His suicide note said that 'I cannot stand it any longer, my brain is too tired to work anymore. It has not had a rest for 20 years except when I am in heavy sleep. It is always on the go like a dynamo and still the work is being piled on to me.' In a fine tribute, City Surveyor Ernest Taylor remembered Simms as a man who had done much for the poorest in Dublin:

> By sheer hard work and conscientious devotion to duty, he has made a personal contribution towards the solution of Dublin's housing problem, probably unequalled by anyone in our time … It is not given to many of us to achieve so much in the space of a short lifetime for the benefit of our fellow men.

Who or What Is a 'Jackeen'?

Donal Fallon

Today the term 'Jackeen' is levelled against Dubliners pri-marily in a sporting context and very much in jest. The popular theory is that it has something to do with pro-British sympathies among Dubliners historically – the 'Jack' in the term is believed to come from 'Union Jack'. Terence Dolan's great work, *A Dictionary of Hiberno-English: the Irish Use of English*, says it is a pejorative term for 'a self-assertive Dubliner with pro British leanings'.

Looking back, however, it seems that the term was first used more generally as a pejorative term for city dwellers of a certain class, and then took on new meaning over time. In the archives, the term appears to have come into popular usage here around the 1840s, when, on the other side of the world, an article in New York's *The Dollar* magazine used it too.

That article is still good for a laugh and a little indignation, describing a 'Dublin Jackeen' as 'a fellow who does very little for a living, and wants to do less'. Across two pages, the article managed to insult almost every aspect of an ordinary Dubliner's existence, noting that:

The dialect of a Dublin Jackeen is as peculiar as every-thing else about him, and as different from that of his countrymen in general, outside of the Circular Roads, as chalk is from cheese, or Bog Latin from Arabic. The Jackeen for instance, says 'dis','dat', 'dough', 'tunder' and the like – while all other manner of Irishmen make a great capital out of the th, and stick it like grim death, shoving it even into such words as 'murther', 'sisther', 'craythure' and every place else where they find a convenient chance.

The Dollar seemed to use the term to describe a certain kind of lawless Dubliner of the lower order, claiming that 'A Dublin Jackeen is the least cosmopolitan of any man in the world', rarely venturing beyond the chaotic and drunken Donnybrook Fair. The piece, which was clearly written for laughs, made no mention of the term having any kind of political connotations.

Before *The Dollar*, the always enjoyable *Irish Monthly Magazine* had given a somewhat different description of what a 'Jackeen' was, describing him or her as 'a personage, who in our metropolitan society, supplies the same place which the conceited cockney does in the great capital of the sister island, or the bourgeois dandy in that of France'. A 'Jackeen' was 'the affected puppy of the middle ranks', though someone 'who will never be mistaken for a gentleman'. Like *The Dollar*, the term was associated with a certain lawlessness, though the social class was different.

One of the earliest references to the term I can find with any kind of British overtones is from *The Kerry Examiner* of February 1854, where it was noted that 'During the last general war, Dublin contributed more than its quota to the ranks of the British army and military records could attest that no better soldiers served than the "Jackeens" of the Irish capital.' Also from Munster, the *Cork Constitution* suggested seven years later that a 'Jackeen' was someone who 'hates his own country, and is forever making vain and painful efforts to imitate the English, for whom he professes a violent admiration, and by whom is cordially despised'.

As time went on, the term began to refer specifically to a pro-British Dubliner. While it may have been used in earlier times to describe city dwellers in general, by the early twentieth century it had taken on one particular meaning. When John Patrick Henry published *A Handbook of Modern Irish* with the Gaelic League in 1911, the term 'Seóinín' was noted to mean a 'Shoneen or Jackeen', described as 'a West Briton who copies the English and cringes to them'.

One of the few Bureau of Military History witness statements that references the term 'Jackeen' comes from Kevin O'Sheil, who also described the peculiarities of those in districts that were more decidedly unionist in outlook:

The typical Rathminesian, and even more so the typical Rathgarian, was a remarkable type. To begin with, he had developed a most peculiar accent which, immediately when he opened his mouth, revealed his venue. It is quite impossible to describe the accent in mere words, and it is greatly to be regretted that it disappeared before the coming of the recording.

In more recent times, 'Jackeen' is primarily a term used in jest between GAA fans, but it has also been used politically on occasion still. In 1990, a Dáil deputy told a meeting in Castlebar that 'The dignity of the people is being trampled on by Dublin "Jackeens" who don't understand how small farmers in the West of Ireland operate.' Just like the tired talk of the 'Dublin media' and 'Dublin establishment', Jim Higgins was merely using the term to differentiate a Dublin-based government from the 'plain people of Ireland'.

In time, the term 'West Briton' (and later 'West Brit') became the preferred insult to level against those deemed unionist in political outlook, or somehow ashamed of Irish identity. Unlike 'Jackeen', it could be applied to anyone on the island. In Westminster, the Unionist MP Thomas Spring Rice had made it clear in 1834 that 'I should prefer the name of West Britain to that of Ireland.' Captain R. Henderson remembered in his Bureau of Military History witness statement that at the time of the Rising, 'the West Britons were resentful at this revolt against English domination, the British Army Separation Allowance element in its then ignorance was infuriated against the soldiers of Irish freedom'.

Regardless of what it may have meant in the past to different people at different times, Dubliners would come to embrace the term ironically. In the glory days of 1970s GAA in Dublin, the homemade banners proclaimed that 'The Jacks Are Back'. While we're not entirely sure where it came from, it's a term that is likely to stick around as a light-hearted jibe towards Dubs.

The Gunrunner in the Four Courts

Ciarán Murray

Ernie O'Malley's works on the War of Independence (*On Another Man's Wound*) and the Civil War (*The Singing Flame*) are easily two of the best books written about the revolutionary period, his descriptive style of prose capable of painting vivid scenes. Covering the period July 1921 to July 1924, *The Singing Flame* commences around the 1921 truce and runs right through to the death of Liam Lynch. As such, the cataclysmic aftermath of the split and all it entailed feature heavily and heartrendingly.

O'Malley has always been something of an enigma to many people. A veteran of the War of Independence and the Civil War, he remained puritanical in his vision for an Irish Republic, and held an uncompromising belief that any violence used in attaining it was soundly and morally justified. His politics never deviated from the creation of the republic, his head never turned, and he was happy to play the part of the consummate soldier. Imprisoned by the Free State, he was elected to the Dáil 1923–27 though as a Sinn Féin member he abstained from taking his seat.

The Singing Flame goes into great detail about the occupation, defence of, and surrender of the Four Courts during the Battle of Dublin. Tragedy would strike the O'Malley family that week: Ernie's younger brother Charles, who had been fighting under Oscar Traynor in 'The Block' on O'Connell Street, was shot and killed at the junction of O'Connell and Parnell streets. He had been due to take the final exams for his first year in veterinary school the next day.

The international complement present in the GPO during Easter Week is well documented, and accounts of them can be drawn down from the Bureau of Military History's witness statements and the Military Service Pensions Collection – perhaps most notable among them were a Swede and a Finn, who, however disastrously, played their parts. Less was recorded about foreign influence in an occupation of similar moment during the Civil War. However, one international participant stands out in a reading of *The Singing Flame* – a well-coiffured American dandy gunrunner who had somehow been taken prisoner in the Four Courts:

Already we had one prisoner near the guardroom. He was a professional gunrunner. He entertained us with stories of Mexico and of the South American republics. He passed comments on the hotels in Dublin; there was only one where a person could eat in comfort. I expect the food from the officer's mess was not much to his liking. He was rather tall, well dressed, with light fair hair and a slight moustache varying between fair and white, well pointed at the ends; he must have used some kind of grease. He was accused of trying to double-cross some of our agents in Belgium and Germany who were attempting to purchase arms. He protested vigorously. This was an outrage; it was the first time he had ever been arrested. He was told it might be the last time, and his smile, showing a few gold teeth, dwindled away. His nasal voice was not raised so often now.

After the Four Courts occupation ended and O'Malley escaped Dublin, he describes making his way to Bray, where he encountered the prisoner again:

> What South Dublin had been doing since the attack on the courts I could not imagine. A man walked over from the hotel door. He was the American gunrunner whom we had released a few hours before the attack on the Four Courts began. He inquired for Liam Mellows and Paddy O'Brien. 'I liked them well,' he said. 'I sure am sorry about O'Brien. They were good boys in there.' He flashed his gold-toothed smile. 'I'm waiting for the next boat, glad to go; this country of yours is too sharp for me.' 'If you send us a consignment of trench mortars,' I said, 'no one will quarrel with you about your excess profits.'

The O'Malley notebooks in the UCD archive name the man as 'Hoover', with no first name and reference that a few years previously he had supplied arms to the Mexicans for their revolution. Sean Lemass' interview with O'Malley notes that 'Hoover sold a cargo of arms from Germany and had come over in advance of its delivery'. How his attempt at double-cross played out, and how he came to be under lock and key in a Four Courts under heavy bombardment, there is unfortunately no mention.

Connolly and Dublin Anarchists

Sam McGrath

In Máirtín Ó Catháin's history of Glasgow anarchism, there is a short but fascinating mention of James Connolly. Connolly's paper, the *Workers' Republic*, was suppressed by the authorities in December 1914 and O'Cathain writes that it was the 'Glasgow Anarchist Group that took over the printing of the paper ... and smuggled it into Ireland'. Apparently, the police in Britain raided several anarchist printing presses, including London's *Freedom Press*, but never caught the Glasgow group. But there are two competing versions of this story, and it's unclear which is correct.

There is also a mention of Glasgow comrades printing the paper and smuggling it into Ireland in Donal Nevin's fantastic 2005 biography of Connolly, *A Full Life*. But Nevin points to Connolly's old colleagues in the Socialist Labour Party. More specifically, Arthur MacManus, who was the one who did the setting, composing and printing, and then smuggled the copies to Dublin using the pseudonym 'Glass'. Belfast-born MacManus, son of an Irish Fenian, later became the first chairman of the Communist Party of Great Britain and was buried in Red Square, Moscow, after his death in 1927. As Nevin backs up his claim with a reference to C. Desmond Greaves' 1971 book *The Life and Times of James Connolly*, the evidence stacks in his favour.

"FREEDOM" MAY BE OBTAINED of

London.—HENDERSONS, 66 Charing Cross Road, W.C. (Wholesale).
NATIONAL LABOUR PRESS, St. Bride's House, Salisbury Square, Fleet
    Street, E.C. (Wholesale).
B. RUDERMAN, 71 Hanbury Street, Spitalfields, E,
J. J. JAQUES, 191 Old Street, City Road, E.C.
QUICKFALLS, 238 York Road, and 61 High Street, Battersea, S.W.
ISENBURG, Cleveland Street, W.
W. REEVES, 83, Charing Cross Road, W.
F. BENDY, 270 York Road, Bridge End, Wandsworth, S.W.
STEVENS, 56 High Street, Islington.
GOLUB, 10 Osborne Street, Whitechapel.
SUGARMAN, 329A Mile End Road, E.
J. YATES, 114 High Road, Willesden Green, N.W.
H. ELLIOT, 329 Lillie Road, Fulham, S.W.
J. WINTERS, 196 Church Road, Willesden, N.W.
J. FLEET, 109 Upper Street, Islington, N.
F. Hahn, 450 Harrow Road, N.W.
Leicester.—H. Holton, 87 Wolverton Road.
Manchester.—H. SEGALS, 99A Great Ducie Street, Strangeways (Wholesale).
HEWKIN, 14A Cannon Street.
M. Robert, 86 Grosvenor Street, Corner of Brook Street.
Burns, New Bailey Street.
Manning, Lower Mosley Street.
Walker, Church Street, Newton Heath.
Collins, 326, Oldham Road, Newton Heath.
Plymouth.—W. Tall, Market Bookstall.
Belfast—W. ROBINSON, 167 York Street.
Falkirk—J. Wilson, 76, Graham's Road.
Leeds—G. Frost, Keeton Street, York Road.
Huddersfield.—H. Francis, 97 Swan Lane, Lockwood.
    A. Wadsworth, Outcote Bank, Manchester Road.
Coventry.—O. Lloyd, Market Stall.
Yeovil—W. R. Fowler, 5 Sherborne Road
Dublin—J. C. Kearney, 59 Upper Stephen Street.
Glasgow.—D. BAXTER, 32 Brunswick Street.
Bristol.—J. FLYNN, Haymarket.
Dundee.—L. MACARTNEY, 203, Overgate.
Cardiff—M. CLARK, 26 Wood Street.
U.S.A.—M. MAISEL, 422 Grand Street, New York, N.Y.

Sellers of *Freedom* newspaper in March 1916 including Belfast
and Dublin. (Image: Libcom.com)

At the time of the post-Rising executions, Antrim-born anarchist and Irish Citizen Army co-founder Jack White was in the Rhondda and Aberdare valleys in South Wales. He did his best to bring the miners out on strike to save Connolly's life. For his troubles, White was charged with trying to 'sow the seeds of sedition in an area which had nothing to do with the grievances of Ireland either real or imaginary', and at a time when 'a peaceful settlement was being arrived at'. He was sentenced to six months in jail for his trouble.

Around the time of the 1916 Rising, it was possible to purchase the anarchist newspaper *Freedom* in Dublin. Printed from 1886 to 2014 in the East End of London, *Freedom* was the stalwart organ of the English-speaking anarchist movement and could boast of links with some of the world's foremost anarchist thinkers, including Peter Kropotkin, Marie-Louise Berneri, and Colin Ward.

A copy of *Freedom* from March 1916, available to read on the *Libcom* website, lists the names and addresses for *Freedom* newspaper sellers in Dublin and Belfast, alongside major cities like London, Manchester, Glasgow and smaller towns such as Plymouth, Yeovil, and Falkirk. They were 'Belfast – W. Robinson, 167 York Street' and 'Dublin – J.C. Kearney, 59 Upper Stephen Street'.

Joseph C. Kearney (*c.*1887 to 1946) was a bookseller and stationer who lived above his shop at 59 Upper Stephen Street his whole life. There are a small number of fleeting references to him and his family in the archives. It could be assumed that he had some sympathy to socialist or anarchist politics, as he was happy to both stock *Freedom* and let the newspaper advertise that fact.

At the time of the 1901 census, Joseph C. Kearney (14) was living at home with his widow mother Lily Kearney (38) née Walsh, and two younger brothers, Thomas (11) and Alfred (10). Lily was a tobacconist and employed an assistant, Mary Callaghan (19) from Cork, in the shop downstairs. Obviously reasonably financially well-off, the family also enjoyed the services of a servant, Ellen Byrne (16), from Carlow.

By 1911, Lily (50) had remarried a Royal Dublin Fusiliers Army Pensioner by the name of Vincent Walter (60). Her three sons, Joseph (24), Thomas (22), and Alfred (20), all still lived at home with her and listed their profession as 'news agent shop men'. Lily's brother Alfred Walsh (52), an 'engine fitter', and a cousin, Louie Wilson (16), a 'draper's shop assistant' from Liverpool, also lived in the house at that time.

In August 1918, Joseph C. Kearney was fined after his wife Louisa Kearney illegally sold matches to a customer. It was the first prosecution, according to the *Irish Examiner* of 28 August 1918, under a new act that 'provided that matches must be sold in boxes and not in bundles under any circumstances'.

Kearney had another brush with the law, but this time for more interesting reasons than selling matches. In April 1928, Joseph C. Kearney was found guilty and fined a total of £60 for selling two 'obscene' publications entitled *Family Limitation* and *The Married Women's Guide*. It could be concluded from this that Kearney was still politically inclined twelve years after he was listed as stocking the *Freedom* newspaper.

In court, the state prosecutor, Carrigan, according to the *Irish Times* of 20 April 1928, said:

> The theories contained in the publications might find support in England or in large communities, but in a comparatively small community, like that in Ireland, he did not think that they would find favour, not that the Irish were superior people, but they, happily, were more old-fashioned than were people elsewhere. The public good in Ireland would not be served by the circulation of these books.

Joseph C. Kearney tragically lost his wife and two children in the 1920s and 1930s. His wife Louisa Kearney died on 8 October 1923. Emily Louisa, his second daughter, passed away on 10 March 1939, aged 22, and was buried in Glasnevin Cemetery. His youngest son, Vincent Joseph Kearney, died on 24 February 1936, aged 15, after a short illness.

Joseph C Kearney himself died on 29 January 1946, and was buried in Glasnevin with his family. After his death, the newsagent at 59 Upper Stephen Street was taken over by a P. Smyth. This house and that whole row at the corner of Upper Stephen Street and South Great George's Street was demolished and replaced by a modern office block (Dunnes Stores head office) in 2007.

The Bolsheveki Bookies

Ciarán Murray

Now more than ever it is possible for those with an interest and an internet connection to study family history. From the online availability of Census data and the Bureau of Military History's pensions and witness statements collections to the newspaper archives, it takes time – and, unfortunately, at times a little money – to delve into the past. In investigating my own history, I came across two interesting associates of my great-uncle William Murray: James and Thomas Redican.

James and Thomas were born to Sligo parents, Thomas and Annie Redican. Thomas Snr was a gardener by trade and had a passion for playing Irish music, and the boys and their siblings Dorothy, Patrick and Lawrence attended school in Donnybrook. On finishing school, James became a bookmaker (under the pseudonym Thomas Casey) and was a Volunteer in E Company, 3rd Battalion, Dublin Brigade. He was active in Boland's Mill during the Easter Rising and would suffer injuries to a hand and an ankle, as well as taking a bullet to a thigh, an injury that would plague him for the rest of his life; he was imprisoned in Frongoch after the surrender. His younger brother Thomas also made an appearance during the Rising, showing up at James' garrison, but De Valera turned him away for being too young.

Sometime after the general release of prisoners from Frongoch, James Redican makes an appearance in Mullingar, as can be read in the witness statements of Michael Murray, captain of the Ballynacarrigy Company IRA, and Michael McCoy, captain of the Mullingar Company. Murray mentions raids for arms 'under the command of James Redican', and a successful raid on the Hibernian Bank in Mullingar. His statement also speaks of Redican and a party of Volunteers, including William Murray, holding up a mail train just outside of Mullingar, destroying communications and removing money from letters. The statement continues somewhat controversially

> It now transpired that Redican was not a member of the Volunteers at all. He was an ex-prisoner from Mountjoy Jail. Apparently while in Mountjoy he got acquainted with some Volunteer prisoners from the Mullingar area and convinced them he was up for political reasons while in reality he was doing time for some criminal offence. On his release, he came to the Mullingar area nosing as staff officer from G.H.Q. and soon was OK with the Battalion O/C and other officers. G.H.Q. now sent down instructions that he was to be put out of the area, much to our surprise … It was really a pity he was of that type because he had plenty of guts and courage and would be an asset to the Volunteers anywhere.

There is no doubt that Redican was a Volunteer so the statement above shows the difficulty with relying on the subjectivity of personal accounts for empirical evidence.

The Hibernian wasn't Redican's only experience of bank raids. By late 1920, he was leading a gang of men (including his brother Thomas and several of those involved in the Hibernian raid) on a series of sorties against banks in Dublin, ostensibly under the orders of Brigadier T.J. Burke of Mullingar, according to Noel Redican's book *Shadows of Doubt*.

In November 1920 and February 1921, the National Bank of Upper Baggot Street was raided, with sums of £2,789 and £1,237 being appropriated. The day after the February raid, the brothers, along with Thomas Weymes (another of the Mullingar men) were picked up and brought to the local police barracks, where they were paraded in front of witnesses, arrested and charged. According to *Shadows of Doubt*: 'They [the IRA] had come to the conclusion that [James] Redican had pocketed the proceeds from the robberies, which were therefore of a criminal nature, and disowned the raiders.' As a result, their arrests may not have been wholly down to sleuth-like police work. Michael McCoy's witness statement would seem to corroborate this, were it not again more than controversial in the nature of its claims, insinuating somehow that Collins was collaborating with the British authorities:

a series of bank robberies occurred around Dublin. David Burke had a suspicion that Redigan [sic] and his party might be the culprits, and so informed Michael Collins. Collins passed on the information to some friends in the D.M.P., and Redigan and a man named Weymes were arrested and sentenced to a term of imprisonment. It was suspected that Redigan then gave information to the British authorities as to the location of the arms in Mullingar. In February, 1921, after David Burke was arrested, an R.I.C. man told him that they had information that arms were stored in a disused oven in McDonnell's bakery in Dominick St. Their information was perfectly correct. Burke got a message out to me and we had them removed shortly before the place was raided.

The three men still regarded the offences with which they were being charged as political, insisting the raids were ordered by superior officers and that the proceeds had been removed by another two of the Hibernian men, Tormey and Murray, for return to their brigadier for dispersal. Their trials were held separately and weren't without controversy – witnesses seemed confused as to who they were meant to be pointing out, and Thomas Redican, though in prison in Arbour Hill for another offence at the time of the February raid, was charged. The three men were sentenced to penal servitude.

Their time in prison was cut short by the signing of the treaty and the subsequent amnesty for republican prisoners in February 1922, but they were re-arrested within weeks for questioning regarding the whereabouts of the money raised through their bank raids – upwards of £5,000 was unaccounted for. They were tried by a republican court at the court of conscience on South William Street in what was widely regarded at the time by the papers as 'an amazing story'. Several newspaper reports, including the 3 June 1922 *Cork County Eagle and Munster Advertiser*, make the point that the money from the raids was used to finance a bookmaking business:

In November, Tormey, James Redican and witness raided the Baggot Street branch of the National Bank. They got about £3,000 there. They went to Tara Street after, taking the money from the bank. Tormey went away that evening. Witness handed over the stolen money to him and he took some of it with him. Witness was acting under Tormey at this time. Witness followed Tormey to Westmeath and there was a division of the money but Witness got none. Witness carried on the book in the meantime. In October, the book was making money. They called themselves the 'Bolsheviki Bookmakers'.

Under the newly formed Free State, the men's stay in prison was far from comfortable, with neither side willing to give concession to the other. Throughout the Civil War they remained guests of the state, who though petitioned, refused to sanction the release of Thomas even though it was proved he could not have been present for the raid that he was charged and sentenced for. The men in turn didn't make it easy for the prison services and until their release in July 1924, frequently engaged in acts of disobedience, refusing to wear uniforms, attacking warders and undergoing several hunger strikes, one of which almost cost James his life.

Their story does not end there. In 1928 Seán Harling, a brother-in-law to the Redican brothers (having married their sister Dorothy), shot and killed Timothy Coughlan, a 22-year-old IRA Volunteer outside the house he was sharing with the Redican family. Harling, a republican interned during the Civil War had joined the secret services of the Free State in part due to economic reasons, and in part due to enormous pressure exerted by Free State agents. He alleged he was ambushed while returning home from work and retaliated in self-defence. However, medical evidence would suggest otherwise. Coughlan's wound looked more like an execution rather than a shot fired in haste while fleeing. The Redican brothers would take the stand once more, this time for questioning in relation to Coughlan's death, having been present in the house during the shooting; the case is almost as inconclusive today as it was at the time.

Bona Fides, Kips, and Early Houses

Sam McGrath

If you knew where to go, it was possible to drink around the clock in 1930s, 1940s, and 1950s Dublin.

When regular pubs closed at 11 p.m., still-thirsty revellers could travel to 'bona fide' pubs on the outskirts of the city. These places utilised a legal loophole, dating back to early coaching days, that allowed a genuine 'bona-fide' traveller 3 miles from his place of residence (5 miles, in Dublin) to drink alcohol outside of normal hours.

A piece entitled 'The Irish "Bona-Fide Traveller" Nuisance' in the *Sacred Heart Review* of 13 September 1902 noted that:

> Travelers, tramps and tourists are common the wide world over, but the so-called 'Bona Fide Traveler' is peculiar to Ireland. Under the curious laws which govern or misgovern Ireland, it has been decreed that when any person 'travels' three miles to a 'public-house' on a Sunday he is entitled to all the drink he can buy, even though the Sunday closing law is in full force there. Thus a man living in the town of Kilronan cannot legally enter a public house to secure a drink,

Photograph of Alma Fawcett (Dolly's daughter-in-law) and 'Danzer' Keaton (local coal man), third and fourth in beside 'Danzer's' sister and her husband outside the Café Continental on Bolton Street in the mid 1950s. (Image: Anne Fawcett)

but let him walk or ride to Knooknagow, three miles away, and he can have all the drink he wants …

There was at least one 'bona fide' on each main road out of Dublin. They included Lamb Doyles (Dublin Mountains), Widow Flavin's (Sandyford), the Dropping Well (Dartry), the Deadman's Inn (Lucan), the Swiss Cottage (Santry), the Igo Inn (Ballybrack), and The Goat (Goatstown).

Throughout the years, a number of late-night revellers, staggering or driving under the influence towards the bona fide, were involved in deadly accidents. This was one of the main reasons for the government abolishing the law in 1960.

If you wanted to keep on drinking after the bona fide closed, you could travel back into the city and visit one of the 'kips' around Capel Street or Parnell Square. A 'kip' was a brothel-cum-speakeasy that sold whiskey or gin from tea cups till the early morning.

One of the city's most famous 'kips' was the Café Continental at 1a Bolton Street at the corner of Capel Street, which was in operation from around the 1930s until the mid-1960s. It was run by the legendary madam Annie 'Dolly' Fawcett (often misspelt as 'Fossett' or 'Fosset').

Dolly, originally from Wicklow, married William Fawcett, who was rumoured to have been a former Dublin Metropolitan Police (DMP) officer from the North, who was discharged because of his relationship with her. The Fawcett family also ran another 'kip' called the Cozy Kitchen on nearby North King Street.

Ostensibly an innocent late-night café, the Café Continental was a haven for revellers who often carried clandestine 'Baby Powers' or miniature bottles of whiskey, which they tipped into their cups of coffee. Dolly also served up 'red biddy' (mixture of red wine and methanol), poitín, and watered-down whiskey.

The *Irish Times* on 7 October 1944 ran a front-page piece about a journalist's visit to an 'all-night drinking den'. My bet would be that it was Dolly Fawcett's.

It was a popular place for ladies of the night, and they'd often find clients there. So Dolly Fawcett's would be better described as a 'prostitute pick up-place', as opposed to a brothel in the traditional sense of the word.

Dolly, who lived over the Café Continental with her family, passed away at home on 12 March 1949. She was 48 years old, and was listed as a 'housewife' on her death certificate. Her funeral, which took place after Mass at the Pro Cathedral, attracted a large attendance as she was highly regarded in the area for her numerous charitable acts.

Her sons Eugene and George continued to run the two businesses after their mother passed away. The family was up in court for 'unlawfully selling intoxicating liquor' in their two cafes in 1947, 1950, 1952, 1953, 1954, and 1963. Inspector McCabe in the *Irish Independent* on 28 November 1963 noted that the Fawcetts had been fined a total of £400 for fifteen separate convictions over the previous fourteen years.

In a newspaper report dating back to 1954, Eugene Fawcett told the judge he would 'retire from business' if he could have 'his family educated'. He eventually did call it a day in 1965. In an article headlined 'Cafe not to trouble the courts again' in the *Irish Independent* on 21 January 1965, Eugene Fawcett's lawyer told the court that a 'phase of the history of Dublin's night life has come to an end'.

There were a number of other late-night cafés, kips, and basements clubs where you could drink after hours. One such place was Toni's Café on 23 Harcourt Road. Its owner was fined for selling whiskey in the early hours of the morning in 1940 and 1941. Changing its name to The Manhattan in the early 1950s, this late-night café was a favourite for taxi men, musicians, and students until its closure in the early 2000s.

The so-called Catacombs in the basement of 13 Fitzwilliam Place was a popular after-hours spot and flophouse in the late 1940s for Dublin's bohemian set. Wild parties were held in a labyrinth of cellars and pantries in a once-fine Georgian mansion. The 'underground' club was opened by Englishman Richard 'Dickie' Wyman, a one-time cruise-liner cocktail maker and a former nightclub manager in London, who moved to Dublin following the death of his British Army officer boyfriend in World War II.

After McDaid's pub closed, Dublin's artist-literary set would head to the Catacombs and drink till the early morning. Regulars included writers Brendan Behan, Patrick Kavanagh, J.P. Donleavy, Anthony Cronin, and Brian O'Nolan; poets Pearse Hutchinson and John Jordan; artists Tom Nisbet and Patrick Swift; actors Dan O'Herlihy, Tony MacInerney, and Godfrey Quigley; musician George Desmond Hodnett; composer Frederick May; socialist activist George Jeffares and sculptors Irene Broe and Desmond MacNamara.

Entrance to the Catacombs was granted by offering Wyman a brown paper bag of half a dozen bottles of stout. In the morning, the porter in McDaid's, John Flynn, would be dispatched on his bicycle to collect the empties from the Catacombs and bring them back. Wyman made a living by selling these empty bottles and renting out basement rooms in the Catacombs. He also apparently made sweets and sold blood to the nearby Blood Transfusion Service when times were tight. A well-loved eccentric, he once walked from Dublin to Catherdaniel, Kerry, where Brendan Behan was helping to restore Daniel O'Connell's house, for a £10 bet.

The Catacombs was renowned for its sexual licence. Brendan Behan infamously recalled that it was a place where 'men had women, men had men and women had women'. Anthony Cronin lived in the Catacombs for a period and described it in his 1976 book *Dead as Doornails* as place that:

> smelt of damp, decaying plaster and brickwork, that smell of money gone which was once so prevalent in Ireland. Off the corridor leading out of the kitchen

were various dark little rooms. Mine, I think, had once been a wine cellar. There was hardly space for a bed in it, and none for anything else except a few bottles and books. The other rooms were variously occupied and people came and went according to need and circumstances ...

What happened to Dickie Wyman? It was revealed in a 2007 RTÉ radio documentary that he got a job as a barman in Welwyn Garden City, England, and then moved to the United States. He kept moving house and his Dublin-based friends eventually lost touch with him. It is believed he died in the early 1980s.

Another late-night café that served alcohol after-hours was the ATS Restaurant at 6 Nassau Street. Ran by Ruby Elizabeth Egan and her husband Patrick, it was raided in 1956, 1957, and 1961 for serving whiskey, stout, and beer in the early hours. When up in court in 1961, Patrick Egan told the judge: 'I plead guilty, there is no point telling you lies.'

From January 1959 to May 1961, the couple were fined fourteen times for liquor offences. Simone de Beauvoir's boyfriend Nelson Algren was witness to one of these Garda raids, as retold in *Who Lost an American?* (1963):

I was reaching for a drop of wine when the glass was snatched from my hand by the proprietor's stout wife, seizing all the glasses empty or full out of the hands of the drinkers, thirsty or dry. Under the tables went the lot. Everyone sat up straight as in church, with nothing before them but ashtrays. Two inspecting officers entered from offstage, where they had been waiting for their cue, inspected the ceiling, flower-pots, table-tops and jukeboxes without finding anything.

While the bona-fide law ended in 1960 and legendary cafés like Dolly Fawcett's closed in 1965, you could still manage to drink around the clock in 1970s and 1980s Dublin if you knew the right people.

Groome's Hotel, opposite the Gate Theatre, was described by Tim Pat Coogan in his 2004 book *Ireland in the 20th Century* as the 'most famous late-night drinking club in Dublin in the sixties and seventies'. Ronnie Drew, in his autobiography, says its regulars included almost 'everybody who worked in the theatre; the newspapers, painters, poets, writers and almost all visiting celebrities'.

The hotel was owned by Joseph Groome, one of the founding members of Fianna Fáil and lifelong honorary vice president. He was involved in Na Fianna Éireann and then the IRA from 1919–23. The hotel was popular with aspiring young Fianna Fáil TDs like Charles Haughey and Brian Lenihan, but also attracted a Labour Party set led by Michael O'Leary. It was frequently referred to as 'a sub-office' of the Dáil, due its popularity with politicians. The hotel was sold in 1973, turned into offices, and then redeveloped as a hotel (Cassidy's) in the late 1990s.

On the other side of the political divide, and probably more difficult to get into, were the republican and left-wing drinking clubs. These included Official Sinn Fein's Club Ui Cadhain at 28 Gardiner Place, the Provisional Sinn Fein's office/drinking club at 5 Blessington Street, and the back of Connolly Books on East Essex Street, which was run by the Communist Party.

If you were able to make it until 7 a.m., you could then make your way to the 'early houses' clustered on the

Northside around Capel Street, close to the old Markets, and on the Southside around the Quays and Pearse Street area. These pubs were given special early morning licences in 1927 for dockworkers, market traders, fishermen, night workers, and those attending early morning fairs.

Since 1962, no new pubs have been added to the list of early houses, and they are considered a dying breed. In 2008, the government put forward legislation to revoke early house licences, but they eventually decided to leave them as they are.

Today the clientele is a little more varied, and, depending on where you go, you are likely to rub shoulders with wired shift workers (taxi drivers, postmen, nurses etc.), thirsty early risers, tourists who have landed into Dublin early, and all-night revellers, who have no intention of going to bed yet. In 2004, there were around sixteen operating early houses in Dublin city. By 2017, this number had been reduced to eleven.

Leaving Her Mark on Kildare Street: the Work of Gabriel Hayes

Donal Fallon

The Department of Industry and Commerce building on Kildare Street is a striking piece of architecture. Designed by Cork architect J.R Boyd Barrett, it was constructed between 1939 and 1942, with the wonderful *Buildings of Ireland* website noting that it was 'greatly delayed by the difficulty of obtaining materials, particularly steel, owing to the outbreak of the Second World War'.

Buildings of Ireland describes the premises as 'one of Dublin's most interesting twentieth-century architectural gems'. Among its finest features are the bas-reliefs by Gabriel Hayes, depicting Irish industry through the ages. They have been described by architectural historian Paula Murphy as being 'carved in a vigorous socialist-realist style', and there is something more East Berlin than Southside Dublin about their style.

Gabriel Hayes was the daughter of a member of the Royal Irish Constabulary, who later became an architect with the Board of Works. Born in Holles Street in August 1909, she was educated at the Dominican College on Eccles Street. Having studied art in Paris and Montpelier, she spent five years in the National School of Art, Dublin. Historian James Durney notes that:

The work of Gabriel Hayes, carved into the Department of
Industry and Commerce bulding (Image: Creative Commons)

In her second year at college she won the teachers-in-
training scholarship, and in 1933 she had five works
exhibited at the Royal Hibernian Academy. In her
master's certificate Gabriel came first in Ireland. She
began exhibiting at the RHA in 1932 and continued
to exhibit there until 1947.

While initially she focused on painting, she would later
establish herself firmly as one of the leading sculptors of her
time in Ireland. Married to Seán Ó Ríordáin, an academic
and archaeologist based in University College Cork, she
moved there in 1936.

That she carried out the works on Kildare Street at all
is interesting, as she was not among the original group of
sculptors invited to submit designs. This group included
Laurence Campbell (responsible for the excellent Seán
Heuston memorial in the Phoenix Park) and Oliver Sheppard
(who gave us Cú Chulainn in the GPO). As Murphy has
noted, 'Hayes was subsequently approached and her designs

and estimated cost of £930 met with approval. This is the work for which Gabriel Hayes is now best known.' Seán Lemass himself inspected the designs and gave them the go-ahead.

When she got down to the business at hand, journalists were impressed by the heights she was willing to scale. A writer with the *Irish Independent* commented on 21 April 1942 that 'when I arrived on a January day of snow and sleet, I was told that she was in the sort of built-up cage slung over the roof to work the keystones over the two toweringly tall windows – 76 feet up. Being built by nature for comfort and not meant for high altitudes I promised to come back.'

That a woman was carrying out the work grabbed plenty of column inches too. 'Mother of two infants, aged 1 and 4, this Dublin-born artist has interrupted her life in Cork for one of the most important sculpturing tasks in Dublin for some time,' the *Irish Press* proclaimed. David Dickson, in his groundbreaking study of Dublin through the ages, makes the point that:

> The prospect of a mother working outside the home was contrary to the whole drift of government thinking in the pre-war years. Opportunities for women to stay at work had been seriously impaired by legislation in 1936 that overturned statutory advances in 1919 and required all women to resign from the public service with no hope of re-employment, even on widowhood, and excluded all women from certain categories of work.

Paula Murphy correctly points out that for the most part, journalists seemed to overlook the quality of her work on the building, instead fixating on trivial things, as 'little was written about this significant work at the time. Journalists seemed more excited that a woman had received the commission and that she was brave enough to work on scaffolding hanging high outside the building.'

The work was designed to show the emerging industries and commercial life of the new Irish state. The *Irish Press*, a newspaper closely aligned with the reigning Fianna Fáil party, noted:

> Her work on the Kildare Street building is original in conception and strongly executed. Beside the head of Eire at the main entrance there is a head of St Brendan, Ireland's first navigator, at the side. Along a 30-foot gallery, Miss Hayes is to carve a further series of scenes in low relief depicting Irish industry and commerce. Her subjects include: the Shannon Scheme, the cement factories, the wool industry and shipbuilding.

Hayes would later design the halfpenny, penny, and twopence coins introduced here in 1971. She died in 1978, recognised in obituaries not as a 'woman sculptor' or a working mother, but a brilliant talent by anyone's definition. Next time you're passing by, stop and have a look at her striking work on Kildare Street.

The Crimean Banquet, 22 October 1856

Ciarán Murray

The Charge of the Light Brigade, an infamous battle during the Crimean War (1853–6), remains one of the worst displays of military recklessness ever recorded. Dublin's links to the fateful event are clear: not only was the bugle that sounded the charge made here, but the bugle call was given by Dubliner William Brittain of the 17th Lancers, orderly bugler to Lord Cardigan, the commander of the Light Brigade. Of the 673 horsemen involved in the charge, over 100 were Irish.

At the time of the war, approximately 30 to 35 per cent of the British army was made up of Irish troops, and somewhere in the region of 30,000 of those Irish troops served in Crimea. They left Dublin with fanfare, the departure of the 50th Foot regiment on 24 February 1854 recorded this way:

> The bands of three other regiments of the garrison led them along the line of route, one of the finest in Europe; and vast crowds accompanied them, vociferously cheering, while from the windows handkerchiefs and scarves were waved, and every token of a 'Godspeed' displayed.

Irish involvement in the war wasn't confined to belligerents though. Civilian medics tended to the wounded, and in a war where 'frontline correspondents' arguably played a role for the first time, Irishman William Howard Russell's first-hand reports on troop welfare led Trinity College to award him an honorary degree on his return. As the war drew on, and casualties mounted (albeit in part through disease, as cholera and malaria were rampant), the support that was granted to it as troops left the country diminished.

Returning victorious, the regiments were not treated to the pomp and occasion they received as they left. Still, the lord mayor of Dublin, at the suggestion of the lord lieutenant, the earl of Carlisle, called together a committee to organise a 'national banquet' to pay tribute to Crimean veterans stationed in Ireland. A subscription list was established, and over £2,000 was collected within the first nine days of its inception.

An *Irish Times* report on the centenary of the event claimed that the merchants and traders of Dublin showed great interest in the project, with offers of assistance coming from different patrons including 'a gentleman, styling himself the Wizard of the North who offered to give a performance for the benefit of the National Banquet Fund'. His offer was kindly declined. Over 3,500 guests were invited to the banquet (3,628 sat down for dinner), along with over 1,000 paying spectators, and such numbers caused large problems with regards to finding a location.

The Rotunda, the Mansion House and several halls in Dublin Castle were examined but deemed too small to fit the purpose. There was a proposal to raise a purpose-built marquee in the grounds of Dublin Castle or Leinster House, but this plan too was dismissed. Finally, a Mr Scovell offered the use of his bonding warehouse near the Custom House (the modern CHQ building in the IFSC). Built as a 'fireproof' tobacco warehouse in 1821, it remains to this day one of the oldest iron-frame buildings in Ireland. The date was set for 22 October, and preparations for the banquet were set underway.

The hall itself, which can still be seen almost in its original state, measures 260 feet long and 150 feet wide, with rows of pillars supporting a magnificent roof of iron framework, which was painted in bright colours for the occasion. During the banquet, the walls of the building were covered in numerous national flags, some bearing the names of the major battles of the war: Alma, Sevastopol, and Balaclava, among others. Decorative field guns on platforms guarded the entrance to the building. The report continued:

> the total length of the tables was 6,172 feet. The viands supplied included 250 hams, 230 legs of mutton, 500 meat pies, 100 venison pasties, 100 rice puddings, 260 plum puddings, 200 turkeys, 200 geese, 250 pieces of beef weighing in all 3,000 lbs; 3 tons of potatoes, 2,000 half-pound loafs, 100 capons and chickens and six ox tongues ... Each man was supplied a quart of porter and a pint of choice port wine. There were guests from every regiment stationed in Ireland, along with 500 pensioners, constabulary and marines, and 60 gentlemen of the press.

Given that Ireland had been in the grips of famine not a decade previously, it is surprising to read of the joy and excitement that the banquet generated. For while across the country people had starved, here you had the gentry feasting what must be the largest number of people to have ever sat down to dinner together in this country, and yet there are several accounts of the vans containing the steaming food being cheered and applauded as they careened down Dublin's North Quays.

Oscar Wilde, Speranza and the Young Irelanders

Donal Fallon

The impressive Independent House on Middle Abbey Street still carries the names of the *Evening Herald* and *Irish Independent* upon it, though today they are mere 'ghost signs', as the Independent News and Media group have relocated in recent years to Talbot Street. Easier to miss than the names of these contemporary newspapers is a small plaque marking the fact that the site was once home to the offices of *The Nation,* an influential nationalist newspaper that began life in the 1840s.

Instigated by the Young Ireland movement, and spearheaded by radical nationalists like Thomas Davis, William Smith O'Brien and John Mitchel, *The Nation* provided a platform not only to nationalist political ideas but to cultural output too. It was within its pages that 'A Nation Once Again' first appeared, the work of Thomas Davis.

Women also contributed to the newspaper, and one such contributor was Jane Wilde. Writing under the pen name 'Speranza', Lady Wilde's poetry was often seditious in nature, calling for armed revolt against British rule in Ireland. In particular, she attacked the British political establishment for creating the conditions that allowed

Lady Wilde from the *Irish Fireside*.

famine to ravage rural Ireland, and called on the peasantry
to revolt:

> Fainting forms, hunger-stricken,
> What see you in the offing?
> Stately ships to bear our food away,
> Amid the stranger's scoffing.

As Christine Kinealy has written, Jane Wilde would come to
be an inspiration to later generations of female nationalists,
including Countess Markievicz and Alice Milligan, one of

the leading lights of the Irish cultural revival. At the time of Jane Wilde's passing in 1896, Milligan wrote of her 'matchless spirit which in a time of doubt, danger and despair, she brought to the service of Ireland'.

The Young Irelanders would ultimately attempt insurrection in 1848, a year synonymous with revolution on the European continent. In an Ireland ravaged by starvation and disease, however, any such rebellion was doomed. John Mitchel, one of the leaders of the movement, would later declare that 'the Almighty, indeed, sent the potato blight, but the English created the Famine'.

Oscar Fingal O'Flahertie Wills Wilde was born in 1854 into a peculiar household, with a mother who was an unrepentant nationalist poet, and a father who had been knighted in the 1860s for pioneering work in his field. Oscar would maintain that the best of his education came from his association with his parents and their remarkable friends. Their Merrion Square home was a hive of discussion and cultural activity.

As a graduate of Trinity College Dublin and Oxford, Oscar Wilde first burst into the public consciousness as a poet ('The poet is Wilde, but his poetry's tame', wrote *Punch*) and a hugely entertaining and engaging public speaker, a recognised figurehead of the aesthetic and decadent movements of the late 1870s and early 1880s. In 1882, Wilde departed for the United States on his first speaking tour there, and he quickly discovered that in many circles his mother's pen name was more recognisable than his own. Promoters began including mention of her on advertisements for Wilde's lectures, and the *Arizona Weekly Citizen* condemned Oscar as being 'so low that he does not scruple to advertise himself for a dollar a ticket as the son of Lady Wilde (Speranza)'.

It was clear to Wilde that some in the US perhaps wished to hear of things other than the aesthetic movement. In San Francisco, he delivered a lecture in which he praised the 'men of forty-eight', and the Young Ireland movement in which his mother had played her own unique part:

> As regards those men of forty-eight, I look on their work with peculiar reverence and love, for I was indeed trained by my mother to love and reverence them, as a Catholic child is the saints of the cathedral. The earliest hero of my childhood was Smith O'Brien, whom I remember well – tall and stately with a dignity of one who had fought for a noble idea and the sadness of one who had failed … John Mitchel, too, on his return to Ireland I saw, at my father's table with his eagle eye and impassioned manner.

He praised *The Nation,* though he avoided reading his mother's poetry on the basis that 'of the quality of Speranza's poems I, perhaps, should not speak, for criticism is disarmed before love'. It was clear that Thomas Davis had had the greatest influence on the young poet:

> The greatest of them all, and one of the best poets of this century in Europe was, I need not say, Thomas Davis. Born in the year 1814 at Mallow in County Cork, before he was 30 years of age, he and the other young men of *The Nation* newspaper had, to use Father Burke's eloquent words, created 'by sheer power of the Irish intellect, by sheer strength of Irish genius, a national poetry and a national literature which no other nation can equal'.

Oscar Wilde would rarely return to the subject of his mother and the Young Irelanders. Indeed, it was perhaps an attempt by a new and emerging public figure (albeit one around which there was enormous fascination, which the *Arizona Weekly Citizen* termed 'Wilde Mania') to win audiences by speaking of a subject he knew held emotional pull among Irish Americans. As editor of *Woman's World* magazine in the late 1880s, however, he would provide a space to those sympathetic to the cause of Ireland, indicating that his sense of nationalism remained. In January 1889, he reprinted an address by the British political activist Margaret Sandhurst, in which she asked: 'Have we, from first to last, ever made a persistent effort to govern Ireland for her good? Have we given up anything for her? Can it be right to tyrannise over any nation committed to our charge?'

When Speranza's first collection of poetry was published, she dedicated it to Oscar and his brother Willie, boasting that 'I made them indeed, speak plain the word COUNTRY. I taught them, no doubt, that a country's a thing men should die for at need!' Oscar would honour his parents in 'De Profundis', writing that 'she and my father had bequeathed me a name they had made noble and honoured, not merely in literature, art, archaeology and science, but in the public history of my own country, in its evolution as a nation'.

Matthew Skwiat has noted that 'many would argue that Wilde is more English than Irish, that none of his plays were set in Ireland, and that his success derived from his time spent in England'. Yet the strength of his mother, and her convictions, played no small part in shaping Oscar Wilde long before he emerged as a household name on the neighbouring island and beyond. Oscar himself would proclaim publicly, 'I am not English; I'm *Irish* which is quite *another thing*'.

Today, Oscar Wilde's Merrion Square home boasts a memorial in his honour and another dedicated to the memory of his father, Sir William Wilde. It is perhaps time Speranza was remembered there too.

Tommy Wood, the Youngest Irish Spanish Civil War Fatality

Sam McGrath

Thomas 'Tommy' Wood (1919–36) was the youngest Irish anti-fascist to be killed in the Spanish Civil War. A Dubliner from a staunch republican family, two uncles on his mother's side were killed during the War of Independence. Patrick 'Paddy' Doyle was hanged in Mountjoy Jail on 14th March 1921. Six weeks after his execution, his brother Seán 'Jimmy' Doyle was killed during the IRA's attack on the Custom House on 25th May 1921.

Wood (often misspelt Woods) joined Na Fianna Éireann at the age of just 7, and was later active with B Company, 2nd Battalion, Dublin Brigade IRA. He left for Spain with Frank Ryan on 11th December 1936 at the age of just 17. Less than three weeks later, he was mortally wounded at the Battle of Cordoba.

Before leaving for Spain, he wrote a letter to his mother, which was republished in the *Irish Democrat* on 31 July 1937:

I am very sorry for not telling you where I was going. I am going to Spain to fight with the International Column. Please forgive me for not letting you know. I got my wages in the Gas. Co. alright. I left a message to be delivered on Sunday. We are going out to fight for the working class. It is not a religious war, that is all propaganda. God Bless you.

He lived with his parents John C. Wood and Sarah Ann Wood (née Doyle) at 16 Buckingham Place just off Amiens Street, with siblings Sean (who died in a workplace accident in 1938), Patrick, Donald, Seamus, Ellis, Kathleen, and Frances.

The *Irish Independent* on 13 January 1937 reported that:

News has reached Dublin that natives of Dublin serving with the Reds at Albacete – T. Woods (aged 17 years), of Buckingham Place, is suffering from shell shock, and C. Gough, of Cabra, is in hospital with a neck wound. Both casualties were sustained in an air raid on Albacete.

The circumstances of Wood's death did not become fully apparent until July 1937, when a letter Frank Ryan wrote to Wood's parents from Albacete was published in the *Irish Democrat*:

He was wounded on the Cordoba Front on December 29 last. I was talking to two comrades who brought him to the dressing station. He was hit above the left knee and then as they were bringing him in, he and one of his comrades were hit again. This time the bullet hit Tommy in the head, but the two lads with him thought it was only a graze as he was conscious all the time. He was brought to Andujar Hospital and the first report from there was very favourable, then we could get no more news of him. It is only now that we have found out why.

Ryan went on to say in the 31 July letter that the name of Wood was confused originally with that of Wools, a Dutch comrade who was also in the hospital. He continued:

> His comrades here wish to be associated in rendering you their sympathy. Tommy was universally liked during the time he was with us here. I want to emphasise that his life was given in a great cause. He did not come looking for adventures nor for reward. He believed in the cause for which the people of Spain, helped by men such as himself, are fighting. He has given his life not only for the freedom of the people of Spain, but of the whole human race, and he will be remembered and honoured equally with those who gave their lives for freedom in Ireland.

Buried in Cordoba, Tommy's name is inscribed on the grave of his parents Sarah and John Wood, and brother Sean, in Glasnevin Cemetery. Tommy was immortalised in Christy Moore's stirring ballad 'Viva La Quinte Brigada':

> Tommy Wood age seventeen died in Cordoba
> With Na Fianna he learned to hold his gun
> From Dublin to the Villa del Rio
> He fought and died beneath the Spanish sun.

Stalin's Star: the Unwelcome Orson Welles

Donal Fallon

In the story of actor Orson Welles, Dublin's Gate Theatre was an important location. While still in his teens he made his professional theatrical acting debut upon its stage in 1931, with Micheál Mac Liammóir recalling that Welles gave 'an astonishing performance, wrong from beginning to end but with all the qualities of fine acting tearing their way through a chaos of inexperience'. Welles remembered the audience's response with great pride, telling his biographer Barbara Leaming that the applause was 'thunderous and totally unexpected ... I got more acclaim for that than for anything I've done since!' He would return to Dublin in 1951, and would be confronted by the sight of protestors at the very same theatre.

By the early 1950s, Welles was an international sensation. He had directed, co-written, produced, and performed in the critically acclaimed *Citizen Kane* (1941), and had followed that up with a number of other successful pictures, including 1942's *The Magnificent Ambersons*. Despite his remarkable talents, he was a controversial figure in the United States, owing to his progressive political inclinations. This was enough to ensure his condemnation in the damning 1950 report *Red Channels: the Report of Communist Influence in Radio and Television*, which has been described as the 'Bible of the blacklist' that swept 1950s Hollywood.

The dossier identified Welles as a dinner sponsor for the Joint Anti-Fascist Refugee Committee, a contributor to the *Daily Worker* newspaper, and a benefit patron for the Medical Bureau to Aid Spanish Democracy. Support for the Spanish Republic, which had been overthrown by Franco's fascist junta with the help of Hitler and Mussolini, was enough to secure the inclusion of many celebrities in the list of suspected 'reds'. The FBI were interested in Welles too, something that is clear from its 149-page file on the actor, which is now available to view online in its entirety.

Welles went to considerable lengths to distance himself from claims that he was a communist, once taking legal action against a gossip columnist who labelled him a Marxist, and maintaining that 'I am not a communist. I am grateful for our constitutional form of government, and I rejoice in our great American tradition of democracy.'

Opposition to Welles in Dublin was organised by the Catholic Cinema and Theatre Patrons' Association, who had been distributing a pamphlet entitled *Red Star over Hollywood*. Even Dublin's archbishop, the imperious John Charles McQuaid, had distanced himself from some of this organisation's actions in the past. Micheál Ó Tuathail, the secretary of the body, was quoted as saying that they were interested in keeping the cinema pure. Throughout the 1930s, the cinema had been routinely denounced in Lenten pastorals and religious publications as a corrupting influence, yet by the 1950s it was evidently clear the cinema was here to stay.

Welles was collected at the airport by Hilton Edwards of the Gate Theatre, who drove him to the venue, and was furious at the sight of demonstrators. He told journalists that 'my only consolation is that I believe this to be a manifestation of irresponsibility backed up by fanaticism and I refuse to believe it represents the opinion of the Irish race. If I might quote W.B. Yeats, this crowd has disgraced itself again.' He recalled that the protestors were led by 'some insane priest', though he would have seen very little of them as he was rushed into the theatre.

Welles was not performing that night – he was there to see *Tolka Row,* a play by Maura Laverty. The actors had to contend with repeated heckling from the small band of demonstrators, and a crowd of the generally curious began to assemble. Newspapers reported that something in the region of a thousand people ultimately gathered outside the theatre. Some carried placards telling Welles to visit Moscow and not Dublin, and condemning him as 'Stalin's Star'. From the stage, the famous visitor denounced the crowd outside for interrupting such a fine work, to tremendous applause from the audience. Welles made his exit via the side door. It was not a night he would remember as fondly as his performance there as a younger man.

Following these events, a war of words played out in the press. Ó Tuathail attempted to justify the demonstration in the letters pages of *The Irish Times,* maintaining that Welles was a supporter of the Friends of the Abraham Lincoln Brigade (the American contingent of the International Brigades that fought in Spain) among other bodies. Others condemned the 'wholly unthinking rabble of witch-hunters', believing the demonstration had brought shame on the city.

The Former Life of a Talbot Street Internet Café

Donal Fallon

Covered in graffiti, the Five Star Internet Café on Talbot Street is an interesting building to look at from outside, but inside it is taken over by computers, telephones, and pool tables, which give no real hint of its former life as a church – a Welsh Presbyterian Church to be precise, and the only example of a purpose-built Welsh chapel in Ireland.

The foundation stone of the church was laid in 1838, and as Howell Evans has written in a history of the community here, the building's 'original intention was not for the Welsh in Dublin, but mainly for the Welsh visiting the city'. Designed by William Murray, an Irish architect who had worked under Francis Johnston, its proximity to the docks meant that it was convenient for Welsh seamen. A contemporary magazine noted soon after its opening that 'in Dublin, English and Welsh seamen hear the gospel preached to them several times a week, in their respective languages'. Another article, in a sailors' magazine, pointed towards a monument not far from the chapel, writing that:

the inhabitants [of Dublin] are friends of seamen, as evidenced by the lofty column erected to the memory

266

The Five Star Internet Café (Photograph by Ciarán Murray)

of Nelson, with its colossal statue of that hero on its summit, which stands in the centre of one of the finest streets in Europe.

Very little has been written on this Dublin church, but Einion Thomas from the University of Bangor has described how the background of the men who visited the church greatly influenced the customs within it:

> The gallery was called the 'quarter deck' and only sailors were allowed to sit there. On the ground floor (or the 'main deck' as it was called), the men sat on the 'starboard side' (the right) and the women

on the 'port side' (the left). It also included some surprising accessories such as spittoons near some of the men's seats, and in the early years smoking was permitted!

The church attracted some Gaelic League advocates owing to the fact that services were conducted in Welsh, and Thomas has noted that Ernest Blythe was one such visitor. Blythe was born into a Presbyterian unionist family near Lisburn, before involving himself in Irish nationalist politics, and later drifting to the right with the Blueshirt movement of the 1930s. Of the Welsh church, he remembered:

> When I joined the Gaelic League and began to learn Irish, one of my fellow members told me, almost with bated breath, that the Welsh community in Dublin had its own church in which services were conducted in Welsh. I went there one Sunday morning to revel in the sound of a language closely related to Irish.

Other Irish nationalists would get a chance to learn and practice Welsh after the Easter Rising, when rebels and suspected radicals were interned in the Frongoch camp in northern Wales. Joseph McCarthy remembered that when conditions were relaxed there the men were allowed to march in the neighbouring countryside, and that 'sometimes a shepherd or two would come to view the scene and Liam O'Briain would engage them in a conversation in the Welsh language, which would be mingled with hearty laughter'. There were certainly some in Wales who sympathised with the rebels in Ireland, such as the Welsh miner Arthur Horner, whose story is told elsewhere in this book, and who remembered that 'as a small nationality ourselves, we had watched with sympathy the Irish people's fight for independence long before the war broke out'.

In June 1944, the *Irish Independent* (nowadays located just across the street from the church) reported that 'a regrettable break in the few remaining links binding the Irish people with their fellow Celts, the Welsh, will follow on the closing down of the Welsh Church, Talbot Street. This church, the only one of its kind in the country, will be offered for sale on June 20.' The paper noted that the last minister in the church was Rev. John Lewis, who had served from 1894 to 1934. The report gives the impression that the building had been scarcely used since then.

What happened in the building between its time as a church and its life as an internet cafe? For many years it served as a shoe shop, operating under the name Griffith's. A ghost sign remains today in the form of the tiling leading into the internet café, which carries that family name. Draig Werdd, the Welsh Society in Ireland, have championed the cause of the building in recent years, highlighting that 'much of the historic fabric still remains in the building, including early nineteenth-century sliding sash windows, a fine plasterwork ceiling, a Welsh slate roof and cast iron gutters'.

Dublin's First Vegetarian Restaurants

Sam McGrath

While plant-based and wholefood diets are increasingly popular today, it may come as a surprise to learn that vegetarian restaurants in Dublin date back to the late nineteenth century. Groups of vegetarians have been organising events in the city since at least the 1860s.

In September 1866, a public meeting on vegetarianism in the Exhibition Rooms, Rotunda Hospital, was disrupted by several members of the public. The *Freeman's Journal* on 28 September 1866 noted that: 'There was a large attendance of respectably dressed persons, but there were many amongst the audience who evidently attended the meeting more for the purpose of disturbing the proceedings and amusing themselves in a very disorderly manner.'

Speakers included Carlow-born social reformer and temperance activist James Haughton, who had become a vegetarian in 1846, Reverend James Clark of Salford, who had helped to establish the American Vegetarian Society in 1850, and writer and campaigner James A. Mowatt from Dublin.

The Dublin Vegetarian Society opened the first vegetarian restaurant in the city, the Sunshine Vegetarian Dining Rooms,

·THE COLLEGE RESTAURANT (VEGETARIAN) HOTEL,

BREAKFASTS, LUNCHEONS, DINNERS, AND TEAS.

Great Variety, Prompt Service, Lowest Prices.

OUR SIXPENNY AND TENPENNY TEAS ARE UNSURPASSED.

DELICIOUS DRINKS
From American Soda Fountain.

THE McCAUGHEY RESTAURANTS, LIMITED,

3 AND 4 COLLEGE STREET, DUBLIN.

Advertisement for the College Vegetarian Restaurant, Dublin
from *The Irish Times*, 11 September 1900.

at 48 Grafton Street in 1891. A short review in the Irish Times on 14 March 1891 stated they it offered 'toothsome food, free from the slightest suspicion of animal matter … at a surprisingly moderate rate'. It was open for less than a year.

In July 1899, Leonard McCaughey from Armoy in County Antrim established the College Vegetarian Restaurant at 3–4 College Street. Food historian Maírtín Mac Con Iomaire explained in his 2008 article 'Searching for Chefs, Waiters and Restaurateurs in Edwardian Dublin' that McCaughey:

had built a chain of successful vegetarian restaurants in Glasgow, Leeds, Belfast and in Dublin … [and that he] owned the Ivanhoe Hotel in Harcourt Street and the Princess Restaurant on Grafton Street.'

The 1911 census lists Leonard McCaughey as a 70-year-old hotel proprietor from Antrim living at 72 Harcourt Street with his wife, three children, a cook, and two servants.

An advertisement for the restaurant in the *Irish Times* on 2 February 1900 proclaimed that 'Vegetarian food is the coming diet', and suggested that 'every man and woman that has suffered from influenza should dine at the College Restaurant as the use of a pure diet is the simplest and surest cure for this woeful disease'.

The restaurant at College Street is mentioned a number of times in the Bureau of Military History witness statements.

Dr Seamus O'Kelly notes (no. 471) that just before the 1916 Rising he was invited to a meeting in the restaurant by Fenian Rory O'Connor, where there was discussion about the upcoming rebellion and attempts made to decode the forged 'Castle Document'. At least four such meetings took place at the restaurant. In addition to O'Kelly and O'Connor, those present included republican solicitor P.J. Little, Francis Sheehy-Skeffington, writer Andrew E. Malone (aka L.P. Byrne), IRB poet Charles Kickham, and playwright Dr Seamus O'Kelly.

Dublin Brigade IRA member Michael Lynch wrote in his account (no. 511) about a waiter in the restaurant who had overheard a group of Trinity College students talking about plans to set fire to the headquarters of Sinn Féin at 6 Harcourt Street on Armistice Night in 1918. This waiter informed Sean MacMahon, vice commandment of the 3rd Brigade, Dublin IRA, who managed to mobilise republicans at the last minute to defend it and other buildings.

In the end, a motley group of 'British soldiers, British ex. soldiers … young men of the tramp class and a proportion of students of Trinity College' did launch some minor attacks on the Sinn Féin headquarters, the Mansion House, St Teresa's Hall on Clarendon Street, and Liberty Hall, but thanks to the waiter, local republicans were able to call up men to repel the attacks.

Irish writer James Cousins and his wife Mary (co-founder of the Irish Women's Franchise League and All-India Women's Conference) in their 1950 joint autobiography *We Two Together* described the restaurant on College Street as a: 'rendezvous for the literary set, of whom AE was the leader. We frequently joined these idealists for lunch, and later met a number of Hindu vegetarians who had come to Dublin.'

Poet and editor of the *Dublin Magazine* Seamus O'Sullivan recalled in the *Irish Times* on 16 October 1943 being brought to this 'famous and well-conducted vegetarian restaurant' by his father in 1901, where they used to see 'the bearded and spectacled features of A.E. and with him, Harry Norman, Paul Gregan … and others of that small, but distinguished, group of workers and writers connected with the Irish Agricultural Organisation'.

The restaurant closed after twenty-three years in business in January 1922.

Frank Wyatt, editor of *Vegetarian News* and secretary of the *London Vegetarian Society*, gave a talk in 1933 on vegetarianism in the Mansion House. The *Irish Times* on 17 January 1933 noted that the meeting was mostly made up of women. Wyatt, a vegetarian of twenty years standing, told the room that he was 'satisfied that he was a healthier man than any flesh eater'.

Moira Henry, a celebrated dressmaker, was a leading figure in the Irish vegetarian movement from the early 1930s onwards. In 1947, she represented Ireland at the 11th International Vegetarian Union Congress in England.

Henry is the first-known named vegan in Ireland, telling the *Irish Press* on 26 February 1949 that she had made the switch from vegetarianism to veganism in 1945. The journalist defined a vegan as a 'vegetarian who not only eschews fish, flesh and fowl but also such by-products as eggs, milk, cheese and margarine'. As honorary secretary of the Dublin Vegetarian Society, she revealed that the membership of the organisation stood at thirty-two.

Patrick Campbell (aka Quidnunc) interviewed Florence Gourlay, honorary treasurer of the Dublin Vegetarian Society for the 5 March 1951 edition of the *Irish Times*. Gourlay said the organisation had thirty-three members (an increase of 1 since 1949!), but that she knew of 104 vegetarians altogether in the Republic. It was noted that while Belfast had a vegetarian restaurant, there was nothing similar in Dublin.

In March 1955 Geoffrey Rudd, secretary to the Vegetarian Society (Britain), addressed a public meeting on the principles and uses of the vegetarian ideals at the Central Hotel, Dublin. An article in the *Irish Times* on 1 March 1955 noted that the Dublin Vegetarian Society had been founded in 1946 and had around fifty members. The original society of the same name had been founded in the 1890s but 'went out of existence during the First World War'.

A member of the society told the newspaper that:

while Dublin had no purely vegetarian restaurant, hotels and restaurants generally were becoming more sympathetic towards their needs and could usually provide vegetarian meals if notice was given before-hand. Most of the members agree that a specialist restaurant would be a step forward but this would take time as well as a 'lot of hard work and some capital'.

Theodora Fitzgibbon in the 7 November 1969 *Irish Times* wrote that she felt sorry for vegetarians, as there was no such thing as a 'purely vegetarian restaurant' in Dublin. Two years later, Sean Doherty wrote a letter to the *Irish Press*, which was published on 18 October 1971, complaining that the country's capital city did not have a vegetarian restaurant and that the 'once thriving' Vegetarian Society was no longer active.

The following year saw the arrival of Good Karma at 4 Great Strand Street. This seems to have been the first purely vegetarian restaurant in the city since the College Vegetarian Restaurant had closed its doors in 1922. As well as a restaurant, a health-food shop called Green Acres operated from the basement.

Elgy Gillespie in the *Irish Times* on 11 September 1972 described the restaurant as having a:

> long room with wooden pillars and a cosily dim glow from candles and firelight. The tables (made by the owners) are high if you like sitting up to your food; low if you prefer to loll across the tie-dyed cushions also made by the owners ... Taj Mahal, Doctor Pepper and Crosby, Stills and Nash provided lush sounds in the background ... it makes a wholesome change from the stagnancy of Dublin eating.

Good Karma only lasted a year, as Gabrielle Williams in the *Irish Times* on 7 December 1973 described it has having being 'recently' closed down by the Eastern Health Board. A reminiscing Sonia Kelly in the same paper on 11 February 1976 described their kitchen as 'immaculate', and said the restaurant was 'closed for tripping over an obscure regulation'.

John S. Doyle, writing in the *Irish Independent* on 16 August 2005 remembered Good Karma as a:

> A 'head' restaurant not everyone knew about, with bare brick walls and no seats, only bean bags, and mellow 'sounds'. Nice food, none of your macrobiotic stuff. The 'staff' were laidback types who said 'all right man', and you were to take it as a privilege to be served by them. This was 1974 [sic] or so. There were numerous Garda raids, and the restaurant didn't last long.

While the restaurant closed, the basement health food shop, Green Acres, remained open. Owner Philip Guiney told Patrick Comerford in the 29 July 1975 *Irish Times* that 'not all the staff, and only a quarter of [his] customers' were vegetarian. An increasing number of older people were visiting the shop, realising that it was 'not just a place for young freaks'. They came to 'supplement their diets with natural foods, and probably a small number had become vegetarian out of economic necessary'.

The journalist also mentioned the Ormond Health Centre on Parliament Street, which sold dandelion coffee, Honeyrose cigarettes, and herbal tea, as well as the Irish Health and Herbal Centre on Trinity Street, which was 'not vegetarian-orientated by any means', but sold a lot of products popular with the vegetarian community.

By the late 1970s, there were a number of wholefood restaurants in Dublin, including Munchies at 60 Bolton

Street, the Golden Dawn on Crow Street and the Supernatural Tearooms at 53 Harcourt Street.

The Golden Dawn, established in 1976, was described by Christy Stapleton of the Vegetarian Society of Ireland in the late 1990s as 'the closest thing to a vegetarian restaurant in Dublin' at the time. Run by showband singer Joe Fitzmaurice and his wife, it used to be a favourite of actors Gabriel Byrne, Vinny McCabe, and Garrett Keogh, and DJ Paul Webb worked there as an assistant cook and Golden Horde frontman Simon Carmody as dishwasher.

A vegetarian restaurant called The Harvest was operating in 1979 on the top of Harcourt Street, and then by 1983 at 1 Lincoln Place. An *Irish Times* journalist visited and wrote in the paper on 14 December 1979 that she had enjoyed her meal of 'Chickpea paté (50p) … a tasty and sustaining … starter. For main course there's a wide choice but the adzuki bean hamburger with rice, salad and a choice of sauce (£1.80) is something to linger over.'

Bananas, a self-service vegetarian restaurant, was opened at 15 Upper Stephen Street by Muriel Goodwin and friends in late 1982. Lorraine Kennedy reviewed it for the *Irish Times* on 15 October 1983, and said she was more than happy with her 'starter of celery soup sprinkled with watercress … for 85p … [and] a vegetable pizza (£1.20) accompanied by a mixed salad of orange, celery and more watercress'.

Also in 1982, Blazing Salads was established as a wholefood restaurant by the pioneering Fitzmaurice family, after they decided to wind down the Golden Dawn. It was based on the top floor of the Powerscourt Centre until 2001, when the family moved operations to a new deli-style premises on Drury Street, where it is still open today.

The Well Fed Café was opened in 1983 at 6 Crow Street as part of the Dublin Resource Centre (DRC) and lasted until at least the mid-1990s. A workers' co-operative, it served delicious veggie food at very cheap prices and won numerous awards.

Cornucopia, arguably Dublin's most well-known vegetarian restaurants began trading on Wicklow Street in January 1986, and has been there ever since. It was established by Neil McCafferty (1952–93) and Deirdre McCafferty, who is still the proprietor of the restaurant.

2016 saw the opening of the Sova Vegan Butchers on Camden Street, Dublin's first permanent vegan restaurant. So began the next chapter of vegetarian dining in the city.

Dublin's Historic Breweries: Watkins' of Ardee Street

Ciarán Murray

The way we drink in Dublin has been changing over the last few years. It's not that it's been evolving, so much as that there has been a restoration of the natural order. Entering any pub you can be almost sure that you can choose from a vastly improved selection of ales, stouts and porters compared to ten years ago. More importantly, our brewers are starting to brew again – Five Lamps, Barrelhead and JW Sweetman's to name but three of many.

For decades Guinness (and, later, its parent company, Diageo) dominated brewing in Dublin, but there was a time when our brewing industry could 'present an unrivalled record to the world', as the 5 June 1908 edition of the *Irish Independent* put it. This city's brewing was said, as far back as the seventeenth century, to be 'the very marrow bone of the commonwealth of Dublin'. The excise list for 1768 showed returns for forty-three brewers in the city, with many of these large operations employing dozens of workers.

In the 1800s, as Guinness rose, Dublin's breweries either amalgamated or closed. By 1850, there were twenty breweries left, by the 1870s there were ten, and by 1920 there were just four breweries including Guinness' operating in Dublin. One

The homes for the workers of Watkins in the latter half of
the nineteenth century have outlasted the brewery itself.
(Photograph by Ciarán Murray)

of the largest during this time was Watkins' Brewery, originally
founded as the Ardee Street Brewery, and later known by the
title of Watkins, Jameson, Pim & Co. Ltd.

A date for the foundation of the brewery is hard to ascertain, but the *Irish Times*, in an article on Dublin brewers in 1922 reported that Watkins' of Ardee Street Brewery held the record for having paid the highest excise duty of any Dublin brewer in 1766. So although there is some evidence to suggest there was brewing on the site as far back as 1536, we can say for sure that the Watkins' Brewery was there since the mid-1700s.

By the 1820s the brewery at Ardee Street was the third largest in Dublin, with an output of 300 barrels per week. It was bettered only by Guinness', with 600 barrels per week and Michael Sweetman's, with 450 barrels per week. Watkins' Brewery's link with our revolutionary past began early: John Devoy's father worked there in the late 1840s, after the Famine, when the family was forced to move from Kildare to Dublin.

By 1865 the brewery was exporting more than 14,000 hogsheads, or approximately 6 million imperial pints of stout. The brewery was bisected by Cork Street, with the brewing house and offices on its south side, and 87 dwellings for workers on its north side. The houses were built for £14,460, with rents ranging from 2/6 (two shillings and sixpence) for a cottage to 6/- (six shillings) for a two up, two down. Many remain occupied today.

The *Freeman's Journal* in 1904 spoke of rumours circulating in Dublin of an amalgamation of two of its more prosperous breweries, namely Watkins' and Jameson, Pim and Co., which would move from their premises between Anne Street and Beresford Street to make way for another Jameson: John Jameson and Son, the whiskey distillers. They also reported that the Watkins family had 'long since disappeared, and the business now carried on by Mr Alfred S. Darley'.

The brewery saw action during the 1916 Rising, when it was occupied by a teetotaller, Con Colbert, and a garrison of twenty men – an outpost under the direct command of Éamonn Ceannt in the South Dublin Union. The outpost was ineffective, and the Volunteers eventually joined up with the Marrowbone Lane distillery garrison.

It was also tragically caught up in the events of the 'Battle of Dublin', a week of clashes at the start of the Civil War that saw more than sixty people killed. A cooper by the name of James Clarke, who worked in the brewery, was shot near Gardiner's Row on the 6 July while walking a friend home. He took a bullet to the face and died half an hour after admission to Jervis Street Hospital.

Towards the end of the 1920s, Watkins, Jameson, Pim and Co. acquired Darcy's Brewery and its trademarks, including O'Connell's Dublin Ale, along with several pubs owned by the company, which they referred to as 'Taps', In March 1937, the *Irish Times* announced that the firm was in voluntary liquidation. The article shows that at the time, the brewery still employed over one hundred men, and blamed rising excise and falling exports for their downturn. While the company outlasted many of its competitors, it closed in 1939.

In 1943, the brewery site was subject to a court wrangle, with a high court judge quashing a warrant issued by a district justice, who, under the Air Raid Precautions Act, 1939 demanded that the Dublin Corporation be allowed to enter the brewery, by force if necessary, to build a shelter in its basement. The demand wasn't met.

After this, things get a little bit hazy regarding the brewery. In September 1951, there was a large fire at the site, and by 1954, advertisements pop up in various papers offering factories premises to let. With a history spanning three centuries, the brewery seems to have gone 'quietly into that good night', along with the rest of Dublin's historic breweries although company records sites suggest there was a 'Watkins, Jameson, Pim & Co. (1976) Limited' set up on 28 April 1976 and that it is still in existence at 10 Ardee Street. Maybe, as Dublin's brewing industry rises again, Watkins' will also be revived.

The 'Denizens of the Slums' Who Looted Dublin

Donal Fallon

The widespread looting that occurred during the Easter Rising is one aspect of the week that participants frequently spoke of in later years when interviewed by the Bureau of Military History. Rebels seemed variously amused, ashamed, and even horrified by the sight of people emptying the shops of Dublin as they proclaimed a republic before the world. It was also an aspect of the week that filled plenty of column inches in the days and weeks that followed, as looters found themselves on trial. Justifying what they had done, a mother and daughter simply told a judge that 'we were looting, like the rest.'

Easter Monday began as a beautiful day, ideal for the Fairyhouse Races, which were getting underway. Seán O'Casey recalled that:

> It was a day on which to make merry, and crowded streets proclaimed that the influences of the sun's geniality was making melody in the hearts of man. Many were climbing joyously on to the trains to seek in nature's bosom a place that would hide them for a few hours 'far from the madding crowd's ignoble

Illustration by Luke Fallon

strife', while distinct gatherings of people stood by near Nelson's Pillar and found happy moments in the contemplation of the passing activities of human life. Curious glances were flung at passing vehicles, burdened with hopeful crews, flashing swiftly by on their

way to Fairyhouse Races, and the pulse of human anxiety was scarcely felt besides the quick-beating pulse of
human enjoyment.

The beginning of the Rising may have taken many people by
surprise, but the breakdown of law and order came almost
immediately. In his entertaining memoir *On Another Man's
Wound*, Ernie O'Malley remembered arriving onto Sackville
Street as the insurrection was in its infancy:

> Diamond rings and pocketsful of gold watches were
> selling for sixpence and a shilling, and one was cursed
> if one did not buy … Ragged boys wearing old boots,
> brown and black, tramped up and down with air rifles
> on their shoulders or played cowboys and Indians,
> armed with black pistols supplied with long rows of
> paper caps. Little girls hugged teddy bears and dolls as
> if they could hardly believe their good fortune.

Where were the police in all of this? The decision of Colonel
R. Johnstone to withdraw the 1,100 Dublin Metropolitan
Police officers from the streets of the city no doubt facili-
tated the widespread looting, and as Brian Barton has noted
in his history of the Rising, 'it soon reached endemic pro-
portions, far beyond the capacity of either the troops or the
insurgents to prevent or contain'. One policeman saw the
humour in it all, remembering that:

> one could see some bizarre sights from the windows
> during that week: corner-boys wearing silk hats, ladies
> from the slums sporting fur coats, a cycling corps of
> barefooted young urchins riding brand-new bicycles

stolen from some of the shops, and members of the underworld carrying umbrellas.

The Beginning of the Spree

The looting on Sackville Street began in broad daylight, and not long after the declaration of the republic. Among those who arrived on the street trying to stop the looting were clergy from the Pro Cathedral. Monsignor Curran, who was serving as secretary to Archbishop Walsh in Dublin at the time of the Rising, told the Bureau of Military History that:

> Before 2 p.m. the crowds had greatly increased in numbers. Already the first looting had begun; the first victim was Noblett's sweetshop. It soon spread to the neighbouring shops. I was much disgusted and I did my best to try to stop the looting. Except for two or three minutes, it had no effect. I went over and informed the Volunteers about the GPO.
>
> Five or six Volunteers did their best and cleared the looters for some five or ten minutes, but it began again. At first all the ringleaders were women; then the boys came along. Later, about 3:30 p.m. when the military were withdrawn from the Rotunda, young men arrived and the looting became systematic and general, so that Fr John Flanagan of the Pro Cathedral, who had joined me, gave up the attempt to repress it, and I left too.

One Volunteer described the scene at Noblett's sweet shop after the windows were smashed in. He remembered the sight of 'a gay shower of sweet stuffs, chocolate boxes and huge slabs of toffee' being tossed about by the young crowd. Desmond Ryan of the GPO garrison also recalled that Seán Mac Diarmada made his way across the street and protested 'vehemently, his hands raised passionately above his head'.

What was the motivating factor in deciding to loot certain shops and not others? One contemporary source made the claim that 'the rougher element that existed in the city' seemed to be targeting 'stores that bore English names or were known to be owned by the foreigners. In this they followed the example set by the mobs in London who raided and looted German stores in that city as an act of retaliation for the Zeplin raids made during the war.' Yet there was little truth to claims that English businesses were being targeted over Irish ones: among the first windows to go were those of domestic companies.

The Arrival of Skeffy on the Scene

Francis Sheehy-Skeffington, the well-known pacifist and feminist campaigner in Dublin, made his way into the city of Dublin early in the uprising to attempt to restore law and order, seeking to establish a citizen patrol to keep the peace among the civilian population. Eileen Costello of the Gaelic League recalled that:

> I saw a man speaking to a crowd of people from the top of an empty tram car near the O'Connell monument. It was Sheehy Skeffington appealing to the people to be quiet and orderly, to go home quietly, to stay in their homes and to keep the peace. I saw people from the slums breaking and looting a shop. It was Laurence's toy shop. I saw the looters inside the shop throwing out toys and cameras to their friends

outside. I felt very great disgust. Later on I saw people in the Gresham Hotel with jewellery they had bought from the looters. I saw a woman with a ring and another with a brooch.

Francis Jones also mentions Skeffy, as he was popularly known, in his *History of the Sinn Féin Movement and the Irish Rebellion of 1916,* published not long after the Rising, during the War of Independence. He recalled that 'a small man, dressed in an Irish tweed knickerbocker suit' appealed to the crowds not to loot, but that 'the rabble merely laughed at him and continued its work of destruction'. Jones claimed that:

> The man who made the appeal was Sheehy Skeffington, one of the best-known figures in Dublin – a man who was not in any way identified with the rebellion or the men who led it. He was, in the first place, just as much opposed to the Germans as to the English in the World War, and was certainly opposed to any revolutionary movement.

This wasn't quite true. While Skeffy was a pacifist, he was also a committed republican, and moved in revolutionary circles. He may have disagreed with the means the rebels deployed, but he certainly shared their goal.

Sheehy Skeffington had not come onto the streets to partake in the Rising, yet he would lose his life that week, murdered in Portobello barracks, having been arrested by the crazed Captain Bowen-Colthurst of the British armed forces. The captain would later be arrested and charged with murder, though he would successfully plead insanity. By

April of 1921, he was found to be cured, and even received a pension. The writer Padraic Colum would pen a fine tribute to his murdered friend after the Rising, remembering that:

> He was not a bearer of arms in the insurrection, he was a pacifist ... But Skeffington is dead now, and the spiritual life of Ireland has been depleted by as much of the highest courage, the highest sincerity and the highest devotion as a single man could embody.

The Dublin Fire Brigade

The fires that spread through Sackville Street created problems for the Dublin Fire Brigade, and DFB historian Las Fallon has noted that:

> apart from the Magazine Fort [in the Phoenix Park], the first two major fires fought by the DFB on the first day of the Rising were in shoe shops, the Cable Shop Company and the True Form shoe shop, both in Sackville Street, which were looted and burned. Dublin's barefoot poor were taking advantage of the rebellion.

In his *Annual Report for the Year 1916*, Dublin Fire Brigade Chief Officer Thomas Purcell captured the madness of it all perfectly. He noted that on the Tuesday of the Rising, as Lawrence's toy shop was burning, 'two persons trapped in an upper room by fire and taken down by fire escape proved to be looters'. Not everyone that stuck around was looting of course – the generally curious were also present. Jones remembered in his history of Sinn Féin that even after the first shots had been fired 'people were walking up and down O'Connell Street in the usual manner, but taking the keenest interest in the work that was being done by the republicans'.

The language used by some participants in the Rising to describe those looting is interesting. In the account of one Volunteer, it's noted that 'despite repeated efforts of the republican forces the looting of shops by denizens of the slums became more general'. In a similar vein, Trinity College Dublin student Thomas Rentol Brown complained in the *Dublin Evening Mail* of 13 May of 'the rabble … breaking plate-glass windows and seizing articles in the shops'. Yet, looting wasn't only the preserve of the 'rabble' or the 'denizens of the slums'. *Irish Life*, published soon afterwards, claimed that 'the looters were by no means confined to the submerged slum population. A remarkable proportion were well-dressed and belonged to the wage-earning working class, or perhaps to classes still more respectable'.

The sheer diversity of the items looted is surprising. Michael O'Flanagan, who had been active with the IRB in Glasgow before taking part in the rebellion, remembered the very unusual sight of a piano passing him by:

> On Wednesday afternoon we noticed four or five men and women coming from the direction of Mary's Lane. Between them they were carrying a piano which we concluded they had stolen from some business premises. We called on them to halt but they refused to do so. We fired a few shots over their heads as a warning and they dropped the piano and made off.

If children were predictable in looting toy shops, adults were predictable too. One victim of the week was Conway's public house, and the presence of drunk people on the street added to the confusion and panic. The looting was so out of control that by the Thursday of Easter Week, the 'provisional government' based in the General Post Office had to acknowledge the actions of the looters, noting that 'the provisional government strongly condemns looting and the wanton destruction of property. The looting that has taken place has been done by the hangers-on of the British forces.' In reality, it was primarily being carried out by the very poor, in a city that was home to horrific tenement squalor, with some of its worst housing only a short stroll from the GPO.

The sheer number of convictions in the aftermath of it all showed that the DMP were committed to tracking down the looters, and the loot. As Joseph O'Brien has noted, 'according to police statistics for 1916, 425 persons were proceeded against for looting during the rebellion and 398 of these were either fined or imprisoned'. Perhaps the last words should go to the *Illustrated Sunday Herald*, which painted maybe the most vivid picture of it all:

> When the fighting started all the hooligans of the city were soon drawn to the spot in search of loot. Half the shops in Sackville Street were sacked. Children who have never possessed two pence of their own were imitating Charlie Chaplin with stolen silk hats in the middle of the turmoil and murder.

The Pagan O'Leary and John's Lane Church

Donal Fallon

John's Lane Church, which sits in the heart of the Liberties, is a masterpiece of architecture. Work on it began in 1862 and it opened in 1874, with Edward Welby Pugin the architect behind the project. Pugin came from a distinguished architectural family. He was the son of Augustus Pugin, who was responsible for the interior design of the Palace of Westminster, and had worked on many striking religious buildings in Ireland and Britain.

However, my interest in John's Lane Church comes not from the architectural history of the building, but rather from a nickname it acquired in its own community, where it was spoken of once as the 'Fenian church'. This was due to the fact that many prominent Fenians worked at the building site, including men like Denis Cromien, Dan Gleason, Michael Lawless, and Michael Malone.

In the midst of the Fenian labourers was a most peculiar radical, known as 'the Pagan' O'Leary. Famous among his peers for his detestation of religion, O'Leary proclaimed to all who would listen that St Patrick had been the worst thing to happen to the Irish nation, because our national saint had 'demoralised the Irish by teaching them to forgive

John's Lane Church, Thomas Street. (Photograph by Paul Reynolds)

their enemies'. When asked in Mountjoy Prison on one occasion if he belonged to the Catholic or Protestant faith, he gloated that he was neither a beggar nor a thief. So his involvement in the construction of a Dublin church was certainly peculiar.

Patrick O'Leary was born near Macroom in the 1820s, and like many young men in the Ireland of the early nineteenth century, he didn't stick around, departing for the United States. We know that O'Leary was studying in an American Catholic college in the mid-1840s, training for the priesthood, and that he made the decision to abandon his studies to partake in the American-Mexican War, which followed the US annexation of Texas. In his eagerness to fire a rifle, O'Leary not only abandoned his religious studies, he scaled the walls of the institution to do so. He enlisted in a regiment destined for the front and fought bravely, with his Fenian contemporary John Devoy remembering that 'he took part in several battles and was hit in one of them by a spent ball in the forehead ... This undoubtedly affected his mind to the extent of making him very eccentric.'

Devoy, who Patrick Pearse would describe as 'the greatest of the Fenians', found O'Leary a curious character:

> His eccentricity took the form of a sort of religious mania. He hated Rome and England with equal intensity, and his queer notion was that after driving out the English, Ireland should return to the old paganism. He was not really a pagan, but an anti-Roman Catholic.

The Fenian movement had erupted into Irish consciousness in the late 1850s. Almost simultaneously, the Fenian Brotherhood in New York City and the Irish Republican Brotherhood in Dublin emerged as interlinked oathbound societies, which advocated the use of physical force to establish the elusive Irish republic. The founders of the movement were undoubtedly radical and internationalist; James Stephens, the father of the Irish Fenian movement, even maintained that 'were England a republic battling for human freedom on the one hand, and Ireland leagued with despots on the other, I should, unhesitatingly, take up arms against my native land'. Being a secret society, many within the Catholic church took a dim view of the Fenians. Paul Cullen, Dublin's Catholic archbishop, would proclaim Stephens to be little more than 'an open infidel'.

The Pagan O'Leary took on one of the most difficult positions within the Fenian movement in Ireland, recruiting men from within the ranks of the British armed forces. He travelled all over the island to do this, and it was said that 'the Pagan swore in soldiers in all sorts of places – not a few in sentry boxes, while yet on duty with rifles in their hands'. Devoy maintained that 'properly utilised [the scheme] would have supplied Ireland with a large body of trained fighting men and correspondingly weakened and demoralised the forces of the enemy at the very outset of the contemplated insurrection'.

Devoy claimed that of the 26,000 British regular troops found in Ireland in the mid-1860s, '8,000 were sworn Fenians'. Of the 6,000 in Dublin, he felt as many as 1,600 were committed to the movement. While Devoy's figures are no doubt exaggerated, the infiltration of the British armed forces was carried out to a significant degree. He remembered, 'they were all over Ireland, but mainly in the chief garrison towns and at the Curragh camp'.

When word of this infiltration eventually reached the upper echelons of the British armed forces, the response was simple but effective: infiltrated units, and those it was feared had been infiltrated, were posted away from

Ireland, and replaced with loyal British units. However, that a revolutionary movement felt confident enough to even attempt the infiltration of the ranks of its political and military opponents was remarkable.

The Pagan O'Leary was ultimately caught in the act, arrested after swearing in a soldier on a bridge in Athlone in 1864, and for his troubles he was sentenced to seven years of penal servitude. When the abortive Fenian rebellion broke out in 1867, O'Leary wasn't in the country, but their radical proclamation did call for 'absolute liberty of conscience, and complete separation of church and state'. It was a sentiment he would have appreciated.

O'Leary lived out his days in the United States, where he died in 1895 in a home for veteran soldiers. It has been said that he changed his ways in the end, and renounced his former views. John Devoy would remember him in his own memoirs:

> This queer, unbalanced man, who was more like a survival of the fifth century than a modern Irishman, was able, in spite of his mental defects, to bring into existence the element in Fenianism that was most really dangerous to England … No Irishman who ever lived was more devoted or self-sacrificing than Patrick O'Leary, who called himself 'the Pagan'.

Number 10 Mill Street, Blackpitts

Sam McGrath

Towards the end of 2014, an application was submitted to Dublin City Council to build a 400-bed student residence on a 2.5-acre site in Mill Street (formerly Tanner's Alley) in the historic south inner-city area of the Liberties, Dublin 8.

The €41 million scheme will provide new retail, restaurant, and office space, extensive landscaping to Mill Street and Warrenmount Lane, and the opening up of a section of the mainly underground Poddle river for public access. Historians and conservators welcomed the planned project, which would also see the complete refurbishment of a dilapidated eighteenth-century townhouse at 10 Mill Street.

Shaffrey Architects, in a 2005 report for Dublin City Council (DCC) entitled 'St Luke's Conservation Plan', described the townhouse as 'perhaps the sole survivor in the area of the gable-fronted house type'. DCC noted in a 2009 report that it 'appears to be the last extant double gabled Dutch Billy' in the city. It continued:

Number 10 Mill Street is extremely important to the entire city both architecturally and historically and it is a failure … on the part of the public authority who owned the building for so many years that it has been allowed to deteriorate to such an extent.

Area History
Following Henry VIII's dissolution of the monasteries in the mid-sixteenth century, land in this area was acquired by William Brabazon, ancestor of the earls of Meath, and became known as the 'Meath Liberties'.

French Huguenots, fleeing religious persecution, settled in the Newmarket and Weavers' Square area from the late seventeenth century, where they contributed substantially to the development of the textile industry. Around 1700, there were seven Huguenot families living in Mill Street, including one called Disney, ancestors of the American cartoonist Walt Disney.

The immediate area, known as the Blackpitts, a name that probably derives from the large black vats used by the tanners and skinners for curing hides, became the hub of the tannery and leather trade in the city. Tanning involved converting animal skin into leather by soaking it in a liquid containing tannic acid.

Number 10, sometimes referred to as Mill Street House, was built in the 1720s by the same Brabazon family. Christine Casey, a senior lecturer in architectural history in Trinity College, has described the house as:

Tall and relatively narrow, of 5 bays and 3 rendered storeys over basement, with a gabled brick porch and brick top floor with a gabled centrepiece. Originally it had a pair of curvilinear [curved-line] gables, flush sash windows and an attenuated [thin] Corinthian doorcase crowned by a vigorous swan-necked pediment … The rooms were wainscoted [lined with wooden panelling] and the stair had three fluted and twisted balusters [decorative pillars] per thread, Corinthian newels [central supporting pillars of a spiral staircase] and a richly carved apron to the landing.

After nearly a hundred years in the possession of the earls of Meath, the house was procured by the Christian Brothers, who opened a school there catering for 500 boys in 1818. In the 1850s, the building began a new life as the Mill Street Ragged School, which was founded by Daniel Molloy. Ragged schools were charitable organisations dedicated to the free education of destitute children.

At the end of the nineteenth century, it was remodelled by architect G.P. Beater as a Methodist Mission and school. The roof and gables were removed and replaced by a hipped roof, and the house was given a Gothic Revival-type makeover.

At the time of the 1901 census, cabinetmaker John Gibson and his wife Lilla lived in the house, along with five elderly female Protestants, who were unmarried or widowed. Their occupations were all listed as 'widows' house – no business'.

At the front of the house, 'A & J 1913', is carved on a blank wall in ornate fashion. Historian Maurice Curtis suggests that this might refer to A & J Clothing.

No. 10 Mill Street was used as a residential house in the 1960s and 1970s. Jean Kelly Carberry wrote on the *Growing up in the Liberties* Facebook page:

I lived in Mill St (No. 10) from '68 till '71. It was
a fine house [with a] grand entrance and [f]ab stair-
cases. The main room on first floor was like a church
with a pulpit. There was a very big garden in the
rear. And if you climbed the wall you were in the
Blackpitts. It had a beautiful front hall door which
I have seen in many books about Dublin. Bang
Bang lived across from us on the left facing up to
Newmarket.

In the 1970s, it was used as a storage facility by the Leyland
and Birmingham Rubber Company, which manufactured
golf balls, wellingtons, and other rubber products.

The Department of Posts and Telegraphs bought the
building in 1981 as part of a parcel of property adjoining
a telex exchange. They had no plans for the building and
neglect led to the house being broken into and vandalised
several times in 1982. Windows were broken, the fireplace
and lead flashing from the roof stolen, and the bannisters
from the staircase stripped.

Amid much protest, the department bricked-up the
windows and door of the house in April 1983. Many felt
that this was a short-term solution to a long-term problem,
and the Liberties Association made repeated demands that
the historic house be restored and turned into a community
centre or museum.

After decades of neglect, refurbishment work began in
early 2015. The website libertiesdublin.ie announced:

Internally, little of No. 10 survives, having fallen
victim over the years to vandalism and theft. This
included the staircase. Some elements of the older

building have been retrieved and reused, including a beautiful large bow-window to the rear and wainscoting panels in the main entrance hall.

It makes a welcome change to see a building been brought back to life.

You'll Never Walk Alone: Heffo's Army and the Question of What to Do With Them

Donal Fallon

Few in the Irish sporting annals command the respect of the great Kevin Heffernan. In addition to his lengthy career with St Vincent's, he enjoyed a successful Gaelic football career with Dublin, which included captaining the capital to an All-Ireland victory in 1948. In May 2004, Heffernan was awarded the Freedom of the City of Dublin at the Mansion House. Someone joked that he was no stranger to the venue, and he quipped that there had been 'many celebratory occasions' there in the past.

Beyond his own achievements on the pitch, Heffernan is best remembered as the manager of Dublin's footballers throughout the glory days of the 1970s. His time as manager is linked with the fierce rivalry that developed between Dublin and Kerry on the pitch, and also with the rise of a youth phenomenon, as the 1970s brought Heffo's Army to Hill 16. Some sports historians refer to the men who took the field as Heffo's Army, but to the media, Heffo's Army were really those who packed the terrace of Croke Park.

Not everyone welcomed the influx of young supporters. In 1975, a letter to the *Irish Independent* complained:

At last year's All-Ireland football final I was standing on Hill 16 in the middle of a huge crowd of Dublin fans. It was a disappointing experience. Gone was the wit, the good humour and the banter of other years. Also, the sportsmanship. Instead, we had silly, tribal chanting, foul language and a terrible attitude of hostility towards the Galway team and its supporters. Just like Old Trafford, White Hart Lane or Highbury! When the match ended the Dublin captain's speech was drowned out by 'You'll Never Walk Alone'. It could have been the Kop or Wembley.

With Dublin taking to the field of play for six consecutive All-Ireland Football Finals between 1974 and 1979, the team brought a certain feel-good attitude to the city, which was reflected even in the pop music charts. If 1966 is remembered in the city for the Go Lucky Four hit 'Up Went Nelson!', then 1974 is remembered for 'The Likes of Heffo's Army', which captured the appeal of Dublin's football stars right across the city:

> They came marching in from Ringsend and from
> Ballyfermot too
> From East Wall and Marino to support the boys in
> blue
> For eleven years we've waited and there's nothing left
> to do
> Now hear it now for Heffo, Heffo's Army's on the move.

In scenes more familiar to soccer stadiums on the neighbouring island, homemade banners appeared on the hill.

Some borrowed from the lingo of British football supporters, insisting that 'Dublin are magic, Kerry are tragic.' A
sports journalist wrote in 1974 that 'the people were there
on the terraces – the real Dubliners, Joxer-like characters
out of O'Casey', but there was also a new and younger
element. Lee Dunne, writing in the *Evening Herald*, captured the new appeal of the team perfectly. From a family
who supported association football, he found himself suddenly enthralled by this sport that had been there all along,
yet hadn't caught his eye. Like the Beatles in Liverpool,
it felt like it came out of nowhere: 'One day, Gaelic was
Gaelic, and suddenly that was changed by the emergence
of Dublin's own team ... The identification with the team
was one of the best things to happen in Bla Cliath since the
Danes bailed out.'

The willingness of Heffo's Army to invade the playing
field caused headaches for GAA officials, and by 1975
the press were reporting that 'Croke Park's notorious Hill
16 may be surrounded by a 12-foot-high barbed-wire
fence'. It was also reported that the GAA were looking
to British soccer clubs for guidance, with approaches
made to Manchester United for information on fencing
arrangements at Old Trafford.

Pitch invaders and drunk terrace-brawlers were frowned
upon, and one Dublin GAA official went as far as to say
that 'a large proportion of the present Dublin following
consists of hooligans, louts and foul-mouthed ruffians who
have absolutely no interest in Gaelic football or the GAA'.
In a similar vein, a man who claimed to have been a regular
at Croke Park for decades was disgusted in 1974 by the
'louts and hooligans who never stood in Croke Park until
this year's Dublin vs. Galway All-Ireland Football Final'. He

attacked their 'absurd flags and banners and their stupid and inane songs and chants'.

Yet many of those who arrived on the scene during this period became committed GAA supporters, which was reflected in the incredible travelling support of Dublin throughout the decade. One regional newspaper was baffled by the huge following brought to Longford on one occasion:

> It was like being in the Kop or at Old Trafford. 'Give me a D, give me a U, give me a B, give me an L, give me an I, give me an N!' roared the conductor perched high up in the steel girders on the roof of the stand and the sound reverberated all around the ground. 'Molly Malone', 'The Likes of Heffo's Army' and 'You'll Never Walk Alone' were followed by 'Go home ye bums, go home'. And then there were provocative chants about the Dubs being the only football team in the land, and 'The rest are no fucking good'.

The GAA, which had been suffering from declining attendance in the capital, had to tread carefully. Although keen to enforce new safety standards in the ground and to control and contain the growing Dublin support, GAA officials certainly welcomed the new revenue generated by the influx of supporters, not to mention the knock-on effect it had on Gaelic football at club level right across the city and county. Fortunes waned in the 1980s, with Dublin taking a single All-Ireland Football Final victory in 1983, but many of those who first experienced the Hill in the glorious 1970s remained.

Heffo's Army was a social phenomenon of a decade marked by new youth cultures and movements. Today, many of those who arrived on the scene in the 1970s remain regulars on the terrace of Croke Park, cheering on a Dublin side capable of bringing similar joys to the city as in those golden days.

The Humours of Donnybrook

Ciarán Murray and Donal Fallon

Look up the word Donnybrook in the dictionary and you'll see something like this:

> **don·ny·brook** [don-ee-brook] noun (often initial capital letter) an inordinately wild fight or contentious dispute; brawl; free-for-all.

For the original Donnybrook Fair was not the supermarket that now carries the name and serves the residents of Dublin 4, but a fair established by the Royal Charter of 1204 'to compensate Dubliners for the expense of building walls and defences around the city'. It lasted an impressive fifteen days, from the end of August until mid-September, was held annually for over 600 years, and by the mid-nineteenth century had become the most important and controversial fair on the island.

Originally billed as a horse fair, the run-up to the event would see traders of everything from exotic fruits to horse manure set up their stalls on Donnybrook Green. Calling it a horse fair was slightly misleading, as horses were rarely on show, and those that were were jokingly said to be fit for little but the glue factory. The actual buying and selling of wares was a cover for what was, in essence, a fortnight-long drinking session.

In the Ould Days at Donnybrook Fair.

A historic postcard celebrating the Donnybrook Fair

By the time it was dissolved by Dublin Corporation in the 1860s, it had become a cacophonous event famed for music, heavy drinking, cockfighting and shillelagh swinging. Walter Bagehot, in his 1867 book *The English*

Constitution, references the event by saying that 'The only principle recognised ... was akin to that recommended to the traditionary Irishman on his visit to Donnybrook Fair, "Wherever you see a head, hit it."' In a similar vein, the English journalist James Grant recounted that 'breaking heads and broken bones were then, indeed, considered an essential part of the fair.'

The *Freeman's Journal* complained nine decades before Bagehot that people visiting the event 'returned to the city like intoxicated savages', a criticism that seemed moderate compared to the description of the event as 'a perfect prodigy of moral horrors, a concentration of disgrace upon, not Ireland alone, but civilized Europe'. Condemnation came from some surprising quarters too, with the influential Young Ireland newspaper, *The Nation*, keen to distance themselves from what they viewed as 'the Donnybrook Fair school of Irish patriotism'. To them, there was nothing for Irish nationalists to be proud of in the spectacle.

Fair attendees were drawn primarily from the working classes, which led one contemporary to quip that 'thieves, pickpockets and swindlers' tended to not be present, 'because there was no money worth stealing, and plenty of emptiness in the pockets of the amateurs'. Yet this account of thieves staying away is at odds with the vast majority of eyewitness accounts: one 1820s visitor was disgusted by the sight of 'all the rabble of Dublin ... thieves, and abandoned women ... while pickpockets followed their avocation'.

Some of the fair was innocent fun. A favourite pastime of younger fair attendees was to buy cheap treacle tarts known as 'treacle tillies' and walk around sticking them to the backs of unsuspecting revellers. 'The Humours of Donnybrook', a song written in the days of the event, captures the diversity and eccentricity of it all:

Oh you lads that are witty, from famed Dublin city
And you that in pastime take any delight
To Donnybrook fly, for the time's drawing nigh
When fat pigs are hunted and lean cobblers fight
When maidens so swift run for a new shift
Men muffled in sacks, for a shirt they race there
There jockeys well booted and horses sure-footed
All keep up the humours of Donnybrook Fair

Still, it cannot be denied that there were major social problems around the event, and not alone in terms of violence or drunkenness. Police complained about 'intemperance orgies', while clergy stated that 'the scenes of immorality, prostitution and the sickness which originate in it are too appalling and too forcible to believe that these proceedings which have led to the destruction of thousands could ever be considered entertainment'.

By the second half of the nineteenth century, the establishment had had enough of the annual bout of debauchery in Dublin's suburbs. Some sort of order was slowly but surely put on proceedings; the creation of the Dublin Metropolitan Police in 1836 had a noticeable effect, with one attendee remembering 'a considerable number of mounted patrols scattered about the place, to be in readiness should any disturbances take place'.

Out of the frustration of the authorities emerged a committee, imaginatively entitled the Committee for the Abolition of Donnybrook Fair. One of the members of the committee was the lord mayor of Dublin, Joseph Boyce, and its central aim was raising £3,000 to purchase the licence for the fair from its holder. When a new Catholic church opened in Donnybrook in 1866, it was 'dedicated to the Sacred Heart of Jesus in order to atone for the riotous antics of the Donnybrook Fair'.

Much had changed during the nineteenth century in terms of public attitudes to drunken gatherings. Father Theobald Mathew's temperance crusade had ensured that Daniel O'Connell's movement for the repeal of the Act of Union could mobilise hundreds of thousands people at events without fear of violence. O'Connell himself would proclaim that 'there is not an army in the world that I would not encounter with my teetotallers. Yes, teetotalism is the first sure ground on which rests our hope of sweeping away Saxon domination, and giving Ireland to the Irish.' It was a long way from the Donnybrook Fair.

Keep Rovers at Milltown

Donal Fallon

In the history of association football in Dublin, Ringsend holds a special place. Shelbourne FC was born there in 1895, and in 1901 it was the birthplace of Shamrock Rovers. The first meeting of The Hoops took place at 4 Irishtown Road. Despite beginning their football-playing days in Ringsend Park, Shamrock Rovers will forever be synonymous with Glenmalure Park, which was commonly known simply as 'Milltown'.

Milltown was home to the club from 1926 until 1987, when it was put on the market by the Kilcoyne family, who had been the owners of the club since 1972. An obituary at the time of the death of Louis Kilcoyne in 2012 noted:

> The Kilcoynes were applauded for digging deep into their pockets and laying a superb pitch before embarking on the experiment of full-time professionalism under their brother-in-law John Giles in 1977. Giles arrived at Rovers from West Bromwich Albion, where he had been player-manager and led the club to promotion to the Football League's first division (then the top tier of English football) in the 1975-76 season.
>
> He signed Eamon Dunphy, Paddy Mulligan, Ray Treacy and former Chelsea captain Bobby Tambling; his

aim was to be a force in European football. Reflecting this ambition, Kilcoyne had plans to redevelop Glenmalure Park into a 50,000-seater stadium.

Giles brought in players like Eamon Dunphy, Ray Treacy and Bobby Tambling, and despite the sneers of some, insisted Rovers could become a challenging side beyond this small island. The Kilcoynes claimed that it was in the face of falling attendances that they lost faith in the Milltown project, and developed ambitions of moving the club across the River Liffey to a ground-share scenario at Tolka Park with Home Farm. *Magill* magazine highlighted at the time, '[the fact that] the Kilcoyne family make their living from a property development company named Healy Homes has led many of their detractors to believe that the decision to leave Milltown had more to do with their entrepreneurial streak than their passion for soccer.'

Out of fan frustration with the proposed move to Tolka Park, in 1987 the Keep Rovers at Milltown (KRAM) campaign was born. Games at Tolka Park were picketed by Rovers supporters, while a sometimes vicious war of words broke out in the press, with Eamon Dunphy claiming in his *Sunday Independent* column that the KRAM campaign was 'unconvincing, funny, sad and in some respects, outrageous.'

The last game Shamrock Rovers played at Milltown was an FAI Cup Semi-Final against Sligo Rovers on 12 April 1987, which brought in a crowd of six thousand spectators. The *Irish Press* called the occasion 'a day of nostalgia and angry protests.' RTÉ asked Rovers fan entering the ground if they would follow the club across the Liffey to Tolka Park. Some were adamant they wouldn't, one man said he 'probably would' but at that moment in time it was a no from him too. The game played out a one-all draw, but is best remembered today for the half-time pitch invasion of Shamrock Rovers fans, some of whom carried banners with slogans including *Fuck Tolka* and *Will Greed Kill The Hoops?*

The journalist Ken Curtin recounted the passionate scenes on the pitch, remembering that 'at one stage, the Rovers fans were joined by Sligo supporters in front of the grandstand. A large force of Gardaí present did not interfere with the protesters and it was left to Rovers player/manager Dermot Keely to persuade them to leave the pitch.'

The halftime protest was front page news the next day. Noel Dunne wrote that while the fans 'were not amused', they were well-behaved, though 'admittedly one of the banners waved aloft carried a rather unprintable slogan, with that four-letter preceding "Tolka Park", and some pretty uncomplimentary remarks were also directed at the directors' box.'

It didn't take long for the frustration of supporters to find an outlet. *Magill* magazine wrote:

> Within days of the announcement of the leaving of Milltown, Rovers fans and former players rallied to form KRAM. They included Brian Murphy, Chief Executive of the Diners Club in Ireland, Gerry Mackey, the former marketing manager of BP – who has subsequently become spokesman for KRAM, former Irish youths coach Liam Tuohy and Paddy Coad. The latter three all played for what most veteran Milltown fans regard as the best Rovers team of all time.

The Tolka Park Boycott

When Rovers moved to Tolka Park in the 1987/1988 season, many supporters boycotted the games there, something that Paddy Kilcoyne admitted in an interview with the *Sunday Press* was 'effective', before stating that 'in real terms there isn't any public interest in this issue and the behaviour of these people had not really affected our determination to succeed at Tolka.' *The Irish Times* wrote too that the KRAM boycott had 'undeniably been successful.' A meeting of fans in the Clarence Hall to discuss the boycott tactic received plenty of press attention. Fans ultimately decided only to boycott home fixtures, and to attend away fixtures. The boycott tactic was aimed at hurting the Kilcoyne owners financially. By attending away matches, fans could continue to voice and display their displeasure.

Boycotts, by their very nature, are divisive affairs. For the fans that chose not to pay in to Tolka Park, however, there was a real camaraderie in it all. Reflecting on the tactic, the *Glenmalure Gazette* fanzine recalled that:

> The first match to be boycotted at Tolka Park was a League Cup match against Athlone where no more than 300 people went in. Louis (instead of giving the crowd as lower than it actually was, as he did when he was on the fiddle at Milltown), inflated the gate. But there was no disguising the fact that Rovers fans hadn't fallen for the lies and the aroma of pretence which surrounded the move to 'The Graveyard.' We certainly had some good craic outside Tolka despite the hardship we had to endure in not going to see the team we loved.

The KRAM campaign had its critics, none more vocal in the media than Eamon Dunphy, who had a history with Shamrock Rovers, having played there under Johnny Giles. Giles had told Vincent Browne in an interview with *Magill* that, 'Ultimately, I want to win the European Cup with Shamrock Rovers. This may sound fantastic, but if you consider the amount of football talent there is [in Ireland], it isn't all that outrageous an ambition.' While the club won the FAI Cup with Giles at the helm, the project was ultimately a failure, and Dunphy came away from his time at Rovers embittered, claiming in his memoirs that:

> It is the kind of people that are in the League of Ireland. There is a breed of person in it that is small town, county councillor, freebie, who contribute nothing and take as much as they can … Nothing is ever allowed to develop here because they don't want anyone to do it. We tried … but they didn't want it … no thanks, because it will interfere with our club.

In May 1987, Dunphy used his column in the *Sunday Independent* to claim that 'it is because domestic football has died that Milltown is closing down.' With Rovers out of it, Milltown was allowed fall into rack and ruin. A year on, *Magill* magazine reported that:

> Glenmalure Park is like a disused set from an old Hollywood movie, gloomy and silent, lacking only the ghostly tumbleweeds. The ground has deteriorated, the crowd barriers on the stone terracing have been sawn off and the pitch – once regarded as one of the finest playing surfaces in Europe– is no longer the hallowed

turf that contributed to many memorable Rovers successes for half a century. The stands have fallen into disrepair and the changing pavilions are wrecked. Only the floodlights, purchased with the financial aid of Shamrock Rovers patrons, remain intact.

Tactically, it wasn't all about boycotting. KRAM marked the first anniversary of the club's decision to leave Milltown 'with a march and an all-night vigil outside Glenmalure Park.' Support was sought from public personalities too, with the Housemartins responding to a letter from Rovers supporters. The iconic band, fronted by football fan Paul Heaton, noted that 'it seems obvious that these people have no genuine interest in the club itself and its history and importance to the community.' A very impressive £2,000 was raised by football fans in Australia in support of the campaign, with the *Irish Press* saying it was the efforts of a young, recently emigrated Hoop that made it happen. Probably the strangest bit of news coverage relating to it all was an article in the *Irish Independent* claiming that Donnybrook businessman Terry Byrne had 'pledged to pick up the tab' for sending Rovers fans to the Vatican, in the hope that they could discuss the issue with the Pope!

In the end, the Kilcoyne family succeeded in selling Milltown, and the *Irish Press* predicted 'war' in November 1988. One newspaper reported that the stadium was sold for £950,000, above and beyond anything KRAM could have hoped to raise. KRAM responded immediately by saying 'the fight goes on.' In the year of the Dublin Millennium, when the city celebrated its history with gusto, Rovers Chairman John McNamara rightly pointed out the irony in a part of Dublin's sporting history disappearing.

Despite legal challenges, the ground was levelled in 1990 for property development. As Rovers fan Macdara Ferris has noted, 'at different stages after leaving Milltown, Rovers played games in Tolka Park, Dalymount Park, RDS, Morton Stadium, Richmond Park and even played one home game 200km from Milltown in Turners Cross in Cork.' A monument today marks the spot where the football stadium once stood, while in recent years an original turnstile from Milltown found a home in Tallaght Stadium, where Rovers play today.

Select Bibliography

Newspapers

An Phoblacht
Catholic Standard
Evening Herald
Freeman's Journal
Irish Democrat
Irish Independent
Irish Press
Irish World and American Industrial Liberator
Latvijas Vēstnesis (Latvian Herald)
New York Times
Sunday Independent
Sunday World
The Guardian
The Irish Times
The Times
The Trinity News

Periodicals, journals and magazines

An tÓglach
Dublin Historical Record
Dublin Penny Journal

Éire-Ireland
Gay Community News
History Ireland
Hot Press
Irish Historical Studies
Magill
New Spotlight
Old Limerick Journal
Saothar
Sacred Heart Review
Studies
The Bell
The Dubliner
The Irish Monthly

Online resources

1911 Census – www.census.nationalarchives.ie/pages/1911/
Archiseek – www.archiseek.com
Brand New Retro – www.brandnewretro.ie
Buildings of Ireland – www.buildingsofireland.ie
Built Dublin – www.builtdublin.com
Bureau of Military History – www.burauofmilitaryhistory.ie
Cork Multitext Project (UCC) – www.multitext.ucc.ie
Dublin.ie – www.dublin.ie
Libcom – www.libcom.org
Liberties Dublin – www.libertiesdublin.ie
Property Losses (Ireland) Committee – www.centenaries.
    nationalarchives.ie/centenaries/plic
Spitalfieldslife – www.spitalfieldslife.com
The Irish Story – www.theirishstory.com

Secondary sources

Amsby, Alan and David Kenny. *Mr Pussy: Before I Forget to Remember*. Dublin, 2016.

Andrews, C.S. *Man of No Property: An Autobiography, vol. 2*. Dublin, 1982.

Bulson, Roy. *Irish Pubs Of Character*. Dublin, 1969.

Coogan, Tim Pat. *A Memoir*. London, 2008.

Coogan, Tim Pat. *Ireland in the 20th Century*. New York, 2004.

Cronin, Anthony. *Dead As Doornails*. Dublin, 1976.

Cousins, James H. and Margaret. *We Two Together*. Madras, India, 1950.

Dickson, David. *Dublin: The Making of a Capital City*. London, 2015.

Dublin City Council. *The Georgian Squares of Dublin: An Architectural History*. Dublin, 2006.

Fallon, Las. *Dublin Fire Brigade and the Irish Revolution*. Dublin, 2012.

Ferriter, Diarmaid. *Occasions of Sin: Sex and Society in Modern Ireland*. Dublin, 2009.

Findlater, Alex. *Findlaters, the Story of a Dublin Merchant Family*. Dublin, 2001.

Fishman, Nina. *Arthur Horner: A Political Biography. 1894 to 1944*. London, 2010.

Geraghty, Tom and Whitehead, Trevor. *The Dublin Fire Brigade*. Dublin, 2004.

Hanley, Brian. *The IRA: 1926 – 1936*. Dublin, 2002.

Harrison, Wilton. *Memorable Dublin houses*. Dublin, 1890.

Healy, Patrick. *Rathfarnham Roads*. Dublin, 2005.

Hopkins, Frank. *Hidden Dublin: Deadbeats, Dossers and Decent Skins*. Dublin, 2008.

Horner, Arthur. *Incorrigible Rebel*. London, 1960.

Kearns, Kevin. *Dublin Pub Life and Lore*. Dublin, 1996.

Kearns, Kevin. *Dublin Tenement Life*. Dublin, 2006.

Kearns, Kevin. *Dublin Voices: An Oral Folk History.* Dublin, 1998.

Kelly, Bill. *Me Darlin' Dublin's Dead and Gone*. Dublin, 1983.

Kinealey, Christine. *Repeal and Revolution: 1848 in Ireland*. Manchester, 2009.

Lacey, Brian. *Terrible Queer Creatures: Homosexuality in Irish History.* Dublin, 2008.

McGuirk, Niall. *Please Feed Me: a Punk Vegan Cookbook*. Dublin, 2004.

Madden, Richard Robert. T*he United Irishmen: Their Lives and Times...* London, 1842.

Nelson Algren. *Who Lost An American?* New York, 1963.

Nevin, Donal (ed.) *James Larkin, Lion of the Fold*. Dublin, 1998.

Nevin, Donal. *James Connolly: A Full Life*. Dublin, 2005.

Norris, David. *A Kick Against The Pricks: The Autobiography*. Dublin, 2012.

O'Brien, Glen. Comin*g Out: Irish Gay Experiences*. Dublin, 2003.

O'Brien, Joseph V. *Dear Dirty Dublin: A City in Distress*. Berkeley, 1982.

Ó Catháin, Máirtín. *With a bent elbow and a clenched fist: A Brief History of the Glasgow Anarchists*. Unpublished.

O'Dwyer, Frederick. *Lost Dublin*. Dublin, 1981.

O'Malley, Ernie. *The Singing Flame*. Dublin, 1978.

O'Regan, William. *Memoirs of the legal, literary, and political life of the late the Right Honourable John Philpot Curran...* London, 1817.

Redican, Noel. *Shadows of Doubt*. Dublin, 2008.

Rouse, Paul. *Sport and Ireland: A History.* Oxford, 2015.

Shafer, David A. *Antonin Artaud.* London, 2016.

Sontag, Susan (ed.) *Antonin Artaud: Selected Writings.* Berkeley, 1976.

Ward, Paul. *Britishness Since 1870. London, 2004.*

Whelan, Fergus. *God Provoking Democrat: The Remarkable Life of Archibald Hamilton Rowan.* Dublin, 2015.

Yeates, Padraig. *A City in Wartime: Dublin 1914–1918.* Dublin, 2011.

Yeates, Padraig. *A City in Turmoil – Dublin 1919–1921: The War of Independence.* Dublin, 2012.